A Play,
A Pie and
A Pint

Volume Two
20th Anniversary Edition

Salamander Street

PLAYS

A Play, A Pie and A Pint Volume Two published in 2024 by Salamander Street Ltd., a Wordville imprint. (info@salamanderstreet.com).

Foreword © Joyce McMillan, 2024

Rose by Lorna Martin © 2024
Fleeto by Paddy Cunneen © 2024
ODIS by Alaedinne Chouiref, Soumer Daghastani, Arzé Khodr, Omar Madkour, Zainab Magdy, Alia Mossallam © 2024
Tír Na NÓg by Dave Anderson © 2024
Storytelling by Oliver Emanuel © 2024
The Great Replacement by Uma Nada-Rajah © 2024
Write-Off by Aodhan Gallagher © 2024
Rachel's Cousins by Ann Marie Di Mambro © 2024

All rights reserved.

All rights whatsoever in this play are strictly reserved and application for performance should be made before rehearsal to Salamander Street, 87 Ivor Court, Gloucester Place, London NW1 6BP.

You may not copy, store, distribute, transmit, reproduce or otherwise make available this publication (or any part of it) in any form, or binding or by any means (print, electronic, digital, optical, mechanical, photocopying, recording or otherwise), without the prior written permission of the publisher. Any person who does any unauthorised act in relation to this publication may be liable to criminal prosecution and civil claims for damages.

This publication was assembled by Laila Noble and Calum O'Brien.

Cover illustration by Calum O'Brien.

PB ISBN: 9781068696237

10 9 8 7 6 5 4 3 2 1

Further copies of this publication can be purchased from www.salamanderstreet.com

CONTENTS

Foreword by Joyce McMillan   iv

Introduction   vii

All plays performed at A Play, A Pie and A Pint   x

Plays:

ROSE *by Lorna Martin*   1

FLEETO *by Paddy Cunneen*   29

ODIS *by various playwrights*   65

TÍR NA NÓG *by Dave Anderson*   96

STORYTELLING *by Oliver Emanuel*   117

THE GREAT REPLACEMENT *by Uma Nada-Rajah*   149

WRITE-OFF *by Aodhan Gallagher*   181

RACHEL'S COUSINS *by Ann Marie Di Mambro*   218

FOREWORD

JOYCE McMILLAN on the 20th ANNIVERSARY OF A PLAY, A PIE AND A PINT

WHEN THE FIRST A Play, A Pie And A Pint season emerged onto Scotland's theatre scene, in the autumn of 2004, no-one had any idea what to expect; although with former Wildcat artistic director David MacLennan leading the project, and his great Wildcat collaborator and co-director Dave Anderson at his side, most people around Scottish theatre knew that whatever happened every lunchtime, at the newly-opened Òran Mór on Great Western Road, it was unlikely to be dull.

The formula was clear from the start. For a modest ticket price, the paying public could enjoy a drink (no spirits, but wine, beer or a soft drink), plus a traditional Scottish meat pie (vegetarian options soon followed), and a new short play every week that was guaranteed to last just under an hour, enabling West End workers—at least in theory—to come along in their lunch breaks.

There was also a definite edge of radicalism to the project. Infuriated by the Scottish Arts Council's decision, back in 1997, to cut the funding of their radical music theatre company Wildcat Stage Productions, MacLennan and Anderson had gone into business with Òran Mór owner Colin Beattie, who was strongly supportive of the project, and were determined, at that time, to make it work on a purely independent basis. The aim was to transform and energise the Scottish theatre scene by getting some 30 or more new short plays onto the Òran Mór stage each year; each one—in the early years—only rehearsed for a week, but performed by professional actors, and written both by brand-new writers trying to break into the business, and by more experienced writers seeking a new direction, or trying out new ideas.

It was a bold concept, and a risky one; but within a year, it became clear that MacLennan's vision was succeeding beyond his wildest hopes, as A Play, A Pie and A Pint rapidly became a vital part of the Scottish theatre scene, attracting a hugely loyal and responsive regular

West End audience, and beginning to find partners and imitators both within Scotland, and far beyond.

Over its first 20 years, A Play, A Pie And A Pint has famously commissioned and produced more than 600 plays, providing countless opportunities for writers, actors and directors to develop their craft, and to try out new ideas in what remains an almost uniquely low-risk environment, by modern professional theatre standards. Productions are simple, rehearsal times remain short, and pay rates are basic, although A Play, A Pie And A Pint works to improve them; it's always worth noting that PPP has never seen itself as an alternative model to Scotland's full-scale new-play theatres, but always as a powerhouse of emerging talent on which they can draw.

For playwrights in Scotland, though—and particularly for emerging playwrights—the presence of A Play, A Pie And A Pint has been transformative, doubling and perhaps trebling their chances of getting a play onto a professional stage in any given year. It has given actors and directors opportunities to extend their range and work with new writers; and it has helped to foster a whole new generation of Scottish music-theatre makers, following in the footsteps of Anderson and MacLennan. It has been a huge asset to its partner theatres across Scotland, at the Traverse and the Ayr Gaiety, in Stirling, Aberdeen and beyond; it has been imitated by theatres from Moscow to Philadelphia, and has staged international seasons on themes ranging—with huge foresight—from Ukraine and Russia to the Arab spring and the Middle East.

And it has been able to do all this, finally, because its late great founder David MacLennan, and those who worked with him, understood that in the end, theatre needs an audience that will give it the freedom to try and fail and try again, to fail better (as Sam Beckett suggested), and sometimes, gloriously, to succeed; and that spirit has survived MacLennan's sad death in 2014, and thrived under succeeding artistic directors Morag Fullarton, April Chamberlain and Jemima Levick.

By inviting its Glasgow audience into Òran Mór, and offering the pie and pint that both offers solace for the shows we don't like, and enhances the joy of those we love, A Play, A Pie And A Pint has built that steady and continuous relationship with its audience that offers artists a huge freedom to play and experiment, while still finding solidarity and support not only from their colleagues, but from a very special paying public.

If there is one secret to A Play, A Pie and A Pint's success, it perhaps lies in that unique and powerful audience relationship. It also depends, though, on the sheer creative energy of a Scottish theatre community that, through good times and bad, has seized every chance to present a play in the beloved "pie dungeon"; and to become part of an extraordinary rollercoaster-cum-powerhouse of fun, reflection, fresh ideas, and profound emotion that rolls on at the heart of Scottish theatre from one week to the next, through nine months of every year.

Joyce McMillan
Theatre Critic, The Scotsman
July 2024

INTRODUCTION

A PLAY, A PIE AND A PINT is delighted to introduce this second volume of plays, celebrating 20 years of the iconic lunchtime theatre company. Throughout the last two decades we have produced over 600 plays, world premieres of original work by some of the most exciting playwrights from across the country, and beyond.

The task of selecting just eight plays from our archive wasn't an easy one and we enlisted the help of past contributors, collaborators, artists, friends and our audience to come up with the plays you'll find within this collection. Each is a snapshot in time, a moment captured from a rich history, and a pointer to the exciting future ahead of us.

We would like to thank everyone who contributed to the collection, the writers themselves and every artist and audience member who has, across the years, made A Play, A Pie and A Pint what it is today.

We hope you enjoy reading and remembering the plays in this volume and that it inspires you to come along to Òran Mór to watch the plays of our future.

A Play, A Pie and A Pint
Glasgow
2024

Team PPP (as of Sept 2024)
Brian Logan—Artistic Director
Laila Noble—Associate Director
Sarah Alice Cruickshank—Producer
Li Kennedy—Producer
Jake Curran-Pipe—Assistant Producer
Calum O'Brien—Communications Officer
Sam Ramsay—Production Coordinator
Zephyr Liddell—Designer
Heather Grace Currie—Designer
Ross Nurney—Technical Coordinator

BOARD OF DIRECTORS

Kevin O'Sullivan (Chair)
Edward Crozier (Vice Chair)
Dave Anderson
Colin Beattie
Juliet Cadzow
David Hayman
Stefan King
Lauren McFarlane
Iona Whyte

ACKNOWLEDGEMENTS

WITH THANKS TO Tina Anderson, Victoria Beesley, April Chamberlain, David Greig, Jemima Levick, Louise Ludgate, Joyce McMillan, Morag Fullarton, Richard Conlon, Susannah Armitage, Diane Carroll and the team at the Òran Mór.

ADDITIONAL THANKS TO OUR CROWDFUNDER SUPPORTERS

Anne Adams
Susannah Armitage
Michael Browning
Allan Cowan
John Dalby
Marion Donohoe
Jacob Dudgeon
Vivian French
Kris Haddow
Lynda Kennedy
Morven Macbeth
Lorna Martin
David McNeish
Helen Morton
Natalie O'Donoghue
Frances Poet
Joyce Sharp
Wilma G Stark
George Walker
Siobhan Walsh

André Agius
Rod Begbie
Gillian Bruce
Alison Cresswell
Scott Davidson
Jim Doran
Caroline Elsey
Jacqueline Gilmartin
Janis Jerome
Kristina Koiak
Joan Macpherson
Alistair McClure
John Mess
Ishbel Morton
Anita O'Hagan
Jacqueline Rinder
Tam Shepherd
Graeme Strachan
Anna Louise Wallace
Morna Young

Mardi Alexander
Martin Breslin
David Cameron
Jackie Crichton
Daniel Donnelly
Claire Dow
Margaret Forbes
Elaine Gorman
Richard G Kay
John Lister
Audrey Marshall
Kenneth J McIntosh
Calum Moore
Felix O'Brien
Kirsty O'Sullivan
Catriona Scott
Chris Spencer
Claire Taylor
Stephen Walls
Frances Yule

FIRST SEASON: AUTUMN 2004

6th—11th Sept: *Hieroglyphics* by Anne Donovan
13th—18th Sept: *Poker Alice* by Greg Hemphill
20th—25th Sept: *Leather Bound* by Chris Dolan
27th—2nd Oct: *The Head of Red O'Brien* by Mark O'Halloran
4th—9th Oct: *Dessert Storm* by Anna Burnside and Jon Pope
11th—16th Oct: *Mobile* by Dave Anderson
18th—23rd Oct: *Laughing at the Fuhrer* by John Bett
25th—30th Oct: *Buridan's Ass* by Steve Plant
1st—6th Nov: *The Genesis Book* by Peter Arnott
8th—13th Nov: *So Long, Sleeping Beauty* by Isobel Mahon
15th—20th Nov: *On the Sidelines* by William McIlvanney
22nd—27th Nov: *My Father's Suit* by Peter McDougall

THE SPRING SEASON: 2005

21st—26th Feb: *Fog* by Bruce Morton
28th Feb—5th Mar: *Casanova's Limp* by S R Plant
7th—12th Mar: *Hot Air* by Robin Sen
14th—19th Mar: *Just the Job* by Ian Black
21st—26th Mar: *Days of the War and Rosie* by Gowan Calder
28th Mar—2nd Apr: *The Price of a Fish Supper* by Catherine Czerkawska
4th—9th Apr: *The Prisoner* by William McIlvanney
11th—16th Apr: *The Brother's Suit* by Peter McDougall
18th—23rd Apr: *Gymnasium of the World* by Anne Downie
25th—30th Apr: *Two Sisters* by Carl MacDougall
2nd—7th May: *A Walk in the Park* by Dave Anderson
9th—14th May: *The White Cliffs* by Suhayl Saadi
16th—21st May: *Two* by Jackie Kay
23rd—28th May: *The Ceremony* by Liz Lochhead
30th May: Three radio sitcom readings & three radio drama readings
    (developed by BBC Scotland)

THE AUTUMN SEASON: 2005

29th Aug—3rd Sep: *The Shedding of the Suit* by Peter McDougall
5th—10th Sep: *The Backpacker Blues* by Douglas Maxwell
12th—17th Sep: *Behind Office Doors* by Claire Hemphill
19th—24th Sep *Undone* by Jamie Havelin
26th Sep—1st Oct: *Wheesht! And Short Spin* by Victor Iriarte
    and Maite Perez Larumbe
3rd—8th Oct: *Night Out* by William McIlvanney
10th—15th Oct: *Triumvirate* by Allan Massie

17th—22nd Oct: *The Importance of Being Alfred* by Louise Welsh
24th—29th Oct: *Double Yella* by Janet Paisley
31st Oct—5th Nov: *Quartet* by Donna Franceschild
7th—12th Nov: *Portable* by Dave Anderson
14th—19th Nov: Orange Playwriting Prize Winner (14-18 year olds)
21st—26th Nov: *Summit* by Davey Anderson
28th Nov—3rd Dec: Orange Playwriting Prize Winner (adult)
w/c 5th/12th Dec: Òran Mór Panto *Cinders*

THE SPRING SEASON: 2006

6th—11th Feb: *The Matinee Idol* by D C Jackson
13th—18th Feb: *Conversations in Havana* by Mike Gonzalez
20th—25th Feb: *Burns of the Solway* by Catherine Czerkawska
27th Feb—4th Mar: *Six and a Tanner* by Rony Bridges
6th—11th Mar: *The Book of Love* by Robert Forrest
13th—18th Mar: *Rain* by Bruce Morton
20th—25th Mar: *Full Blown Rose* by Roz Hammond
27th Mar—1st Apr: *Night Hawks* by John Bett
3rd—8th Apr: *Broken* by Selma Dimitrijevic
10th—15th Apr: *54% Acrylic* by David Harrower
17th—22nd Apr: *Forbidden Fruit* by Kirsten Thorvall
24th—29th Apr: *Ida Tamson* by Denise Mina
1st—6th May: *Moldova* by Sean Hardie
8th—13th May: *Pro-ActiveMon 13 R* by Alma Cullen
15th—20th May: *The Above* by Simon Macallum

THE AUTUMN SEASON: 2006

28th Aug—2nd Sep: *Side Affects* by Raman Young
    (Young National Theatre of Scotland)
4th—9th Sep: *Drawing Bored* by D C Jackson
11th—16th Sep: *Sea Change* by Lewis Hetherington
18th—23rd Sep: *Tír na nÒg* by Dave Anderson
25th—30th Sep: *A Fortnight on the Seychelles* by Maite Perez Larumbe
2nd—7th Oct: *Hedy Lamarr and the Easter Rising* by Michael James Ford
9th—14th Oct: *Goodbye Jimmy* by Alasdair Gray
16th—21st Oct: *Angels' Wings* by Grace Barnes
23rd—28th Oct: *The Tarot Reading* by Eleanor Yule
30th Oct—4th Nov: *Tequila Sunset* by Elizabeth MacLennan
6th—11st Nov: *Excuse My Dust* by Terry Wale
13th—18th Nov: *Byre Dogs* by Callum Smith Lawrence
20th—25th Nov: *Ae Fond Kiss* by Ann Marie Di Mambro
27th Nov—2nd Dec: *Rocketville* by Liam John Hurley
4th—24th Dec: Òran Mór Panto: *Jack and the Beanstalk* by
    Dave Anderson and David MacLennan

THE SPRING SEASON: 2007

5th—10th Feb: *Piece of My Heart* by Liz Lochhead
12th—17th Feb: *Velvet Love* by Simon Maccallum
19th—24th Feb: *GBH* by Adrian Wiszniewski, music by Gordon Rigby
26th Feb—3rd Mar: *Lie Down Comin* by John Mortimer
12th—17th Mar: *The Date* by Claire Hemphill
19th—24th Mar: *This Time I Promise* by Marcella Evaristi
26th—31st Mar: *Burning Your Boats* by Sean Hardie
2nd—7th Apr: *Metrosexual* by Sandy Nelson
9th— 14th Apr: *Turning the World Upside Down* by Mike Gonzalez, music by Dave Anderson
16th—21st Apr: *Loss of the Golden Silence/Midgieburgers* by Alasdair Gray
23rd—28th Apr: *23756* by Rony Bridges
30th Apr— 5th May: *Melody* by Deirdre Kinneghan
7th—12th May: *I Of The Needle* by Adrian Osmond
14th—19th May: *Father Son and Holy Smoke* by Jane Duncan

THE AUTUMN SEASON: 2007

27th Aug—1st Sep: *Digging up Dad* by Vivien Adam
3rd—8th Sep: *Ha Ha Ha* by Tom Tabori
10th—15th Sep: *The Frock* by Kate Donnelly
17th—22nd Sep: *Elf Analysis* by Morna Pearson
24th—30th Sep: *The Inquisitor* by Peter Arnott
1st—6th Oct: *Targets* by Alma Cullen
8th—13th Oct: *Meeting Matthew* by Clive King, music by Hilary Brooks
15th—20th Oct: *Hue and Cry* by Deirdre Kinhan
22nd—27th Oct: *Being Norwegian* by David Greig
29th Oct—3rd Nov: *Crazy Love* by Che Walker
5th—10th Nov: *Between Dog and Wolf* by Sean Buckley
12th—17th Nov: *The Dirt Under the Carpet* by Rona Munro
19th—24th Nov: 100th Play by various writers
26th Nov—1st Dec: *Fleeto* by Paddy Cunneen
3rd—22nd Dec: Òran Mór Panto: *Rumplestiltskin* by Andy Gray

THE SPRING SEASON: 2008

4th—9th Feb: *Maria of my Soul* by Julie Fraser
11th—16th Feb: *Resurrection* by Nicola McCartney
18th—23rd Feb: *Hephaestos* by Chris Dolan
25th Feb—1st Mar: *Hidden Worlds—Litter of Sandals* by Stuart Delves
3rd—8th Mar: *Dough* by David Ian Neville

10th—15th Mar: *Flowers of the River* by Dave Anderson
17th—22nd Mar: *Out on the Wing* by D C Jackson
24th—29th Mar: *The Apprentice* by Martin McCardie
31st Mar—5th Apr: *God's Hairdresser* by Sean Hardie
7th—12th Apr: *An Advert for the Army* by Kieran Lynn
14th—19th Apr: *Gods are Fallen and All Safety Gone*
      by Selma Dimitrijevic
21st—26th Apr: *A Drunk Woman Looks at the Thistle* by Denise Mina
28th Apr—3rd May: *The Tobacco Merchant's Lawyer* by Iain Heggie
5th—10th May: *Death Story* by Alma Cullen
12th—17th May: *Zarraberri* by Maite Perez Latumbe/*Limbo* by
      Victor Iriarte
19th—24th May: *The Last of Us* by Pamela Cartner
26th—31st May: *Call it Sleep* by Brian Pettifer

CLASSIC CUTS 2008

2nd—7th June: *The Way of the World* by William Congreve
9th—14th June: *King Lear* by William Shakespeare
16th—21st June: *The Shoemaker's Wonderful Wife* by
      Federico Garcia Lorca
23rd—28th June: *Anthony and Cleopatra* by William Shakespeare

THE AUTUMN SEASON: 2008

1st—6th Sept: *Mums and Lovers* by Ian Pattison
8th—13th Sept: *Speak the Speech* by Alma Cullen
15th—20th Sept: *Sweet Home Balmaha* by Tom Urie, Matthew
      McVarish and Donald Cameron
22nd—27th Sept: *When Clarence Calls* by Ford Kiernan
29th Sept—4th Oct: *Killing Brando* by Alexis Zigerman
6th—11th Oct: *Godzilla Vs Mechagodzilla* by Lydia Adetunji
13th—18th Oct: *Videotape* by Oliver Emanuel
20th—25th Oct: *Moonwalking* by Nicola Wilson
27th—1st Nov: *Stage Fright* by Eleanor Yule
3rd—8th Nov: *Raspberry* by Gary Robson
10th—15th Nov: *Washed Up* by Laura Neal
17th—22nd Nov: *Under My Skin* by Ali Muriel
24th—29th Nov: *The Bones Boys* by Colin MacDonald
1st—20th Dec: Òran Mór Panto: *Babes in the Woods* by
      Dave Anderson and David MacLennan

THE SPRING SEASON: 2009

2nd—7th Feb: ***The Pipes! The Pipes! / Voices in the Dark*** by Alasdair Gray
9th—14th Feb: ***Fifteen Minutes*** by Kim Millar
16th—21st Feb: ***Nigerian Story*** by Simon McCallum
23rd—28th Feb: ***Will Shu*** by Jacqueline Clark
2nd—7th Mar: ***The Waltz of The Cold Wind*** by Paddy Cunneen
9th—14th Mar: ***Kyoto*** by David Greig
16th—21st Mar: ***The Ching Room*** by Alan Bissett
23rd—28th Mar: ***Poem in October*** by Robert Forrest
30th Mar—4th Apr: ***Lucky Box*** by David Harrower
6th—11th Apr: ***An Apple A Day*** by Jo Clifford
13th—18th Apr: ***Djúpid (The Deep)*** by Jon Atli Jonasson
20th—25th Apr: ***Too Clever By Half*** by Andrew Dallmeyer
27th Apr—2nd May: ***A Drop in the Ocean*** by Dave Anderson
4th—9th May: ***The Oddest Couple*** by Clare Hemphill
11th—16th May: ***Waterproof*** by Andy Duffy
18th—23rd May: ***What the Animals Say*** by David Ireland
25th—30th May: ***According to Ben*** by John Bett

CLASSIC CUTS 2009

1st—6th June: ***Medea*** by Euripedes'
8th—13th June: ***Lady Windermere's Fan*** by Oscar Wilde
15th—20th June: ***Cyrano De Bergerac*** by Edmund Rostand
22nd—27th June: ***Romeo and Juliet*** by William Shakespeare

THE AUTUMN SEASON: 2009

31st Aug—5th Sept: ***Old Girls*** by Zoe Strachan
7th—12th Sept: ***Eat Your Heart Out*** by Renato Gabrielli, translated by Ann Marie Di Mambro
14th—19th Sept: ***La Befana*** by Adrian Wiszniewski, music by Gordon Rigby
21st—26th Sept: ***Clara*** by Wilma Stark
28th Sept—3rd Oct: ***About a Goth*** by Tom Wells
5th—10th Oct: ***Long Player*** by Heather MacLeod
12th—17th Oct: ***The Glimmering Nymph*** by Sandy Nelson
19th—24th Oct: ***A Perfect Child*** by Lewis Hetherington
26th—31st Oct: ***Arguments for Terrorism*** by David Ireland
2nd—7th Nov: ***10,000 Meters Deep*** by Laura Lomas
9th—14th Nov: ***Life of Wylie*** by Sean Hardie
16th—21st Nov: ***Gabriel*** by Catherine Grosvenor
23rd—28th Nov: ***An Incident at the Border*** by Kieran Lynn

30th Nov—19th Dec: Òran Mór Panto - *A Christmas Carol*
    by Dave Anderson and David MacLennan

THE SPRING SEASON: 2010

1st—6th Feb: *The Secret Commonwealth* by Catherine Czerkawska
8th—13th Feb: *Crunch* by Gary McNair
15th—20th Feb: *Company Policy* by D C Jackson
22nd—27th Feb: *Heaven* by Simon Stephens
1st—6th Mar: *The Shattered Head* by Graham Eatough and Maggie Rose
8th—13th Mar: *Soup* by Ella Hickson
15th—20th Mar: *Battery Farm* by Gregory Burke
22nd—27th Mar: *The Garden* by Zinnie Harris
29th Mar—3rd Apr: *A Prayer* by Selma Dimitrijevic
5th—10th Apr: *Tonight David Ireland will Lecture, Box and Dance*
    by Sandy Grierson
12th—17th Apr: *Bear on a Chain* by Sue Glover
19th—24th Apr: *Casablanca (The Lunchtime Cut)* by Morag Fullarton
26th Apr—1st May: *Turbo Folk* by Alan Bissett
3rd—8th May: *Songs of Joyce*
10th—15th May: *Please, Mister b*y Patrick Harkins
17th—22nd May: *Before I Go* by Ian Pattison
24th—29th May: *Federer Versus Murray* by Gerda Stevenson
31st May—5th June: *The Sunday Lesson* by Cathy Forde

CLASSIC CUTS 2010

7th—12th June: *The Seagull* by Anton Chekov, adapted by
    Mary McCluskey
14th—19th June: *Tartuffe* by Molère, adapted by Liz Lochhead
21st—26th June: *Fuenteovejuna* by Lope de Vega, adapted by
    Philip Howard
28th June—3rd July: *Lysistrata* by Aristophanes, adapted by
    Dave Anderson and David MacLennan

THE AUTUMN SEASON: 2010

30th Aug—4th Sep: *Fly Me to the Moon* by Marie Jones
6th—11th Sep: *In the Pipeline* by Gary Owen
13th—18th Sep: *The Uncertainty Files* by Linda McLean
20th—25th Sep: *Calais* by April de Angelis
27th Sep—2nd Oct: *Good with People* by David Harrower
4th—9th Oct: 200th Play by various writers
11th—16th Oct: *Changing Lines* by Alan Massie
18th—23rd Oct: *One Gun* by Ian Low

25th—30th Oct: *Elysium Nevada* by Barry McKinley
1st—6th Nov: *Wee Andy* by Paddy Cunneen
8th—13th Nov: *Baltamire* by Sandy Nelson
15th—20th Nov: *Face to Face* by Iain Heggie
22nd—27th Nov: *The House* by Steven McNicoll
29th Nov—18th Dec: Òran Mór Panto: *Sleeping Beauty* by
  Dave Anderson and David MacLennan

THE SPRING SEASON: 2011

31st Jan—5th Feb: *Bunnies* by Kieran Lynn
7th—12th Feb: *The Company Will Overlook A Moment of Madness* by Rodolfo Santana, adapted by Morna Pearson
14th—19th Feb: *Instructions for a Butterfly Collector* by
  Mariana Eva Perez
14th—19th Feb: *The Archivist* by Hector Levy, adapted by
  Lewis Hetherington
21st—26th Feb: *Four Parts Broken* by Fernanda Jaber adapted
  by Abigail Docherty
28th Feb—5th Mar: *A Dead Man's Dying* by Esteban Navajas Cortes,
  adapted by Davey Anderson
7th—12th Mar: *The Confidant* by Gilberto Pinto, adapted by
  Alan Bissett
14th—19th Mar: *The Soap Hour* by Marianella Yanes
21st—26th Mar: *One Night in Iran* by Oliver Emanuel
28th Mar—2nd Apr: *St Catherine's Day* by Michael Marra
4th—9th Apr: *What Love Is* by Linda McLean
11th—16th Apr: *The Dacha* by Helen Kluger
18th—23rd Apr: *The End of Hope, The End of Desire* by David Ireland
25th—30th Apr: *Paisley to Paolo* by Martin McCardie
2nd—7th May: *Miracle* by Nicola McCartney
9th—14th May: *Thank God for John Muir* by Andrew Dallmeyer
16th—21st May: *Top Table* by Rob Drummond
23rd—28th May: *I Heart Maths* by James Ley
30th May—4th June: *Sin of the Fathers* by Patrick Harkins
Òran Mór Summer Panto - *Goldilocks & the Glasgow Fair* by
  Dave Anderson and David MacLennan

CLASSIC CUTS 2011

6th—11th June: *Daphnis and Chloe* by Longus, adapted by Hattie Naylor
13th—18th June: *Wind in the Pines* by Kanami, adapted by
  Paddy Cunneen
20th—25th June: *A Midsummer Night's Dream* by William Shakespeare,
  adapted by Andy Gray

Kenny Ireland, Sharon Small and Bill Paterson in *Astonishing Archie* (2012). Photo: Leslie Black.

Elaine C Smith and George Drennan in *The Sweetest Growl* (2019). Photo: Leslie Black.

27th June—2nd July: ***Don Giovanni*** by Lorenzo Da Ponte, adapted by Mary McCluskey

THE AUTUMN SEASON: 2011

5th—10th Sep: ***God Bless Liz Lochhead*** by Martin McCardie
12th—17th Sep: ***Angels*** by Ronan O'Donnell
19th—24th Sep: ***Supply*** by Cathy Forde
26th Sep—1st Oct: ***Watching the Detective*** by Paddy Cunneen
3rd—8th Oct: ***Dig*** by Katie Douglas
10th—15th Oct: ***You Cannot Go Forward Where You Are Right Now*** by David Watson
17th—22nd Oct: ***Eternal Source of Light*** by Leo Butler
24th—29th Oct: ***McAdam's Torment*** by Audrey Devereaux
31st Oct—5th Nov: ***Connected*** by Will Irvine and Karl Quinn
7th—12th Nov: ***The Murder of Geoffrey Robbins*** by John and Gerry Kielty
14th—19th Nov: ***The Kiss*** by Murry Watts
21st—26th Nov: ***Bite the Bullet*** by Sandy Nelson and Keith Warwick
28th Nov—3rd Dec: New Voices
5th—24th Dec: Òran Mór Panto: ***Snow White and the Seventh Dwarf*** by Dave Anderson and David MacLennan

THE SPRING SEASON: 2012

30th Jan—4th Feb: ***Sex, Chips and the Holy Ghost*** by Jo Clifford
6th—11th Feb: ***Born to Run*** by Gary McNair
13th—18th Feb: ***Spirit of Adventure*** by Oliver Emanuel
20th—25th Feb: ***Serov's People*** by Peter Arnott
27th Feb—3rd Mar: ***The Jean-Jacques Rousseau Show*** by various writers
5th—10th Mar: ***Rolls in their Pockets*** by Rob Drummond
12th—17th Mar: ***Facegone*** by Will Gore
19th—24th Mar: ***Slice*** by Mel Giedroyc
26th—31st Mar: ***The Last Great Dictator*** by Kieran Lynn
2nd—7th Apr: ***Cold Turkey at Nana's*** by Ben Tagoe
9th—14th Apr: ***Forfeit*** by Alan Wilkins
16th—21st Apr: ***Would You Please Look at the Camera*** by Syrian playwright
23rd—28th Apr: ***Dear Glasgow*** by various writers
30th Apr—5th May: ***Hadda & Hassan Lekliches!*** by Jaouad Essouani
7th—12th May: ***Damascus Aleppo*** by Syrian playwright
14th—19th May: ***Sleeping Beauty Insomnia*** by Abdelrahim Alwaj
21st—26th May: ***One Day in Spring*** by various writers
28th May—2nd June: ***Sweet Dreams*** by Ron Butlin
4th—9th June: ***The Brothers' Keeper*** by Peter MacDougall

CLASSIC CUTS 2012

11th—16th June: ***Pygmalion*** by George Bernard Shaw
18th—23rd June: ***Ubu Roi*** by Alfred Jarry, adapted by Marcus Roche
25th—30th June: ***King John*** by William Shakespeare, adapted by Philip Howard
2nd—7th July: ***Private Lives*** by Noël Coward, adapted by Jennifer Hainey
9th—28th July: Òran Mór Summer Panto: ***Alice in Poundland*** by Dave Anderson and David MacLennan

THE AUTUMN SEASON: 2012

3rd—8th Sep: ***Dead Famous*** by Keith Temple
10th—15th Sep: ***The Room in the Elephant*** by Tom Wainwright
17th—22nd Sep: ***Chalk Farm*** by Kieran Hurley and A J Taudevin
24th—29th Sep: ***And The Children Never Look Back*** by Salka Gudmundsdóttir
1st—6th Oct: ***The Great Disappointment of Santa Muerta*** by Amanda Monfrooe
8th—13th Oct: ***Remember You Are Beauty Full*** by Matthew McVarish
15th—20th Oct: ***Faith Fall*** by Frances Poet
22nd—27th Oct: ***Demons*** by various writers
29th Oct—3rd Nov: ***Princess for a Day*** by Jack Dickson
5th—10th Nov: ***Astonishing Archie*** by Bill Paterson
12th—17th Nov: ***Loyalty/Phantom Force*** by Mike Gonzalez and Paul Laverty
19th—24th Nov: ***This Little Piggy*** by Jamie Laing
26th Nov—1st Dec: ***Take Me If You Need Me*** by GCU Students
3rd—22nd Dec: Òran Mór Christmas Panto: ***Aladdin and Jeannie*** by David Anderson and David MacLennan

THE SPRING SEASON: 2013

28th Jan—2nd Feb: ***Only the Lonely*** by Ann Marie Di Mambro
4th—9th Feb: ***Thank You*** by Catrin Evans
11th—16th Feb: ***3 Seconds*** by Lesley Hart
18th—23rd Feb: ***A Respectable Widow Takes to Vulgarity*** by Douglas Maxwell
25th Feb—2nd Mar: ***Most Favoured*** by David Ireland
4th—9th Mar: ***Clean*** by Sabrina Mahfouz
11th—16th Mar: Òran Mór/Channel 4 Comedy Drama Award Winner
18th—23rd Mar: ***Diving Manuel*** by Denise Mina
25th—30th Mar: ***In the Heart of Darby Park*** by Suzie Miller
1st—6th Apr: ***Old Blood*** by Morna Pearson
8th—13th Apr: ***Margaret and Ken and the End of the World*** by Sean Hardie
15th—20th Apr: ***Butterfly Kiss*** by Dave Anderson
22nd—27th Apr: ***Secrets*** by Lin Weiran, adapted by Rona Munro
29th Apr—4th May: ***Sweet Silver Song of the Lark*** by Molly Taylor

Juliet Cadzow in *God Bless Liz Lochhead (2011)*.
Photo: Leslie Black

Sarah MacFarlane, Colin Beattie and Susannah Armitage.
Photo: Douglas Timmins.

6th—11th May: *Thieves and Boy* by Hao Jingfang, adapted by Davey Anderson
13th—18th May: *Marco Pantani - The Pirate* by Stuart Hepburn
20th—25th May: *Mortal Memories* by Liz Lochhead
27th May—1st June: *Fox Attack* by Xu Nuo, adapted
    by Catherine Grosvenor

CLASSIC CUTS 2013

10th—15th June: *Volpone* by Ben Johnson, adapted by Andy Clark
17th—22nd June: *The Changeling* by Thomas Middleton & William Rowley
24th—29th June: *The Taming of the Shrew* by William Shakespeare,
    adapted by Sandy Nelson
1st—6th July: *Three Sisters* by Anton Chekhov, adapted by Viv Adam
8th—27th July: Òran Mór Summer Panto 2013. *A Bit of A Dick…
Whittington* by Dave Anderson and David MacLennan

THE AUTUMN SEASON: 2013

2nd—7th Sep: *Trouble and Shame* by David Ireland
9th—14th Sep: *Divided* by Ian Pattison
16th—21st Sep: *The Great Train Race* by Robert Dawson Scott
23rd—28th Sep: *Woman of the Year* by Stef Smith
30th Sep—5th Oct: *The Jazz Club Murder* by James Runcie
7th—12th Oct: *The Trouble with Double* by D C Jackson
14th—19th Oct: *Saint One* by Lesley Hart
21st—26th Oct: *Doras Duinte* by Catriona Lexi Campbell
28th Oct—2nd Nov: *Grace Undertaking* by Paddy Cunneen
4th—9th Nov: *The Deficit Show* by OTT
11th—16th Nov: *Janis Joplin: Full Tilt* by Peter Arnott
18th—23rd Nov: *Guilty* by Rona Munro
25th—30th Nov: *Home* by Jenny Knotts
2nd—21st Dec: Òran Mór Panto: *The Uglies* by Dave Anderson
    and David MacLennan

THE SPRING SEASON: 2014

27th Jan—1st Feb: *Frank's Dead* by Stewart Thomson
3rd—8th Feb: *Rough Island* by Nicola McCartney
10th—15th Feb: *Fishwrap* by Kieran Lynn
17th—22nd Feb: *Wake Me in The Morning* by Jeremy Raison
24th Feb—1st Mar: *Save the Lap Dance for Me* by Morag Fullarton
3rd—8th Mar: *The Friends of Miss Dorian Gray* by Marcella Evaristi
10th—15th Mar: *Between The Thinks Bubble and The Space Balloon*
    by Liz Lochhead
17th—22nd Mar: *Auntie Agatha Comes to Tea* by George Milne
24th—29th Mar: *Love With a Capital 'L'* by Tony Cox

31st Mar—5th Apr: *A Perfect Stroke* by Johnny McKnight
7th—12th Apr: *The Last Bloom* by Amba Chevannes
14th—19th Apr: *Skeleton Wumman* by Gerda Stevenson
21st—26th Apr: *The Queen of Lucky People* by Iain Heggie
23rd Apr—3rd May: *Helen* by Thomas Eccleshare
5th—10th May: *The Tale of Fanny Cha Cha* by Joyce Falconer
12th—17th May: *Voices From the Black That I Am* by
    Karl O'Brian Williams
19th—24th May: *Nine Lives* by Zodwa Nyoni
26th—31st May: *Fred and Alice* by John Sheehy
2nd—7th June: *Fast Cuts and Snap Shots* by Inua Ellams

CLASSIC CUTS 2014

9th—14th June: *The Call of the Wild* by Jack London, adapted
    by Dominic Douglas
16th—21st June: *The Misanthrope* by Molière, adapted by Frances Poet
23rd—28th June: *Don Quixote* by Miguel de Cervantes Saavedra,
    adapted by Ben Lewis
30th June—5th July: *Ophelia: Shakespeare's Hamlet*, rewritten by
    Alan McKendrick
7th—26th July: Òran Mór Summer Panto: *Maw Goose* by Dave Anderson
    and David MacLennan

THE AUTUMN SEASON: 2014

1st—6th Sep: *Faster, Louder* by Steven Dick
8th—13th Sep: *A Terrible Beauty* by Ian Pattison
15th—20th Sep: *Miss Shamrock's World of Glamorous Flight*
    by Martin Travers
22nd—27th Sep: *It's Only Words* by Sylvia Dow
29th Sep—4th Oct: *Flame Proof* by Lesley Hart
6th—11th Oct: *Mary Barbour's Daughters* by AJ Taudevin
13th—18th Oct: *Squash* by Martin McCormick
20th—25th Oct: *Crash* by Andy Duffy
27th Oct—1st Nov: *Flying with Swans* by Jack Dickson
3rd—8th Nov: *The Happiest Day of Brendan Smillie's Life*
    by Catherine Grosvenor
10th—15th Nov: *Bridge* by Donna Franceschild
17th—22nd Nov: *Theatre Uncut* by various writers
24th—29th Nov: *The King's Kilt* by Rona Munro
1st—20th Dec: Òran Mór Panto: *The Emperor's New Clothes* by
    Dave Anderson

THE SPRING SEASON: 2015

26th—31st Jan: *Butterfly* by Anne Hogg
2nd—7th Feb: *Hooray for All Kinds of Things* by Sandy Nelson
9th—14th Feb: *We Can All Agree to Pretend This Never Happened*
    by Emma Goidel
16th—21st Feb: *Netting* by Morna Young
23rd—28th Feb: *Flower, Bird, Wind, Moon* by Paddy Cunneen
2nd—7th Mar: *Lifesaving* by Rob Drummond
9th—14th Mar: *Leviathan* by Matthew Trevannion
16th—21st Mar: *The Day the Pope Emptied Croy* by Martin McCormick
23rd—28th Mar: *Take the Rubbish Out, Sasha* by Natalia Vorozhbyt,
    translated by Sasha Dugdale
30th Mar—4th Apr: *Fat Alice* by Alison Carr
6th—11th Apr: *Broth* by Tim Primrose
13th—18th Apr: *Whisky Galore/Uisge-Beatha Gu Leór* adapted by
    Iain Finlay MacLeod
20th—25th Apr: *No Nothing* by Alan Spence
27th Apr—2nd May: *Vlad the Impaler* by Richard Crane
4th—9th May: *The War Hasn't Started Yet* by Mikhail Durnenkov,
    adapted by Davey Anderson
11th—16th May: *Tommy's Song* by Lou Prendergast
18th—23rd May: *The Head in the Jar* by Deb Jones
25th—30th May: *Thoughts Spoken Aloud From Above* by Yuri Klavdiev,
    adapted by Peter Arnott
1st—6th June: *Sunset Boulevard (The Lunchtime Cut)* by Morag Fullarton

CLASSIC CUTS 2015

8th—13th June: *The Yellow Wallpaper* by Charlotte Perkins Gilman,
    adapted by Sandy Nelson
15th—20th June: *Philoctetes* by Sophocles, adapted by Benny Young
22nd—27th June: *Moby Dick; or, The Whale* by Herman Melville, adapted
    by J.C. Marshall
29th June—4th July: *Andromaque* by Jean Racine, adapted by Frances Poet
6th—25th July: Summer Panto: *The Pie Eyed Piper of Hamilton* by
    Dave Anderson and Gary McNair

THE AUTUMN SEASON: 2015

31st Aug—5th Sep: *The Cameo* by Kieran Lynn and D C Jackson
7th—12th Sep: *The Quiet Land* by Malachy McKenna
14th—19th Sep: *To Hell and Back* by DM Collective
21st—26th Sep: *Kontomble (The Shaman and The Boy)* by Nalini Chetty
28th Sep—3rd Oct: *140 Million Miles* by Adam Peck

12th—17th Oct: *Descent* by Linda Duncan McLaughlin
19th—24th Oct: *A Word with Dr Johnson* by James Runchie
26th—31st Oct: *The Wakeful Chamber* by Rebecca Sharp, composed by Pippa Murphy
2nd—7th Nov: *After the Cuts* by Gary McNair
9th—14th Nov: *Happy Hour* by Anita Vettesse
16th—21st Nov: *John Gabriel Barclay* by John Carnegie
23rd—28th Nov: *The Course of True Love* by David Leddy
30th Nov—23rd Dec: Òran Mór Panto: *Ali Bawbag and the Four Tealeafs* by Dave Anderson and Gary McNair

THE SPRING SEASON: 2016

25th—30th Jan: *Causeway* by Victoria Bianchi
1st—6th Feb: *Frances & Ethel* by David Cosgrove
8th—13th Feb: *Face - Isobel* by Peter Arnott
15th—20th Feb: *Face - Morag* by Peter Arnott
22nd—27th Feb: *The Angel and The Manse* by George Docherty
29th Feb—5th Mar: *Mr. and Mrs. Laughton* by Michael-Alan Read
7th—12th Mar: *Some Other Stars* by Clare Duffy
14th—19th Mar: *Billy (The Days of Howling)* by Fabien Cloutier, translated by Nadine Desrochers
21st—26th Mar: *Prom* by Oliver Emanuel
28th Mar—2nd Apr: *Neither God Nor Angel* by Tim Barrow
4th—9th Apr: *Ringroad* by Anita Vettesse
11th—16th Apr: *There Is Someone Who Hates Us* by Michelle Ferreira, adapted by Lynda Radley
18th—23rd Apr: *Flo* by Martin McCardie
25th—30th Apr: *Selkie* by Kay Singh
2nd—7th May: *Second Hand* by Paul Charlton
9th—14th May: *The Love I Feel is Red* by Sabrina Mahfouz
16th—21st May: *Role Shift* by Lesley Hart
23rd—28th May: *Arsehammers/Bonfire Night* by Claire Dowie
30th May—4th June: *Del Gesu's Viola* by Hector MacMillan

MINI MUSICAL SEASON: 2016

6th—11th June: 400th play! *The Day I Found The Blues* by Dave Anderson
13th—18th June: *Mack The Knife* by Morag Fullarton
20th—25th June: *Frances & Ethel* by David Cosgrove
27th June—2nd July: *Vinyl Idol* by Debbie Hannan and Andy McGregor
4th—23rd July: Òran Mór Summer Panto: *Rumple Still-Skint* by Gary McNair and Dave Anderson

THE AUTUMN SEASON: 2016

29th Aug—3rd Sep: *The Real Mrs. Sinatra* by Clive King
5th—10th Sep: *Behind The Barrier* by Muriel Gray
12th—17th Sep: *The Letter* by Stuart Paterson
19th—24th Sep: *Miss Veitch's Roses* by Jane Livingstone
26th Sep—1st Oct: *Breaking The Ice* by Kieran Lynn
3rd—8th Oct: *Mischief* by Ellie Stewart
10th—15th Oct: *Walking on Walls* by Morna Pearson
17th—22nd Oct: *One Thinks of It All As A Dream* by Alan Bissett
24th—29th Oct: *Dr Johnson Goes To Scotland* by James Runcie
31st Oct—5th Nov: *Snout* by Kelly Jones
7th—12th Nov: *Hameldaeme* by Damian Mullen
14th—19th Nov: *On The Sidelines* by William McIlvanney
21st—26th Nov: *Moving Pictures* by Philip Differ
28th Nov—23rd Dec: Òran Mór Panto: *The Princess and The Pie*
  by Morag Fullarton

THE SPRING SEASON: 2017

6th—11th Feb: *Dusty Won't Play* by Annie Caulfield
13th—18th Feb: *Dirt Under The Carpet* by Rona Munro
20th—25th Feb: *An Tango Mu Dheireadh An Partaig/Last Tango
  in Partick* by Alison Lang
27th Feb—4th Mar: *World Domination* by Lesley Hart
6th—11th Mar: *The Beaches of St Valery* by Stuart Hepburn
13th—18th Mar: *Gap Years* by Gavin Smith
20th—25th Mar: *Jocky Wilson Said* by Jane Livingstone and
  Jonathan Cairney
27th Mar—1st Apr: *Ding-dong (A Bit of a Farce)* by Hilary Lyon
3rd—8th Apr: *Channeling Jabez* by Giles Croft
10th—15th Apr: *His Final Bow* by Peter Arnott
17th—22nd Apr: *Voices in Her Ear* by David Cosgrove
24th—29th Apr: *Safe Place* by Clara Glynn
1st—6th May: *Confessional* by David Weir
8th—13th May: *Beg Borrow Steal* by Anita Alexander Rae
  (The David MacLennan Award Winner)
15th—20th May: *But That Was Then* by Peter McDougall
22nd—27th May: *Small World* by Sean Hardie

MINI MUSICAL SEASON

29th May—3rd June: *I Love You, in Danish (Jeg Elsker Dig)* by Dave Anderson
5th—10th June: *Brigadoom* by Tony Cox
12th—17th June: *Wee Free! The Musical* by Hilary Brooks and Clive King

19th—24th June: ***Spuds*** by Andy McGregor
26th June—1st July: ***TOSCA: The Henchman's Tale***, music
    by Giacomo Puccini, script by Alexander Tarbet
3rd—22nd July: Òran Mór Summer Panto: ***PUNochhio*** by Gary McNair

THE AUTUMN SEASON: 2017

28th Aug—2nd Sep: ***The Empty Charcoal Box*** by Stuart Hepburn
4th—9th Sep: ***Late Sleeper*** by Simon Macallum
11th—16th Sep: ***The Witches of West Fife*** by Jane Livingstone
18th—23rd Sep: ***Disturbed*** by Ian Cowell
25th—30th Sep: ***Pleading*** by Rob Drummond
2nd—7th Oct: ***Love and Death in Govan and Hyndland*** by Ian Pattison
9th—14th Oct: ***Hysteria!*** by A J Taudevin
16th—21st Oct: ***From the Air*** by Anita Vettesse
23rd—28th Oct: ***#71*** by Karen Dunbar
30th Oct—4th Nov: ***The Burton Taylor Affair*** by Steven Elliot
6th—11th Nov: ***Meat Market*** by Chris Grady
13th—18th Nov: ***Kind Stranger*** by Matthew McVarish
20th—25th Nov: ***The Weir Sisters*** by Lynn Ferguson
27th Nov—30th Dec: Òran Mór Panto: ***Cinderella 2: I Married A***
    Numpty by Morag Fullarton

THE SPRING SEASON: 2018

12th—17th Feb: ***It's Behind You!*** by Alan McHugh
19th—24th Feb: ***Party Politics*** by Lorna Martin
26th Feb—3rd Mar: ***Aye, Elvis*** by Morna Young
5th—10th Mar: ***Rishta*** by Taqi Nazeer
12th—17th Mar: ***The Greatest*** by Alan Muir
19th—24th Mar: ***For The Love of Chekov (The Dating Game)***
    by A.S. Robertson
26th—31st Mar: ***McGonagall's Chronicles*** by Gary McNair
2nd—7th Apr: ***Rachel's Cousins*** by Ann Marie Di Mambro
9th—14th Apr: ***Margaret Saves Scotland*** by Val McDermid
16th—21st Apr: ***Eulogy*** by Rob Drummond
23rd—28th Apr: ***The Persians*** by Meghan Tyler
30th Apr—5th May: ***Where's Lulu*** by Danny McCahon
7th—12th May: ***Hot Water*** by Steven Dick
14th—19th May: ***Chic Murray: A Funny Place For a Window***
    by Stuart Hepburn
21st—26th May: ***The First Dance*** by Martin McCormick
28th May—2nd June: ***The Vampire Clinic*** by Peter McDougall

Ryan Fletcher and Mel Giedroyc in *A Midsummer's Night Dream* (2011).
Photo: Leslie Black.

David Anderson, Brian James O'Sullivan and Maureen Carr in *Chic Murray: A Funny Place for a Window* (2019).
Photo: Leslie Black.

MINI MUSICAL SEASON: 2018

4th—9th June: ***The Thinkery*** by Brian James O'Sullivan
11th—16th June: ***Melania*** by Hilary Brooks and Clive King
18th—23rd June: ***The Edge of The World: A Digital Detox Musical*** by Richard Ferguson
25th—30th June: ***Cranhill Carmen*** by Benny Young
2nd—21st June: Òran Mór Panto: ***Pure Freezin'*** by Andy McGregor

THE AUTUMN SEASON: 2018

27th Aug—1st Sep: ***Losing The Rag*** by Alan Muir
3rd—8th Sep: ***Outside In*** by Chris Grady
10th—15th Sep: ***Tap Dancing with Jean-Paul Sarte*** by James Runcie
17th—22nd Sep: ***The Lottery Ticket*** by Donna Franceschild
24th—29th Sep: ***Tipping The Hat*** by John Bett
1st—6th Oct: ***It Wisnae Me*** by Alan Bissett
8th—13th Oct: ***The Last Picture Show*** by Morag Fullarton
15th—20th Oct: ***A Change In Management*** by Dave Gerow
22nd—27th Oct: ***King Turd*** by Louise Welsh
29th Oct—3rd Nov: ***The Biscuit*** by Donald Mcleary
5th—10th Nov: ***We Interrupt This Programme*** by DM Collective
12th—17th Nov: ***Oscar Slater - The Trial That Shamed A City*** by Stuart Hepburn
19th—24th Nov: ***Turns of The Tide*** by Lynn Ferguson
26th Nov—29th Dec: Òran Mór Panto: ***The Lying Bitch and The Wardrobe*** by Morag Fullarton

THE SPRING SEASON: 2019

11th—16th Feb: ***Tartuffe*** by Moliére, adapted by Liz Lochhead
18th—23rd Feb: ***A Respectable Widow Takes To Vulgarity*** by Douglas Maxwell
25th Feb—2nd Mar: ***Spuds*** by Andy McGregor
4th—9th Mar: ***Coming Clean*** by Alma Cullen
11th—16th Mar: ***Ringroad*** by Anita Vettesse
18th—23rd Mar: ***The Scurvy Ridden Whale Men*** by Steven Dick
25th—30th Mar: ***Chic Murray: A Funny Place For A Window*** by Stuart Hepburn
1st—6th Apr: ***Aye, Elvis*** by Morna Young
8th—13th Apr: ***Lion Lion*** by Sue Glover
15th—20th Apr: ***The Mack*** by Rob Drummond
22nd—27th Apr: 500th Play: ***Casablanca*** by Morag Fullarton
29th Apr—4th May: ***The Origins of Ivor Punch*** by Colin MacIntyre
6th—11th May: ***Toy Plastic Chicken*** by Uma Nada-Rajah

13th—18th May: ***Jocky Wilson Said*** by Jane Livingstone & Jonathan Cairney
20th—25th May: ***Cool Dads*** by Simon Macallum
27th May—1st June: ***Tír Na NÓg*** by Dave Anderson
3rd—8th June: ***What The Animals Say*** by David Ireland
10th—15th June: ***Ida Tamson*** by Denise Mina
17th—22nd June: ***Dusty Won't Play*** by Annie Caulfield
24th—29th June: ***Last Ferry To Dunoon*** by Peter McDougall
2nd—20th July: Òran Mór Summer Panto: ***Dracula Re-Vamped*** by John and James Kielty

THE AUTUMN SEASON: 2019

26th—31st Aug: ***Crocodile Rock*** by Andy McGregor
2nd—7th Sep: ***From Paisley to Paolo*** by Martin McCardie
9th—14th Sep: ***Number One Fan*** by Kim Millar
16th—21st Sep: ***Mack The Knife*** by Morag Fullarton
23rd—28th Sep: ***The Signalman*** by Peter Arnott
30th Sep—5th Oct: ***Fly Me to the Moon*** by Marie Jones
7th—12th Oct: ***The Sweetest Growl*** by Claire Nicol
14th—19th Oct: ***Divided*** by Ian Pattison
21st—26th Oct: ***A Walk in the Park*** by Dave Anderson
28th Oct—2nd Nov: ***Marco Pantani: The Pirate*** by Stuart Hepburn
4th—9th Nov: ***Good With People*** by David Harrower
11th—16th Nov: ***Do Not Press This Button*** by Alan Bissett
18th—23rd Nov: ***Cranhill Carmen*** by Benny Young
25th Nov—28th Dec: Òran Mór Panto: ***Dixie Whittington: The Hamecoming*** by Morag Fullarton

THE SPRING SEASON: 2020
(interrupted due to COVID-19)

10th—15th Feb: ***Camino*** by Sean Hardie
17th—22nd Feb: ***When The Penny Drops*** by Catriona Duggan
24th—29th Feb: ***Lessons in Love*** by Kate Donnelly & Clare Hemphill
2nd—7th Mar: ***Daniel*** by Isabel Wright
9th—14th Mar: ***Paring Off*** by Alma Cullen
16th—17th Mar: ***The Beaches of St. Valery*** by Stuart Hepburn

THE AUTUMN SEASON: 2021

8th—11th Sep: ***Celestial Body*** by Morna Pearson
13th—18th Sep: ***Rose*** by Lorna Martin
20th—25th Sep: ***Joke*** by Johnny McKnight
27th Sep—2nd Oct: ***A New Life*** by Andy McGregor
4th—9th Oct: ***The Tale of Typhoid Mary*** by Marty Ross
11th—16th Oct: ***My Name is Sarah, And...*** by Brian James O'Sullivan

18th—23rd Oct: *Exquisite Corpse* by Conor O'Loughlin
25th—30th Oct: *The Silver Superheroes* by Morna Young
2nd—6th Nov: *My Name is Sarah, And...* by Brian James O'Sullivan
  (replacing *Opening Time* by Dave Anderson due to cast illness)
8th—13th Nov: *The Storm* by Owen Whitelaw
15th—20th Nov: *Mary & Ada Set The World To Rights* by Jane Livingstone
30th Nov—31st Dec: Òran Mór Panto: *Cinderella 2: I Married A Numpty* by Morag Fullarton

THE SPRING SEASON: 2022

14th—19th Feb: *Oscar* by Brian James O'Sullivan
21st—26th Feb: *The Ticket Meister* by Peter McDougall
28th Feb—5th Mar: *Ten Things to do Before You Die* by Dani Heron
7th—12th Mar: *I'm Dissolving My Love in A Bath of Acid* by D C Jackson
14th—19th Mar: *Milkshake* by Rob Drummond
21st—26th Mar: *Man's Best Friend* by Douglas Maxwell
28th Mar—2nd Apr: *Daniel Getting Married* by JD Stewart
4th—9th Apr: *My Doric Diary* by AyeTunes!
11th—16th Apr: *Mooning* by Erin McGee
18th—23rd Apr: *Opening Time* by Dave Anderson
25th—30th Apr: *Mr Moonlight* by Kim Millar
2nd—7th May: *Absolute Bowlocks!* by Graeme Rooney
9th—14th May: *Hello in There* by Cathy Forde
16th—21st May: *Not Now* by David Ireland
23rd—28th May: *Infernal Serpent* by David Gerow
30th May—4th June: *Alright Sunshine* by Isla Cowan
6th—11th June: *The Body Electrician* by Patricia Panther
13th—18th June: *Inheritance* by Belle Jones
20th—25th June: *The Words* by Maryam Hamidi
27th June—2nd July: *Scots* by Noisemaker
5th—23rd July: Òran Mór Summer Panto: *Goldilocks Goes to Greece* by Andy McGregor

THE AUTUMN SEASON: 2022

5th—10th Sep: *Sally* by James Ley
12th—17th Sep: *Impromptu at Òran Mór* by Morna Pearson
19th—24th Sep: *Break My Windows* by Dave Gerow
26th Sep—1st Oct: *He Who Opens The Door* by Neda Nezhdana, translated by John Farndon with Anatole Bilenko
3rd—8th Oct: *Made in China* by Alice Clark
10th—15th Oct: *The Peace Piece: Live From Òran Mór!* by Joe Douglas and Faisal Abualheyja
17th—22nd Oct: *The Golden Rage* by Johnny McKnight

24th—29th Oct: *Alföld* by Joe McCann
31st Oct—5th Nov: *Jinnistan* by Taqi Nazeer
7th—12th Nov: *The Prognostications of Mikey Noyce* by Frances Poet
14th—19th Nov: *BABS* by Morna Young
21st—26th Nov: *Kiki* by Hilary Brooks & Clive King
29th Nov—31st Dec: Òran Mór Panto: *Rab Hood And The Sheriff of Shettleston* by Morag Fullarton

THE SPRING SEASON: 2023

20th—25th Feb: *Until It's Gone* by Alison Carr
27th Feb—4th Mar: *Burning Bright* by Áine King
   (winner of David MacLennan award)
6th—11th Mar: *The Worm Who Turned* by Kim Millar
13th—18th Mar: *Write-off* by Aodhan Gallagher
20th—25th Mar: *Variant* by Peter Arnott
27th Mar—1st Apr: *The Spark* by Kathy McKean
3rd—8th Apr: *Scots* by Noisemaker
10th—15th Apr: *Storytelling* by Oliver Emanuel
17th—22nd Apr: *Welcome to Bannockburn* by Lesley Hart
24th—29th Apr: *Faye's Red Lines* by Ian Pattison
1st—6th May: *Davina & Goliath* by Dave Anderson & David Baillie
8th—13th May: *Quietus* by Matthew McVarish
15th—20th May: *Leopards Ate My Face* by Grant O'Rourke
22nd—27th May: *The Merry Wives of Wyndford* by Linda McLaughlin
29th May—3rd June: *The Devil Drinks Cava* by JD Stewart
5th—10th June: *Meet Me at the Knob* by Johnny McKnight
12th—17th June: *Bloodbank* by Meghan Tyler
19th—24th June: *The Great Replacement* by Uma Nada-Rajah
26th June—1st July: *Keepin' the Heid* by Rachel Flynn
5th—23rd July: Òran Mór Summer Panto: *Jack and the Bean Pie* by Andy McGregor

THE AUTUMN SEASON: 2023

4th—9th Sep: *Forever Home* by Pauline Lockhart and Alan Penman
11th—16th Sep: *Ship Rats* by Alice Clark
18th—23rd Sep: *Coast* by Annie George
25th—30th Sep: *The Sheriff of Kalamaki* by Douglas Maxwell
2nd—7th Oct: *Stay* by Isaac Savage and Jonathan O'Neill
9th—14th Oct: *Meetings with the Monk* by Brian James O'Sullivan
16th—21st Oct: *Disfunction* by Kate Bowen
23rd—28th Oct: *An Act of Union* by Andy McGregor
30th Oct—4th Nov: *Playthrough* by Kenny Boyle
6th—11th Nov: *Castle Fallon* by Peter Stewart

Martin Donaghy and Francesca Hess in *Storytelling* (2023). Photo: Tommy Ga-Ken Wan.

Saint Diane Carroll. Photo: Daniel McAvoy.

13th—18th Nov: *Fleg* by Meghan Tyler
20th—25th Nov: *The Guns of Johnny Diablo* by Philip Differ
28th Nov—6th Jan: Òran Mór Panto: *Snow White and the Seven Maws* by Johnny McKnight

THE SPRING SEASON: 2024

19th—24th Feb: *JACK* by Liam Moffat
26th Feb—2nd Mar: *Bread and Breakfast* by Kirsty Halliday
4th—9th Mar: *Starving* by Imogen Stirling
11th—16th Mar: *Pushin' Thirty* by Taylor Dyson and Calum Kelly
18th—23rd Mar: *Hotdog* by Ellen Ritchie
25th—30th Mar: *The Scaff* by Stephen Christopher and Graeme Smith
1st—6th Apr: *Tamám Shud* by Thomas Jancis
8th—13th Apr: *Ness* by Hannah McGregor
15th—20th Apr: *Who Pays the Piper* by Jen McGregor
22nd—27th Apr: *Bridezilla and the Orchard of Sin* by Maired A. Martin
30th Apr—5th May: *Lewis Capaldi Goes Tropical* by Raymond Wilson
7th—12th May: *Looking for the One* by Sylvia Dow
14th—19th May: *Roost* by Laurie Motherwell
21st—26th May: *Dungeons, Dragons and the Quest for Dick* by Laila Noble
27th May—1st June: *The Way, the Truth and the Life* by Mike O'Donnell
3rd—8th June: *The Funeral Club* by Éimi Quinn
10th—15th June: *Medea on the Mic* by Nazli Khatambakhsh
17th—22nd June: *Party of the Century* by Ross MacKay
25th June—20th July: Òran Mór Summer Panto: *Mumbelina* by Johnny McKnight

THE AUTUMN SEASON: 2024

2nd—7th Sept: *Poker Alice* by Greg Hemphill
9th—14th Sept: *The Last Cabaret on Earth* by Brian James O'Sullivan
16th—21st Sept: *The Wolves at the Door* by Jack Hunter
23rd—28th Sept: *Armour: A Herstory of the Scottish Bard* by Shonagh Murray
30th Sept—5th Oct: *Anna/Anastasia* by Jonny Donohoe
7th—12th Oct: *Lost Girls/At Bus Stops* by Róisín Sheridan-Bryson
14th—19th Oct: *Detained* by Michelle Chantelle Hopewell
21st—26th Oct: *Cassie and the Space Cowboy* by Paul F. Matthews
28th Oct—2nd Nov: *Ghost Off!* by James Peake
4th—9th Nov: *Blast Off, Starburst* by Catriona MacLeod
11th—16th Nov: *Miracle on Deanston Drive* by Katharine Williams
18th—23rd Nov: *Jellyfish* by Katy Nixon

Dave Anderson in *A Walk in the Park* (2019). Photo: Leslie Black.

David MacLennan. Photo: Julie Bull.

A Play,
A Pie and
A Pint

Volume Two
20th Anniversary Edition

Lorna Martin

Rose

Public Choice

Rose was selected by our audience, who nominated their favourite plays from across the years and then voted on a shortlist.

Lorna is an award-winning scriptwriter and playwright. She co-created (with Sharon Horgan) and wrote the critically acclaimed comedy drama series ***Women on the Verge*** for UKTV and RTE. Her first stage play, ***Party Politics***, was performed as part of A Play, A Pie and A Pint's 2018 season.

Lorna is also an award-winning journalist. She worked at The Herald and was formerly Scotland Editor of The Observer. She travelled across the world in search of good stories and won an Amnesty International Media Award for human rights journalism.

Her interests as a writer span comedy and drama, and her journalistic instincts draw her to true stories. She is writing a feature film based on Rose Reilly's incredible life.

Rose was first performed in September 2021 at Òran Mór.

CHARACTERS

ROSE REILLY
PIERRE
EDNA
SFA OFFICIAL
MALE JOURNALIST
MANAGER
BARBER
ROSE'S MUM
SCOUT
JOHN
BRIDGET
ELSIE
RECEPTIONIST
STAN
IAN RUSH
COMMITTEE MEMBER
SIBLINGS AND KIDS

NOTE ON TEXT

Pauses, beats and moments are indicated by spaces between lines.

The play is set in a football changing room with a couple of benches and some football jerseys hanging up.

It is a monologue for a female who can play the main character of ROSE REILLY as well as the other small parts.

ONE

Play song 'Rose' by Lynnie Carson.

Muffled and indecipherable snippets of people talking.

ROSE enters.

ROSE: It's mad through there. Press and Scottish Football Association all over us like a bloody rash.

We're getting presented, here at Hampden, with our Scotland caps.

Me and four of my former teammates are finally getting a wee nod from the SFA. For a match we played against England 47 year ago.

Forty... seven... years.

They must've been awfully busy... The men... At the SFA.

Don't get me wrong. I'm honoured and I'm proud. But at the same time, I can't stop thinking about my sidekick. My wee mucker, Edna Neillis.

Edna was something else. Gifted with natural talent. Not only did she play like Celtic's Jimmy Johnstone, she was a dead ringer for him as well. Skinny wee legs and wild red hair.

We called her Jinky. Which she hated. Cos she was Rangers daft.

Not long after the 1972 Scotland/England game—the one we're finally getting capped for—me and Edna went to play for the French side, Reims.

We won the league and the owner, Pierre, invited the two of us up to his big executive suite to celebrate. That sounds a bit dodgy. But it was nothing like that. He was a true gentleman. And a great champion of the women's game.

Me and Edna are sitting on these big sofas and Pierre pops open a bottle of champagne... probably the most expensive in France.

He fills our glasses and chats away.

I'm nodding along even though I haven't a clue what he's on about.

PIERRE: Quel jeu incroyable. Tu as joué fabuleux. Je ne comprends pas l'écossais. Ils sont fous.

ROSE: Edna goes over to him.

EDNA: Excuse moi, Pierre. Have you not got any lager? Cos this champagne's pure mingin.

(A beat.)

ROSE: He kept looking at Edna after that. Like, what the hell's this? Like he'd never met anybody like her.

I'd never met anybody like her.

47 years.

Too late for Edna.

And too late for my mum and dad... to see that Scotland is actually proud of us.

Out there today, the press and SFA are calling us pioneers and trailblazers.

But we didn't want to be pioneers and trailblazers. We just wanted to play football.

****

It's November 1972. And it's baltic. We're at Ravenscraig Park in Greenock for the Scotland / England match. It's being played here cos the SFA wouldn't let us use an official pitch. Or official changing rooms. Or referees. They probably wouldn't even let us use one of their balls.

It's no surprise really.

The previous year, 1971, UEFA asked all its 32 member countries to lift the ban on women's football, which had been introduced after the first world war.

Nearly every nation agreed: England, Ireland. Even Russia and Albania.

Only one country opted to keep the ban.

Scotland.

Scotland.

Football-daft Scotland is the only country in UEFA to keep the ban on women's football.

SFA OFFICIAL: It's simply not a game for ladies. And we're not saying that to stop the ladies having fun. On the contrary. We're saying it to protect them. It's for their own good.

(A beat.)

ROSE: Lucky us, eh? Having the men... at the SFA... looking out for us like that.

The ban doesn't stop us playing. It just makes everything much more difficult.

Unlike the England squad, who're well-funded and supported, we've nothing. No backing. No money. No transport. No kit.

We have to raise money for strips. Sew the numbers and badges on ourselves. Borrow shorts. Stick the Sunday Post down our socks as shin pads.

On the day of the match, we flag down a removals lorry and bribe the driver to take us to Greenock. Sixteen of us sit on sofas, beds, under lampshades. The Scotland international squad travelling in style.

We're the underdogs. The minnows. But we're convinced we're gonna hammer them.

As we run onto the frozen pitch, in our home-made jerseys, we couldn't be any prouder.

Twenty minutes in, Edna crosses the ball and Mary Carr goes for a low-flying header.

GOAL!!

One nothing to Scotland. Ya beauty!

Ten minutes later, I take a corner.

Flies right to the back of the net.

(A pause... she eyeballs the audience.)

Did you not hear that? I scored from a corner! Against England!

Yussss! It doesn't get any better!

We go wild.

Two-nothing up.

Get it right up you!!!!

Just before half-time they pull one back. The dirty bastards.

Talking of dirty bastards...

The press had a slightly different attitude towards us back then.

Now these aren't their exact words but they're not far off...

MALE JOURNALIST: They're not as good as the men and never will be. It's a bit like men knitting. Oh, now young Rose Reilly's got the ball. What a magnificent physique. I wonder if she's got a boyfriend. Oh, was that a goal I missed?

ROSE: Naw, they certainly weren't calling us pioneers and trailblazers.

In the second half, everything changes. One player takes command of the game. She holds the England midfield together and sets up their equaliser.

It's Paddy McGroarty. She's as Scottish as Irn Bru.

She'd been sent—by her mother—to a convent in Ireland... to stop her playing football!

She obviously escaped. Then defected to England. Who could blame her?

In the dying minutes, she sets up another goal. They beat us 3-2.

Oh, Paddy McGroarty, if only you'd been playing for Scotland. We'd have annihilated them.

Everybody kept saying we should feel proud of ourselves; that we did well under the circumstances.

But I didn't want to 'do well under the circumstances'. I wanted to win. I wanted to hammer them.

I wasn't proud. I was heart-broken.

I wanted to be able to burst into my house, tell my mum and dad that we beat England. That *I* beat England.

(Pause.)

I suppose I wanted to make them... proud.

(A moment. ROSE is emotional but fighting it. A long beat. Then, she snaps out of it.)

****

Thing is, all I've ever wanted to do is play football.

When I'm three I get a doll for Christmas.

I swap it for a ball.

It goes everywhere with me.

When I go messages for my mum, I do keepy-uppies all the way.

(She does two.)

That's all you're getting.

We live next door to a creamery factory. It's where I hone my skills. Left foot. Right foot. Head it on to the roof. Left foot. Right foot. Head it on to the roof. Repeat. For hours. And hours. And hours. Making a complete racket.

Mr Mair, the manager, comes out every so often.

MANAGER: For christsake Rose Reilly. Would you get to hell with that bloody ball?

ROSE: I even sleep with it. Cos I'm scared my mum or one of my brothers will take it off me.

At primary school, boys and girls have separate playgrounds. Every day, I ignore their daft rules and run for a game of football with the boys.

And every day, I get the belt.

The first time, I can't help it. I cry. But I hear some wee shit laughing. I turn and stare him out.

He's laughing at me for crying.

From that day on, I don't flinch. Even though it's agony. I just eyeball Mr McGurk or whoever's turn it is that day.

(ROSE does it now. Hands out, as if she's getting the belt, staring straight ahead, or eyeballing an audience member. Only the very slightest imperceptible grimace.)

(As if a mantra) To show emotion is to show weakness.

I learn that at five.

Five.

(A beat.)

And I've never ever forgotten it.

Physical punishment doesn't stop me.

I keep playing. Everywhere and anywhere. And at seven, my talents are finally spotted.

John Roy who runs Stewarton Boys' Club asks if I'd like to play with them.

I'm at the barbers for a short, back and sides before you can say: is the Pope a Catholic.

BARBER: Does your mammy know you're here?

(A beat.)

YOUNG ROSE: Aye. Totally. It's her idea. She'll drop the money in later.

ROSE: ROSE becomes ROSS.
I burst into the house with my new hair-do. My mum drags me right out again. Straight back to the barbers.

BARBER: Hello, Bridget!

ROSE'S MUM: What. In the name of God. Have you done. To. My. Daughter's. Hair?

ROSE: My mum's raging. The barber's shaking. And all I'm thinking is... I'm gonna be playing for Stewarton Boys' Club. Ya beauty!!!

(A brief pause.)

One game, I play a blinder. Score eight goals. A Celtic scout approaches John. Says he wants to sign the wee number seven.

SCOUT: I want to sign that wee number seven.

JOHN: Ah sorry it's actually a wee lassie.

SCOUT: No. Him there. The one with the dodgy hair cut who scored all the goals.

JOHN: Aye. Still a wee lassie. I know it doesn't look like a wee lassie. And it certainly doesn't play like a wee lassie. But it honestly is a wee lassie. (*Shouts*) Hoi Ross. Come here.

(A beat.)

YOUNG ROSE: Awright, mister?

(He looks her up and down. Then a bit closer. Up and down again.)

SCOUT: Jesus Christ, you're right. It is a wee lassie.

JOHN: I know. It's bloody heart-breaking.

ROSE: Aye. It is bloody heart-breaking. For me! That's my Celtic career over before it's even started.
But what am I meant to do? Start greeting?

Instead, I just keep on going. Keep trying to better myself.

I even get a book from the library about one of the greatest players ever, Stanley Matthews. It says he has a steak every night for his dinner. So, I'm straight downstairs

YOUNG ROSE: Mammy, I need a steak every night for my dinner.

BRIDGET: You'll eat mince and tatties or whatever's put down to you!

YOUNG ROSE: But Stanley Matthews has a steak every night!

ROSE'S MUM: Oh, is that right? Well, you're not Stanley Matthews, are you? You're Rose Reilly. So here's your options:
1. You can ask Stanley to buy you a steak every night.
2. You can eat whatever's put down to you. And that's what you'll choose.
Or 3. You can starve?

ROSE: I think it's borderline neglect!

(A beat.)

The book also says Stanley Matthews rises at the crack of dawn, flings open all the windows and inhales the fresh morning air.

So next morning, I'm up at five. Fling open the windows. Inhale the fresh morning air.

(Inhales and exhales deeply.)

There's six of us in the room.

My twin, Mary, and my older brothers, Jack, Tom and Gerard, and my sister, Ebeth. Another set of twins, Anne and Bridget, are in another room.

I'm filling my lungs... oblivious to everything. When I hear:

SIBLINGS: ROSE. ROSE! What are you playing at?! Mammy. She's trying to freeze us all to death.

ROSE'S MUM: ROSE REILLY!!!!

ROSE: *(Tongue in cheek)* I can't understand why my whole family's so against me playing football.

But it doesn't stop me.

At nine, I join the local women's football team Stewarton Thistle. Formed by local woman Elsie Cook, her mum Betty and her aunties. The rest of the players are from Stewarton's many wool factories.

I'd asked Elsie when I was seven if I could join the team. I'd just had my short back and sides. She looked at me.

ELSIE: It's a lassies' team. For, you know, lassies!

ROSE: I told her I was a lassie, I was just pretending to be a boy so I could play. She told me to come back in two years.

So, I counted down the days.

Two years and 30 seconds later, I'm in my first changing room. I was never allowed in with the boys.

All the other players are much older than me and they're all wearing these big Playtex bras. Which makes me think that they're all mammies!

Over the next few years, a group of hardcore Scottish girls and women defy the ban and form teams like the Fife Dynamites, Aberdeen Primadonnas and the Cambuslang Hooverettes. Guess where they worked?

(A beat.)

And travelled the length and breadth of the country to play the beautiful game.

At one charity tournament at Butlins I notice this wee lassie with wild ginger hair. She struts onto the pitch, singing:

EDNA: Wake up Maggie, I think I've got something to say to you.

ROSE: No idea why she's singing that. But she is.

It's Edna Neillis.

Everybody watches her. And she hasn't even kicked a ball yet.

When she does (phew), poetry in motion. She's got it all: incredible ball control, a natural feel for the game as if she plays with her brain as well as her legs.

She's brilliant. And she knows it. It's like the word 'gallus' was made up just for her.

The two of us end up in the same team, West Thorne. And become good pals.

I go to all the Rangers matches with her, cos I love the game so much. Edna says she'll come to Celtic Park with me. But every time... she comes down with a mystery bug... that only ever lasts 90 minutes.

I never did pull her up for that.

When Edna was a teenager the Celtic manager, Jock Stein, saw her play and said to her, 'if you were a boy I'd sign you right away'. You know what she said?

EDNA: Nae offence Jock but naw you wouldnae. Cos I wouldnae be seen deid in a green and white jersey!

****

ROSE: When I'm not playing football. I'm out running. And, at 15, I'm invited to a training camp for the 1970 Commonwealth Games.

It's mostly private school girls. And I'm there in my wee black sannies held together with rubber bands.

We're just about to do the 400m run when one of the girls takes me aside:

VERY POSH KID: I don't know if you heard the coach earlier. But he said you should go much slower than you feel you want to at the start. It really helps you save your energy for the final 100.

TEENAGE ROSE. Oh. OK. No, I didn't hear that. Thanks very much.

ROSE: My new best pal.

The starting pistol goes.

I fight my instinct to bolt. And instead jog off, conserving my energy. The others belt it.

I realise what she's done. The sneaky wee bitch.

(Running) Your money might be able to buy you good results and a fancy PE kit. But here's what you can never buy: Passion. Grit. Raw fucking talent.

I beat them all!

And I'm picked to represent Scotland. In the Commonwealth Games.

My mum and dad are thrilled.

So am I. Until the coach says I need to quit football—cos I'll get 'fooballer thighs'—he said I had to focus 100% on athletics.

For the first time in my life. I do as I'm told. And stop playing football.

I last a week.

I can't do it. Can't live without it. That's when it really hits me... football is everything to me. It's who I am. Take it away from me... you might as well kill me.

Before I get a chance to tell my mum I'm not doing athletics and the Commonwealth Games, we get called up to the school.

The head-teacher Mr Matthews says he has no option but to expel me. It's not that I'm a bad kid. Just that other pupils had complained because I was allowed to skip classes to do gym.

My mum digests this bombshell.

BRIDGET: Well, Mister Matthews... luckily Rose has a brilliant career lined up. She's just been selected to represent Scotland, at the Commonwealth Games. So, in a way, it's the school's loss. Rose can focus all her energy into her athletics career. Can't you Rose?

(A beat.)

Can't you? ROSE?

ROSE: She glares at me. When I tell her there isn't going to be any athletics career, because I'd quit to focus on football, she's furious.

She's straight round to Elsie's mum. She needed somebody to blame.

(Bridget raps the door...)

BRIDGET: My daughter won't be playing football anymore. She has a very good career lined up. In athletics. So she won't be kicking another ball. Ever. Is that clear? To everybody? ROSE REILLY WILL NOT BE KICKING ANOTHER FOOTBALL. EVER.

(A beat.)

And that's the final word on the matter!

ROSE: The final word on the matter. Aye right, mum.

*****

ROSE: At 17, there's nothing on the horizon. No prospects. No future. No job. I did have one—briefly—in a carpet factory. But I took an extended lunch-break... to play football.

It was with Johnny Walker's, the team from the whisky factory. They're a really, really good team.

I explained it to the manager as if they were Real Madrid. He wasn't impressed. Said I clearly wasn't committed... to the carpet industry.

He was probably right. Sacked after a fortnight.

One day not long after that, I'm reading the back page of my dad's Daily Record. I see the name Stan Shivas and I have a genius idea.

YOUNG ROSE: Edna, if Scotland doesn't want us. To hell with them. Let's go to Europe. France or Italy. Be professionals.

(A beat.)

EDNA: Hang on a minute. France or Italy? They're foreign countries, Rose. They speak a totally different language.

YOUNG ROSE: Aye. I know. The language of fitba'

ROSE: Next thing, I'm at the Daily Record in Glasgow.

RECEPTIONIST: Can I help you?

YOUNG ROSE: I'm here to see Stan Shivas.

RECEPTIONIST: You mean Stan Shivas?

YOUNG ROSE: Aye, that's what I said.

RECEPTIONIST: Do you have an appointment?

YOUNG ROSE: No. I mean aye. I mean yes.

ROSE: Eventually, I'm escorted through to this huge noisy newsroom. It's nearly all men. They're all smoking, shouting, bashing away at typewriters.

Stan Shivas is in a long trench coat. Puffing away on a cigar.

STAN: Fit can I de for you?

YOUNG ROSE: Me and my pal want to go to Europe to be professional footballers.

STAN: And I want to marry Sophia Loren and work at the Washington Post.

ROSE: To his credit, he doesn't tell me to get lost. He hears me out. I leave a scrapbook of cuttings and Elsie's mum's phone number. We never had a phone. He says he'll see what he can do.

A few weeks later, me and Edna are round at Elsie's. Her mum gets a phone call. It's Stan Shivas at the Record!

ELSIE'S MUM: *(mouths)* It's Stan Shivas! At the Record!

(ELSIE'S MUM shoos them away, gestures 'sshhhh!')

Mmhmm... mmhmm... okay... right... okay... (*as if on phone*)
hold on a minute, Mister Shivas.

He's got you a trial! At Stade de Reims! In (*to them*) France!

ROSE: Edna, cocky as ever, says:

EDNA: Tell him we don't dae trials.

ROSE: She changed her mind as soon as she heard the Record were going to fly us to Paris.

At the match, we play as if our life depends on it. We run riot. The two of us against the rest of the world.

(A beat.)

We're signed at half-time.

Back then, I never gave it a second thought. I was 17. I just thought, hmm, this is how life goes. But when I think about it now... signed at half time!? Not bad eh. Not bad at all.

That night we fly back home to pack.

Edna quits her job and heads straight to "What Every Woman Wants" for her Parisienne wardrobe. And her pals arrange a farewell party for us.

('Bye Bye Baby' by the Bay City Rollers plays)

*****

ROSE: Edna turns up at the airport like one of the Bay City Rollers: huge green flares, bright orange top, platforms. And her curly red hair.

I turn up in my tracksuit with my wee suitcase and my mum and dad.

It doesn't enter my head what might be going through theirs.

My mum had always been so against me playing football. As passionately opposed to it, as I was in love with it.

I think it was fear. A lassie playing football in the 70s was a freak, a weirdo, a lezzie. 'Normal' girls got married to the boy next door and had weans. They didn't get on a plane and go to Europe to play football.

At the airport my little cardboard suitcase bursts open. My dad takes off his belt and braces and ties them round the case. Making it the most secure suitcase on the plane. As if it contained the European Cup! Instead of a tracksuit and a pair of knickers.

Maybe it was my dad's way of saying: 'I love you and I'm proud of you'.

It was so different back then. Nobody told their kids they loved them 100 times a day. Or even once a day. They certainly didn't say they were proud of them.

And we're off. Two gallus Scottish teenagers. Following our dream.

Bye Stewarton. Bye Scotland. Cheerio SFA (*gives them the 'v' sign*)

Bonjour Paris!

*****

ROSE: In the end, we don't stay long at Reims. Just six months. Because... wait till you hear this: Scouts from AC Milan saw us play and bought us. Reims couldn't afford to keep us.

Edna says:

EDNA: Can you put that in writing and send it recorded delivery to the SFA?

ROSE: We don't even tell our families we're moving to another country.

We just do it.

Don't think. Just do. That's always been my motto.

At 18, 1973, Rose becomes... Rosa.

(*Italian music plays...*)

*****

It's love at first sight. I love everything about Milan—the smell, the food, the people. Even their bin men look like models.

We go to fancy restaurants. Order steaks—finally! And spaghetti.

The first time it comes we're like: what the hell's this. We thought spaghetti was bright orange hoops, out a tin.

(*A beat.*)

On our first night, I take a walk inside the San Siro stadium. Home of AC Milan!

It's enormous. Holds 80,000 fans. Dressing rooms like a 5-star hotel.

I step onto the pitch.

Completely alone.

I take in everything.

Walk to each corner. I'm going to score from here.

I walk to the 18-yard box. And I'm going to score here!

You can do this Rose Reilly.

It's massive. Holds 80,000 fans.

You can do this, Rose Reilly... You can do this.

After all... it's just two goals and a ball.

Just like back home.

But at the same time... nothing like back home.

(A silent moment... as if ROSE is mulling over it all. Almost getting emotional but then composes herself again.)

In our first season we win the Serie A title and the Italian Cup. And we're not just there to make up the numbers.

In the final league match against Lazio, which we needed to win, I score a hat-trick in a 3-0 victory.

Not a game for ladies!

(A beat.)

*****

Everything's going brilliantly in Milan. Until... about three months in...

Edna says she's home-sick. She misses Scotland. Her mum. Her family.

I do too, but... maybe not as much. Maybe I'm tougher.

Don't think. Just do.

Maybe I'm more like my mum than I ever realised.

I tell Edna: 'There's nothing for us in Scotland. This is the opportunity of a lifetime.'

But it's no use. Her mind's made up. She leaves Milan for Ruchazie, one of the roughest parts of Glasgow.

It'd been the two of us against the world.

I'm a bit lost without my partner in crime, my sidekick. And the next year is one of the hardest of my life.

It's like that Welsh striker, Ian Rush, said, when he moved from Liverpool to Juventus:

IAN RUSH: It's really difficult... in Italy... it's like living in a foreign country.

ROSE: And that was with a £3.2 million transfer fee.

It is hard.

But what am I meant to do? Greet? What's that ever achieved?

Instead, I put my head down and I work... obsessively hard. The rest of the squad train in the evening, to avoid the mid-day heat. I do extra sessions—in the blistering afternoon sun. Often to the point of making myself sick.

The thing is, to do something like this, you have to be a bit weird. It's not a normal life. Whatever that is. It's certainly not an easy life. But then, is it ever, if you're trying to achieve your dream?

At the age of 18, I live alone in a hotel for a year. I talk to myself in the mirror.

ROSE: Awright Rose? How are you doing? Not bad, thanks. How are you? Aye good, thanks. How was training today? It was hard. Pushed myself to the limit. What did you have for your dinner? Steak! Are you missing home? Shut up. You missing Edna? Shut up.

Don't think. Just do!
Emotion is weakness.

Don't think. Just do.
Emotion is weakness.

I buy La Gazetto dello Sport every day.

At first, I don't understand much, the odd word: AC Milan. Juventus. Lazio.

So, I buy a dictionary. I learn three words a day. After a while. And a bit of perseverance... just saying, Ian Rush

ROSE: Uno... Due... Tre...

becomes

ROSE: Che bella giornata e non riesco a credere di poter parlare fluentemente italiano mi fai un cafe per favore, come stai oggi? Ciao bella.

*****

Meanwhile, back home in sunny Scotland...

The SFA finds itself under pressure—both from UEFA and politicians who want to introduce an equality law—to lift their ban on women's football. So eventually they do. In 1974. Only three years after everyone else!

I'm still playing in Italy when they call Edna and Elsie to a meeting. They assume it's to apologise. Maybe ask for their input on how they can support, nurture the girls' game.

They sit opposite about half a dozen committee members.

COMMITTEE MEMBER: The ruling body of the Scottish Football Association has carefully considered a report on your recent conduct, taking into account any and all mitigating circumstances. We have now voted on the most appropriate course of action. It is the decision of the SFA that you, Elsie Cook, Edna Neillis and Rose Reilly... are all hereby sine died.

ROSE: Banned from the Scottish game. For life.

For talking to the press. And bringing the game into disrepute.

(A very long beat. ROSE just stares at the audience for a long time.)

Banned for life? For bringing the game into disrepute.

Elsie Cook—who, with her mother, did so much to organise girls' and women's football. Whose husband constantly told her to be more like a 'normal woman' and 'play bingo'. Yes, she talked to the press. But only to get the SFA to take the women's game seriously.

Banned for life?

Edna Neillis, one of the most talented female footballers Scotland has ever seen.

After the ban, Edna had no option but to leave Scotland again. She returned to Italy. But it was hard for her. She never settled. All Edna ever wanted to do was play football **in** Scotland.

Banned for life?! For bringing the game into disrepute?

Fuck. That.

Me? Banned for life? For what?

For not playing by their rules?

For leaving Scotland, to better myself?

For being a girl who dared to have a dream?

How dare you Rose Reilly?

Who does she think she is, that Rose Reilly?

No. No, you weren't calling us pioneers and trailblazers then.

*****

Over the next decade, all through my 20s—despite the Scottish Football Association—I thrive on the European pitch.

I play for 10 Italian teams—and am made captain of every one of them. Win eight league titles, four Cups, and the Serie A Golden Boot for top goal scorer in 1978 and 1981, with 43 and 45 goals.

In one season, I play for the Italian team Lecce on Saturdays then fly to France to play for my old team Reims on Sundays. Both sides win their leagues that year.

Nobody's ever done that before.

Nor will they.

In 1984, I'm 29, and I'm asked to play for Italy in the Mundialito Femminile, pre-cursor to the women's World Cup.

I was the only one out of 40 foreign players selected to join the national squad.

Don't ask me how they managed to get me Italian nationality. But, in Italy, if they want something to happen (like winning the World Cup), it happens.

Next thing, I'm running out the tunnel in an Italian jersey for a match against... England.

While they're belting out 'God Save the Queen', I'm belting out 'Oh, Flower of Scotland'. It was a Scottish heart beating under an Italian jersey.

We beat England. Finally! Ya beauty!

And we reach the World Cup final against West Germany.

The minute the whistle goes, I play as if my life depends on it. I'm everywhere.

Eight minutes in, I'm pelting down the left-wing. I get the ball. I see Caroline Morales coming in from the right. I whack it across.

Lands right at her foot. She blasts it past the keeper. Yuss! We go wild. Italy one. Germany nil.

Ten minutes later, Betty Vignotto's flying down the wing. She takes a shot. I'm following the ball. Don't take my eyes off it. It comes off the cross-bar. I'm in the perfect spot. I blooter it. Right into the back of the net. Italy two Germany nil.

I've scored in a world cup final!!!

Thirty minutes, Betty Vignotto takes a penalty. Three nil.

Early in the second half they pull one back, dirty bastards! The pressure is on, 10 mins to go they get a free kick... goes wide! Two mins left I take a shot from 40 yards... flies over the bar. Final whistle goes... we've won!

The stadium erupts.

Forza Azzuri!!!

(A long beat, savouring the moment but also tinged with pain...)

I should've been able to do that for Scotland!

The following year we play at a big international tournament in China, in front of 90,000 fans. I score 10 goals in five games and, at 30, I'm voted the best female footballer in the world.

(Turns to an audience member...)

What did you get for your 30th?

Not bad for a wee lassie from Stewarton who was belted, expelled, sacked, banned, and told time after time after time...

It's. Not. A. Game. For. Girls.

It's. Not. A. Game. For. Girls.

It's. Not. A. Game. For. Girls.

YES. IT. FUCKING. WELL. IS. A. GAME. FOR GIRLS.

****

In 2000, I get a phone call. My mum's had a severe stroke.

I'd had one of these calls years earlier about my lovely wee dad. He'd had a heart attack and I was to come home right away. Only I couldn't because my passport had expired. For three weeks, I prayed for him to hang on. And he did.

When I eventually got to see him, I held his hand and told him I loved him.

I also thanked him.

For securing that suitcase as if it contained the crown jewels. But there was something else. My dad secretly gave Elsie a Provy cheque to buy our jerseys for that Scotland England match. He swore her to secrecy cos my mum would've killed him. But Elsie told me. I thanked him for that. And for everything. For being my dad.

Of course, he was proud of me. He didn't have to spell it out. I knew it. And he knew I knew it. And that's all that matters.

He died later that day.

Now, my mum.

I'm 45 now, retired from the professional game for five years. Not long after I hung up my boots, I was playing an amateur game with Sicilian cops. I injured my calf and one of them recommended this Argentinian doctor. Norberto.

I hadn't been looking for anything. Nor had he.

But he spoke Italian like Maradona. And that was that. We fell in ... you know... love. And were married on Christmas Eve.

No-one told me you can get pregnant at 45. But you can!

When I told my mum, it was the happiest day of her life. She was shouting it from the rooftops. To her, I think it meant I was normal. Unimpressed by 100 goals. She only ever wanted 100 weans.

Valentina Bridget was born.

The baby's 8-months when I get the call. I put her in a sling and return to Stewarton immediately.

At the hospital, my mum takes my hand, and asks me not to leave her.

I quietly ask the doctor, how long she's got. He says... about a week.

So I say to her... 'Don't worry Mammy, I won't leave you'.

That week passes.

Then another.

Then another. Then a month. Then a year.

Nine years! She hangs on for.

I told you she was a determined and strong-willed woman.

But thank God she was. Cos I think she passed quite a lot of it on to me.

I never did leave her.

You can't get your mammy back, can you?

I'm not an emotional person.

(*Like a mantra*) Emotion's weakness. Learned at five. Ingrained at five.

But... what I'd give for my mum and dad to see this. To see that it wasn't me there was something wrong with. That it was... out there. A society that still doesn't know what to do with women who don't fit into a box. Who don't fall into line. Do as they're told. Who don't look and think and behave the 'right' way.

To hell with that. To hell with that.

(*A moment... trying not to get emotional...*)

Right, enough about me.

I better move myself.

I don't want to keep the SFA waiting. Cos that would be rude wouldn't it? To keep them waiting.

(*Checks watch*)

I mean... that's nearly an hour. Still... At least it's not...

47 years!

I'd also give anything for Edna to be here. To see this. My wee mucker.

(*Looks up to heaven*)

We should never have faced the obstacles we did.

We should never have been belted at school.

We should never have been banned.

We should never have had to leave Scotland...

Just because we were girls who wanted to play football.

Aye... I think they're finally right...

We were pioneers and trailblazers,

   Mary Anderson
   Mary Carr
   Jane Haughton
   Jean Hunter
   June Hunter
   Linda Kidd
   Margaret McCauley
   Marion Mount
   Edna Neillis
   Rose Reilly
   Sandra Walker
   Linda Cooper
   Liz Creamer

Mary Davenport
Diane McLaren
Irene Morrison

We were pioneers, and trailblazers.

Pioneers and trailblazers.

THE END

Paddy Cunneen

Fleeto

Spirit of David MacLennan

Fleeto was nominated by those who knew and worked with David as a representation of David's love of language and his belief in the power of theatre to explore issues of social and political importance.

Prior to relocating to Glasgow with his family in 1999, Paddy Cunneen worked as a composer for theatre, television and film. When A Play, A Pie and A Pint launched at Òran Mór he was impressed with the range of plays, their subjects and styles, and the wide variety of first time playwrights, so he decided to try writing a play. He spoke to David MacLennan about this ambition, and sent him a few sketched lines for the emerging idea of *Fleeto*. David's response was typically enthusiastic and supportive. Not only did he insist that Paddy keep going with the idea and the style, but also promised that he would confidently put it onstage at Òran Mór.

Fleeto was Paddy's first play. He subsequently wrote a total of five plays for Òran Mór which have been performed throughout Scotland and abroad.

Fleeto and *Wee Andy* won awards at the Edinburgh, Adelaide and Brighton Fringe Festivals. These awards include Pauline Knowles winning Best Actress at The Adelaide Festival for her roles in *Fleeto* and Wee Andy.

Another of his plays, *Watching The Detective*, saw Stuart Bowman nominated as best actor in the 2012 Critics Awards for Theatre in Scotland, for his solo performance as the detective.

Fleeto was first performed in November 2007 at Òran Mór.

CHARACTERS

MACKIE
A young lad from a housing scheme

POLICE OFFICER

KENZIE
Leader of a gang of young men

THE MOTHER

LIST OF SCENES

SCENE 1	SLASH AND INVOCATION
SCENE 2	SERGEANT CUNT
SCENE 3	THE NED ILIAD
SCENE 4	FLIGHT FROM THE SCENE
SCENE 5	FORENSICS
SCENE 6	WHERE NOW?
SCENE 7	THE KNOCK ON THE DOOR
SCENE 8	THE BOOK
SCENE 9	WHOSE TRAGEDY?
SCENE 10	NO REASONS
SCENE 11	DOG BORSTAL
SCENE 12	PETROL STATION
SCENE 13	THE BURGER BAR
SCENE 14	FUNERAL PYRE

SCENE 1

SLASH AND INVOCATION

MACKIE: No, not Wee Andy, No. Ya bastards. No.

POLICE OFFICER: With heavy heart I stand here once again
 To tell you yet another Glasgow lad
 Was slashed and stabbed last night upon our streets.

MACKIE: Ah, Jesus Fucking shit, this can't be true.

POLICE OFFICER: Young Andrew Graham...

MACKIE: Wee Andy, he's been killed!

POLICE OFFICER: ...While walking home alone just after school.
 Was by a gang of mindless youths with knives,
 Most viciously attacked and left for dead.

MACKIE: Wee Andy never done naebody harm.
 He never got in trouble or a fight.

POLICE OFFICER: At first we feared that he would lose his life;
 So grievous were the injuries sustained..

MACKIE: He hardly even went outside his house.
 The two of us just hung out at his place.
 And played Olympus War Gods on PC.
 And noo my pal's been stabbed. Fur whi'?

POLICE OFFICER: ..But Glasgow has such skill in stab wound care—
 For all too much we practise now this craft—
 That surgeon's blade and stitch has saved that life
 Which thuggish blade last night put under threat.
 I want to introduce his mother now, who will
 Appeal for public help in tracking down
 The perpetrators of this sickening deed.

MACKIE: His maw is greeting sore, she cries and howls.

ANDY'S MA: (*Recorded Voice Over*)
 See now they've slashed and scarred ma poor boy's face?

All swollen like a ham hock tied wi' string,
He's marked for life. He might as well be dead.
Who's gonnae gi' him work, or teach him skills
'Cept dealers, druggies, thieves and life's sick dregs?

MACKIE: She's right! She's fuckin' right. Who cares 'bout him?

POLICE OFFICER: We have some footage from CCTV
Which shows a group of four young men that hour
Close to the scene of crime—all walking past.
And here we must say categorically,
That they are clearly not involved in this.
Now, most of them are Asian, it would seem.
We simply need to speak/

MACKIE: Power of man and manhood, roar and yell
Across grey tenements, as on that day
When Kenzie and his troops broke running free,
Pured petrol on the cinders of their shame,
And blazed their way, unstoppable and strong,
In brotherhood and clans of valiant troops
Imposing on the place their Ways of War—
And made the toon respect them by dread deeds
Of wrath and blood let loose upon its streets;
Bellow in me now and fill my veins
Wi' rage and lust for vengeance, since the state,
Wi' haughty hand and ASBO law enforced,
Would sty me in these schemes of filth and grime,
Wherein I will, enslaved, fast waste away
Unless, wi' fearless chib, I stake their hearts
And teach those cunts who slashed Wee Andy's face,
Tae fear my kind and count me as a man.

SCENE 2

SERGEANT CUNT

POLICE OFFICER: I feared the worst would happen in this case.
See, we have here so many gangs of youths
Which gather in large groups and carry knives
And seek revenge according to their Code—

A cruel code, requiring blood for blood.
I made appeal for calm on TV news.

KENZIE: So, on ma fucking screen, some Sergeant Cunt
Calls out to me and asks me to stay calm.

POLICE OFFICER: I ask for calm maturity today
Especially from those young men in our town
Who take the law, and knife, in their own hands
And rampage through the streets in violent gangs.

Come out and meet the world, full man-to-man
Not cowering in ranks of hooded thugs.
It's only what a man can face alone
That is the truest measure of his worth.

KENZIE: *(to POLICE OFFICER)* " Ya fuckin prick, ya! Bawbag of the law!"

(to audience) Who hides, beneath a chibproof vest of black,
A heart still blacker yet—it throbs
In frustrate rage tae pan my fucking face.
He rants at me now, "Braveheart, stand alone!"
Whilst on his collar sits a radio
Wi' access tae full powers of the State
And reinforcements swiftly motioned in.

(to POLICE OFFICER) "Then stand alone yersel, ya cuntin' fuck!"

POLICE OFFICER: I'm sick at heart for what will happen next,
There's little that can stop young men like him.
He's smart, he's sharp. He'll organise a gang
Of running youths for violent revenge.

KENZIE: *(running off)* You're a fucking wanker!

POLICE OFFICER: Enraged by injured pride and out for blood,
They'll go berserk with knives on city streets
Till someone pays a forfeit—with their life.

SCENE 3

THE NED ILIAD

MACKIE: Next. Kenzie came and found me by the shop,
   He walked right up wi' can of brew in hand
   And eyeballed me tae let me know the score.

KENZIE: So you're wee Andy's pal. Here. Come wi' me.

MACKIE: He threw away the fag from aff his lips
   And beckoned me tae follow wi' his hand.
   So round behind the wall we went as one.

KENZIE: We're gonnae sort those cunts who hurt your pal—
   Cos they deserve whatever comes their way
   For cutting up Wee Andy's face wi' knives.
   Naebody gets away wi' shit like that,
   See, naebody touches naebody from our scheme.
   We take care of our own, we get them back.
   Come and join wi' us and get them cunts.
   I'll teach ya how tae break their fuckin heids.
   If it's Asylum that those fuckers seek,
   We'll put them in a madhouse right enough.

MACKIE: And then he reached inside his trackie top
   And pulled, wi' skillful hand in deadly grip,
   That Blade—most mortal of all blades on Earth—
   It sliced the air apart, like shrieking ice,
   The way a plane will scrat the bastard sky.

KENZIE: This blade we grabbed from poxy Eastend hands,
   When proudly came a gang of Fuckin' Neds
   From Dennistoun tae mix it on our patch;
   They took sore blows that day, some fuckin wounds.
   Not one big man of theirs escaped our wrath
   But left Infirmary sheets stained black wi' blood.
   It greeted from the slashes in their flesh—
   As if their meat be-wept their sorry luck
   Tae war 'gainst such BraveHeart lads as we.
   And homewards were they sent tae think again.

MACKIE: Is this the blade that sliced up that guy's hand?

KENZIE: Aye, fuckin' Jezza came from South Nitshill
Tae spray his bastard menchie on our walls.
That cunt he tried his best tae save his face
Against my slashing rage last August night.
Two fingers from his haun' he lost right there
When savage blade in righteous anger ripped
That haun' apart, and severed bone from bone.
Two dying digits left upon the street...
Which Div and Stu picked up in mocking fists
And gave, in scornful glee, the finger back
Tae that cunt greetin' on the ground in pain.

MACKIE: Then Kenzie, holding high this vengeful blade,
Began tae call the brothers tae his side.

KENZIE: Come on!

A GANG of six young men suddenly appears onstage, shouting.

MACKIE: And wi' his other haun' aloft he crossed
A carving knife, as lethal as the first,
So made a metal saltire of the pair.
This filled the troops wi' joy,..

The GANG shouts aloud in malevolent joy.

MACKIE: ...and then he spoke
In these proud words of war—for all tae hear.

KENZIE: We're gonnae stick these blades into those cunts,
Deep in their chests, right through their fuckin hearts

GANG: (*shouting*) " Right!" "Bastards" *etc...*

KENZIE: We're gonnae let their scummy lifeblood drain
Into the mingin' Clyde, whose filthy flow
Will retch and vomit up in rank distance
At foreign life-juice, polluting foul
The manky turds and condoms in her flood.

GANG: (*shouting*) "Great" "Wa-hey!" *etc...*

MACKIE: And so he spoke—or words tae that effect,
  At which, like monkey hordes in war-lust thrill,
  The chatter and the patter sounded out
  From all the troops now ready for the fray.

GANG: (*shout out their readiness for the battle*) " Yeah" "Fuckin' right" etc...

MACKIE: So Stu proclaimed aloud of how he would,

  "Wi' Timbie boot, stamp on some wanker's face
  And spread his nose in bright red bloody smear
  Across his mooth, when emptied of its teeth."

The GANG gives a short burst of wild laughter.

One gang member jumps up onstage and mimes as MACKIE describes BISCUIT's actions.

MACKIE: Then up rose Biscuit, he that can out-run
  The fastest footed polis, or his dug,
  And round the troops his dance of war began—
  Wi' arms a while of menace round his heid—

GANG: (*All shout*) Ya fanny!

MACKIE: And though some shouted "fanny" as he danced,
  Yet all were full of joy within their hearts.

The GANG roars and shouts approval.

MACKIE: Then Dunky, Stevo, Whacker, Coyle and Div,

The GANG points at one of their number and calls out to him.

GANG: Divvv-oh!

MACKIE: Whose fame extends frae Greenock tae Lyndale
  For "Causin It at every fuckin chance",
  Began tae chant,

GANG: (*Under MACKIE's speech, quietly begin to sing following to the tune of Auld Lang Syne*)

  "Go hame, ya cunts, Go hame, ya cunts.
  Away tae fuck, Go hame!!"

MACKIE: ...which stirred the Fleeto Hearts
  Til all were pure dead mento for the deed—
  Tae slay the needy, piss-bag foreign scum.
  The locusts in our homeland—on our broo.
  This song they sang, and all the troops joined in—

The GANG suddenly bursts into a deafening chorus:

GANG: "Go hame, ya cunts, Go hame, ya cunts.
  Away tae fuck, Go hame!!"

MACKIE: Then, straight away, wi' combat mind and will—
  As being brothers all in Burbry's clan—
  Bright helmets of pale Tartan we put on,
  Their peaks turned skyward in a jaunty slant
  That gives the finger tae the Gods above;
  And some their cowls and hoods of war raised up,
  Tae veil their visage from the Cyclops Eye—
  That keeps its snidey watch, by video,
  From pillars and tall masts about the toon.

The GANG make mocking cries as they make obscene gestures at the camera.

MACKIE: And checked we then our weapons for the job—
  Our breadknives, chisels, hammers, stanleys, clubs,
  Our apple corers—fit tae punch a hole

GANG: (*A loud unison shout of visceral pain*) Owwwwwffff..

MACKIE: From which some fucker's blood would drain in floods
  Of liquid death on tarmac under him.
  Some said hot machetes they could get
  Whose weight, when swung in battle's fiercest rage,
  Will server flesh and veins and shatter bone,
  But some said they would never carry knives—
  Tae risk four years of life in Polmont Jail?
  When they, wi' boot or fist, could haud their own
  And crack some mad cunt's skull or gouge his eye.
  So chibs and claymores—all were then concealed
  In Jaket, trackies, socks, or Chantelle's purse—
  Like sgian dubh in ancient times—obscured
  In deadly hiding place from rival's eye.

GANG: (*mockingly*) "Come Ahead!" " Ya Bas!" *etc…*

MACKIE: And next we searched, through darkened Glasgow streets,
Tae find a leech on Caledonia's heart.
A Black Watch we would keep until we found
Some foreign cunt, who'd left his own backyard,
Tae live the bluebell life wi' Scotland's best?

GANG: (*Shout out threateningly*) "Aye Right!" "No Way!" *etc…*

MACKIE: Through Merchant Streets we prowled and bayed like wolves,
That, wi' the scent of blood, will leave behind
Their natural habitation tae commit
Their darkest deeds in city's darkest lanes.

And driven wi' this hunger, we raced on
Tae hunt and harry down, in rightful wrath,
Stray members of that evil Asian breed.
Then, finding one such cunt alone, we swarmed
Tae pann his stupit melt right there and then…

GANG: (*war cries of*) "Ya Bas!" *etc…*

MACKIE: But when he saw our troops amass in force,
He shat himself in fear and ran like fuck,

The GANG make mocking shouts.

MACKIE: All cowardly in sobbing, shrieking voice—
Where once his kind had braved our Andy's face.

So, proudly then, once more, through Albion ran
The Brother-hooded Bravehearts. Full of fight.
From Albion tae Ingram, Candleriggs,
And down towards the Broomielaw we sped.
But nowhere could we find that fearty cunt.

The GANG roar in frustrated disappointment.

One gang member jumps up onstage and mimes out MACKIE's account of DUNKY's actions.

MACKIE: Then Dunky says "I cannae understaun

How such a muppet could gie' us the slip—
Cos he's a refuge newboy on the block
But we've lived here for years and know the place."

GANG: (*Shout in one great chorus*) Aye!

The gang member who played BISCUIT jumps up onstage and mimes again.

MACKIE: Then Biscuit pipes up loud tae all the troops—
"See back on Stockwell Street? I saw a pair
Of lads that we should take, one black, one white,
Who looked at me, or gave me eye it seemed,
When I had passed them by wi' roasting speed."

BISCUIT jumps back into place.

MACKIE singles out another gang member, STU, who pounds his palms as MACKIE recounts...

Then Stu, his voice all rage, gave out tae us,
And clearly could we hear his boiling wrath,
That now we must "those fucking cunts sort out.
Teach them tae eyeball us on Glasgow's streets."

But. Even as he spoke tae spur us on,
Before we could turn round and hunt them down,
The very two we sought now crossed our path
By turning out from back the alley's way.

And straight away, in reflex tae their sight,
So, Kenzie launched a devastating fist,

GANG: (*In horror and admiration at the violence*) Wooaahhhh!

MACKIE: Which struck the darker coloured of the two,
And smashed the foreign structure of his face—
So blood poured out through shattered nose and mouth—
Enough tae drown the fucker where he stood,
Tho' he, instead just gasped and choked for breath.
Then, suffered Kenzie's boot into his baws

GANG: *(sounds of pain)* Euuuhhhh!

MACKIE: Wi' such a mortal cry of pain and grief
That several of our troop were stunned quite still,

The GANG bursts out in laughter..

But soon laughed loud, and cheered Great Kenzie's deed.

KENZIE: He's no so fucking sun-tanned handsome now
I've re-arranged the ugly fucker's face.

MACKIE: At which the troops, as one, took great delight
And made afresh their chants of mocking hate.

GANG: *(screeching out)* Go hame, ya cunts! Go hame, ya cunts!

MACKIE: Now, in that moment whilst we were distract,
The white one—Jesus why did he do this?—
Pulled up his stricken pal and pressed his ear
Wi' calming words tae ease the gory pain
He salvaged from our midst his hurtmost friend—
And ran the pair of them way up the street.

So, racing after them, we ran like wind,
Which fanned afresh our red-hot fires of rage
Tae all-consuming hatred in our minds.
A trail of flame and smoke we left behind
As comet-like, we rushed at fright'ning speed.

GANG: *(war cries of)* Ya Bas! Fuuuuccckkkk! *etc...*

MACKIE: Now—Kenzie's awe-inspiring flaring eyes
Sought out, intae the streetlit darkness world.
And led us on, as leaders do, wi' words.

KENZIE: They're here! He's here! I smell his fucking stench—
I'll tear the cunt apart when I lay hands.

MACKIE: Now. As he spoke, his hand pulled out The Blade
Which glinted through the dark in grievous spite:
And scored a thrill of terror in us all.

The GANG race around the stage, looking for their victim.

MACKIE: So round we ran, and round, and round again
All calling, screeching out in bloodlust thirst.

The GANG members freeze in threatening poses.

MACKIE: It wasnae us that ran—it was a force
Which in our hearts just had tae be obeyed.
Some thing, it was, in wild control a' us,
Which urged us on tae grave deeds of our fate.
Some God. Some Devil. Some fucking crazy power.
The spirit of Mad Dogs howled in our veins.

With a terrifying howl, the GANG members race back to position.

And, filled wi' it, I too ran fast along
While keeping closest touch tae Kenzie's side
Who all the time was raving on wi' this:

(through this next speech the gang echoes some of KENZIE's obscenities, adding their own too)

KENZIE: "He's here! he's here! No, fuck, he's gone! The cunt!
I'll fucking kill ya cunt, I'll slash your face.
I'll take your fuckin heid off where you stand,
You Cuuuunnnnnnt!"

GANG: *(joins in with this last word in a terrifying roar)* Cuuuunnnnnnt!

MACKIE: And now: the darkened world turned darker still.
As if the Gods would veil the dreadful night
In hope of blotting out what would occur.

For suddenly the white lad of the two,
Who blocked our path tae let his pal escape,
Now found himself wi' nowhere left tae hide—
Cos round him on all sides the troops stood firm.
So, in a desperate act tae break out free
He runs at me, as being tae his mind
The least, and weakest, of our warrior clan.
But, even as he raced tae where I stood
I felt a hand place lethal steel in mine
And in my ear was said—

KENZIE: "Now here's your chance
Tae stick that cunt for good, he's coming now
He's coming at you now. HE'S COMING! NOW!!!

MACKIE: And all I did was lift my hand up... So.

MACKIE lifts his hand up suddenly, revealing the knife, and freezes at the moment of fatal impact.

The GANG run away, as fast as possible.

The POLICE OFFICER walks onstage as MACKIE maintains his position, holding the knife with outstretched arm.

POLICE OFFICER: (*to audience*) What we have here is a knife that's penetrated the lad's chest between his ribs, and gone deep into the apex of his heart—an inch into the right ventricle, severing a coronary artery. In a matter of seconds his strong young heart will pump two pints of blood into his chest and lungs. He'll kind of drown.

(*to MACKIE*) You hear the gurgling. You feel every twitch and spasm as he slumps to the floor.

He's groaning and writhing, he's grabbed your blade. You feel his weight, don't you?

MACKIE: I don't feel nothing.

POLICE OFFICER: Don't you?

MACKIE: I didn't do nothing.

POLICE OFFICER: Didn't you? He's young, and strong, isn't he?

MACKIE: I don't know.

POLICE OFFICER: Make sure you look at him. LOOK AT HIM!

MACKIE: He's too fucking heavy.

POLICE OFFICER: LOOK AT HIM! He's looking straight at you.

MACKIE lifts his eyes to meet those of his victim

POLICE OFFICER: You didn't know that when you stab someone, they look you right in the eye. Did you? What's he trying to say? He can't speak, his lungs are full of blood. He's asking you why is it that someone can take a knife and stick it in another person, without any care for what will happen?

MACKIE: I didn't do it. I swear. It wasn't me.

POLICE OFFICER: Feel it? That dance of death on the end of your blade?

MACKIE: It's no my blade.

POLICE OFFICER: You've made it yours. DO YOU FEEL IT?

MACKIE nods

POLICE OFFICER: All that trembling and jerking. Travels up the blade, doesn't it?

MACKIE: (*nods*) Uh-huh.

POLICE OFFICER: The convulsions of death, they are.

MACKIE: Ah Jesus, I can feel it.

POLICE OFFICER: You should be ashamed of yourself.

MACKIE: It's inside me!

POLICE OFFICER: I hope it's right inside you! I swear to God, you'll feel his heart jump and kick like a knackered washing machine.

MACKIE: No!

POLICE OFFICER: Doesn't matter what you've imagined beforehand or even how you've been trained, nothing can prepare you for the smell, or the sound, or the strange brotherly embrace of it once the blade's ripped Death into him.

MACKIE: He's eyeballing me.

POLICE OFFICER: He's eyeballing you alright. You're the last person he's ever going to see.

MACKIE: Shut up!

POLICE OFFICER: What's his poor mother going to say?

MACKIE: Shut up! Shut the fuck up!

POLICE OFFICER: What you going to do?

MACKIE: I don't know

POLICE OFFICER: Are you going to leave it stuck in him or pull it out?

MACKIE: I don't know

POLICE OFFICER: We'll find it if you leave it in him.

MACKIE: I'll pull it out.

POLICE OFFICER: He'll bleed buckets if you do.

MACKIE: I'll leave it in.

POLICE OFFICER: It's got your prints on it now.

MACKIE: I'll pull it out.

POLICE OFFICER: Make your fucking mind up.

(*Beat.*)

If you've got a fucking mind.

MACKIE drops the knife.

It sticks in to the floor with a sickening thud and stands on its point.

MACKIE runs away, as fast as he can.

SCENE 4

FLIGHT FROM THE SCENE

MACKIE: I ran and ran and ran and retched dry puke.
 I ran in sick'ning sweat and choking fear.
 I ran, I fuckin ran as fast as dogs,
 Wi' stabbing pains of stiches in my side.

 But when I heard the distant sirens howl—
 I gasped for breath and froze stock-still in fear.

 Oh, get him tae that fuckin hospital!
 And pull that knife from out his bleeding heart.
 Don't let the fucker die. Don't let him die.

I never meant tae stab him. No. No way.
Kenzie put the knife... It wasn't me..
He just... He ran straight at me... I... I..

It's not the way you see it in the films—
A jab wi' blade, some blood, a wound that heals...
I felt the fucker's shattered heart explode;
He coughed his fuckin' lifeblood over me.

Don't let the fucker die. Don't let him die.
Don't let him die. Oh please. Don't let him die.

SCENE 5

FORENSICS

POLICE OFFICER puts on a pair of forensic gloves.

POLICE OFFICER: His life was gone, of that there was no doubt,
No reflex in his pupils could we find,
No beat of life, nor any vital sound
Which might have murmured softly in his frame
To plead with us for paramedic aid.
So we left him laid out on the street
And wrestled with the despond of our minds.

Right.

First we had to move the public back.
For tho' they were distressed and keen to help,
We have to keep you back—with plastic tape—
In case you should the evidence destroy.

So. Biologists arrived, from Scenes Of Crime,
Some fifteen minutes later, at the site.
They caref'ly laid out metal stepping stones,
Which keep the clues from damage underfoot.

Their touch on him was light, by glove and brush,
It was as if they thought he might awake
From slightest sensing of their careful hands.
But he lay still, insensible to all.

I couldn't help but stare at his young corpse—
What waste of life. For what? Just thrown away.
Thank God forensic tent was put in place
And swiftly hid his broken heart remains
From tearful eyes, and darkest thoughts of death,
And the prying fucking gaze of tabloid lens.

Great beams of light shone bright, around the tent,
From lanterns which we keep as part of plans
For nuclear war, or death of our young men.
They shine without the sunlight's warming grace,
And somehow make the night seem blacker yet
With ruthless beams of darkness visible.

Our work progressed with practised speed and skill
And detailed horror of this brutal act
Was brought from shadow into reason's light
Amid this callous glare of night made day.

Then, with conclusion reached, by expert team,
That all the evidence was now secured,
We moved him from the cold unyielding ground
To colder slab in city mortuary.

His phone and wallet spoke of who he was.
And gave his name to us indifferently
In Ozymandian facts of life now gone.
James.
Fairgrieve.
Student.

And so came time to do what we most dread.

For now the Crime Scene Manager had name,
A D.O.B. address and next of kin;
And, as we always do in suchlike case,
Two officers were quickly put in post,

Informed of that night's brutal act of death,
And swiftly sent to break the news to all
Unwitting family members at the home.

No matter what the time of day or night
Such news as this we tell immediately—

Even if its three a.m. we go.
Before the carrion press descend to feast
In howling packs at doors of grieving kin.

He pulls the knife out of the floor.

So, armed with new-honed details of events,
We went to pierce the heartfelt happiness
Which dwells within the breast of parent's love.

SCENE 6

WHERE NOW?

MACKIE: I ran and ran until my fuckin' heart
Was bursting in my chest and in my ears.
I walked, I crawled, I tried tae pull in air—
Which made the bastard fires inside my lungs
Erupt, in flames of red hot agony.

He's dead. He must be stone cold fuckin' dead.
I've killed that poor bastard—I don't know why.
I should have stayed—I might have saved his life.

I can't run any more, I just can't breathe.
My legs are pure dead fucking weights,
Afire wi' burning acid in my veins.

Ah Jesus Christ, the knife went in his heart!
I've got tae run and run and never stop!
I've got tae get away. I've got tae run.

But where? Oh, Fuckin' Hell where can I go?
They'll come and get me if I go back home.

Oh Jesus cuntin' Christ, just fuckin' run!

SCENE 7

THE KNOCK ON THE DOOR

The MOTHER sits in a chair onstage.

POLICE OFFICER: I've lost count of how many times before
I've chapped on doors to bring this dreadmost news.
It must be more than nine or ten this year.
Experience, it seems, will never teach
An easy way to break a person's heart.

I'll go up to the house and say, quite calm,
"There's been a body found, and we believe
That it's your young son James, and that he's dead."
And she'll say "No, oh God, this cannot be."

The MOTHER stands.

POLICE OFFICER: I'm DCI Martin Booth from Pitt St Police station. Are you Mrs. Alison Fairgrieve?

MOTHER: Yes. Is this about the Neighbourhood Watch?

POLICE OFFICER: I'm afraid not, this is in relation to another matter. Do you have a son James Fairgrieve?

MOTHER: He's not in trouble is he?

POLICE OFFICER: I'm sorry to say I've got some news for you. Would you please sit down.

(*to audience*) So now you wait and try your best to speak
With clear and simple words, of mortal woe.

(*to MOTHER who is now seated*)

As I say we've got some news, and I'm afraid it's very bad news, and there's no easy way to say this, but, I believe that your son's been killed.

(*to audience*)

No-one ever understands those words
Which say the thing that every parent dreads.
She'll answer straight away "this cannot be.."

MOTHER: This must be a mistake. He's just gone into town with his friend.

POLICE OFFICER: Unfortunately we have strong cause to believe that is the case and that he is dead.

MOTHER: No, you've got it wrong. I spoke to James earlier this evening.

POLICE OFFICER: I'm afraid we know that. We checked his mobile and it shows he dialed your number here, just after six this evening? There was an incident at seven fifteen.

MOTHER: Incident? What incident? Where is he?

POLICE OFFICER: As I say, there was an incident and at the moment, Mrs. Fairgrieve, I'm sorry to have to tell you, James has been moved to the city mortuary.

MOTHER: No, that's not true. Take me to him. Please. I want to see him. I need to see him.

POLICE OFFICER: Of course.

(to audience) It is, in fact, required by law, that now
Post mortem should take place with speed,
To ascertain the cause of James' death.
And, this requires that people of his kin
Identify the body where it lies.
So now I have to take her to the morgue
To make her see, when I pull back the shroud,
That image of his face—bereft of life.
Then by her sob, or screams, or silent stare,
We'll know for sure exactly who he was.

(To MOTHER) I need to ask you to come and identify him.

MOTHER: Oh God.

POLICE OFFICER: I'm so sorry.

MOTHER: *(suddenly shrieking and screaming)* No! No! What's happened? Oh God, not James! No! James! James! Oh please God, no.

SCENE 8

THE BOOK

MACKIE: I managed tae get home, back tae my house,
  But thought the fuckin' police might be there
  And so I hid, in fear and sweat, behind
  The rubble of the knocked down factory.

  Kenzie came and found me lying low
  In trembling dread behind the concrete wall.
  He hissed out, in the darkness, it was him—
  I had no need tae fear his coming by.

  (*to KENZIE*) Is he dead?

KENZIE: He's fuckin' dead as shit, I tell you mate,
  He had a metal hard-on on his chest—
  That knife stood up, erect and proud as fuck.

MACKIE: Ah Jesus, Jesus Christ, what can I do?

KENZIE: Get yer arse away from round this place.
  The polis'll come for ye sure as fuck.
  Some cunt'll grass, and blame it all on you
  Cos they'll be feart in case they get the jail.

MACKIE: (*to audience*) Once more he reached inside his trackie-top
  But now, pulled out a book, and no a blade.
  A black book, small and hard, wi' 'lastic band,
  All splattered brown and scarred wi' crusted blood.
  (How quickly does blood turn from red tae brown?)

KENZIE: I picked this up, from where you stabbed that cunt.
  It must have fallen out his pocket, mon.

MACKIE: O Jesus Christ, this book belonged tae HIM!
  If only it had sat against his heart
  And stopped the blade, he might be still alive.

KENZIE: It's full of writing! Aye! There's loads of shit;
  Some fucking crap about the Greeks and Troy,
  And other writing there—I read it all,

He's wrote in here the story of his life;
About his Maw and what she means tae him,
And stuff about him shagging this hot burd—
That's all wrote down here too. It's fucking cool.

MACKIE: And now, I felt some force inside me move.
It bled, like ice, deep down inside my guts—
A cold, clear rage that frosted up my heart
But left my mind as sharp as any knife.
That book was mine; I did the shameful deed
And, like the Spartans say in Gods Of Troy:
"The spoils of war belong tae those who slay".

(to KENZIE)

Hey, Kenzie, gi' it here tae me, that's mine.

KENZIE: Away and shite, it's me that picked it up.

MACKIE: But only 'cos he lay dead on the ground. I'm the one who stabbed him in the heart, So anything of his—belongs tae me.

KENZIE: Go fuck yersel', I'm keeping this, awright?

MACKIE: *(to audience)* And saying this, he stepped in shadow's way,
Which, like a hoodie pulled across his face
Concealed him from the lost look on my own.

But, as he went tae leave me there, so I
Was sudden filled wi' overwhelming need—
Like junkies, who will do all desperate shite
Tae get their fix: That's how I was.

So when his back was turned, I ran at him,
And smacked him tae the floor wi' one hard skelp,
Then grabbed his head, and bounced it on the ground,
And found myself wi' knee pressed on his throat,
Which made him gasp and choke, wi' face all blue.

So mad was I wi' hunger and wi' fear,
I panned his face, full whack, wi' knuckled fist,
Again, again, again, I hit him hard,
Cos I knew I was dead if he got up.
I pushed my knee, full force, tae burst the veins
That stood out on his fearsick face and neck,

Till blood and phlegm all gurgled down his throat.
Then, as I punched his face for one last time,
My thumb got jabbed, full deep intae his eye
Which burst, and sprayed it's gunge all over me.

KENZIE screams.

And he, in broken agony, lay still.

But I just took the book from out his grip,
And left him, barely breathing, on the ground.
Kenzie. Cunt. Who couldnae gi' a shit.
Well, I don't give a fuck about him now
I've got the book. This book. The life I took
All written down right here. Right in my hand.

SCENE 9

WHOSE TRAGEDY?

POLICE OFFICER: (*to audience*)
You NEVER, ever leave someone alone
To whom you've had to give such news as this.
You always ask for someone close to them
To sit in mournful shock, attempting care.
But if that can't be done, you stay yourself
To keep them talking all the dark night long
In forlorn hope that it might do some good.
And so it was I stayed through night's long hours
In listening to her grief-stained words of woe,
Until the ill-judged song of birds announced
Unwelcome greeting to the useless dawn.
Then came despairing friends and grieving kin,
Inept attendants on her sore distress.
Their clumsy silence brought her no relief.
I headed home.

He gets up, trying to contain his angry tears.

Listen.

These things that happen they're... horrific, they're tragic, but they're no ma tragedy. That's the bottom line. You have empathy for people, compassion for them, but you don't take it home with you. My ex-wife told me that.

Jesus, imagine if you took this home with you.

SCENE 10

NO REASONS

MACKIE is now despairingly drunk with a can of brew in hand.

MACKIE: I strayed into the land of NoReasons,
   Tae scavenge on its empty plenty shelves
   And stacks of sugared fats—pure fuckin filth—
   That kills our pauperised, untutored kin
   More surely than does knife or chib or blade;
   Past dykes of wine and lager, ground tae sky,
   All straining tae hold back their toxic flood;
   Through sandbagged walls of crisps, and tartrazine
   And EisenBrau and shit that we devour.
   And easy fuckin' pickings did I snatch,
   So walked wi' brew in jaket stashed away
   Right up tae face security's old prick
   Who, none the fuckin' wiser, let me pass.

   And looking back inside I saw a troop
   Of old and glaikit bampots, stupit men
   Who wander round the store wi' self-same walk,
   The eunuch's shattered stumbling baw-less gait.
   They, waiting for bitch matriarchal word
   Tae push their trolleys round from aisle tae aisle,
   Do lumber in a sleeping scooby state,
   Whilst she wi' full control directs his life.

   "Ya fuckin Hyena ya, ya bitch, ya cow!"

   Those neutered pricks wi' dead unseeing eyes,
   In dead unliving bodies shackled so.

All ambling like the numpties in that film
Where, in a shopping Mall, some cunts get locked.

"Ye fuckin' fearty pricks, ye shitebags ye."

Are these real men? These Fathers? Leaders? Kings?
Who even on the telly are reviled
And mocked by adverts all—as bawless cunts.
What loss tae us if gelded sheep like these
In drunk or drugged up daze fall down and die?
If such moronic dreeks should come near me
They'll feel my blade burn through their bloated guts.

I've chibbed at nobler meat than theirs, and chewed
Through tougher of their fuckin' stupit kind
In burger bun;

"Ye useless fuckin' cunts!"

SCENE 11

DOG BORSTAL

POLICE OFFICER is in the pub, he has the remains of a pint of Guinness in his hand.

POLICE OFFICER: Dog Borstal, have you seen that on your screens?
I love that bloody program. Tell you why.
It's mostly 'cos it says if you've a dog
But fail to treat it right, around it turns
And makes your life an abject misery
Of whining, barking, biting, howling rage.
That's not the poor dog's fault, the fault's your own;
Who would not treat the beast with due respect,
Nor tender to its needs nor give due care,
But made a toy of him, as you saw fit.
So now you find he's pissing on your chips,
And bites yer arse when e'er he gets the chance.
Which tells you more than words of mine can say
About the need for care and for respect.

See...

There's this... grave... on Tumbledown. And in it is a... white, shrouded body. No coffin. But when you open the shroud—it's a beautiful Patagonian shroud—there's no corpse either, just two eyes. Pick up the eyes and you'll see the pupils are dilated wide with death. If you turn the eyes under the cold grey sunlight you can just make out a strange image inside. It's my ugly nineteen year-old face, screaming in rage as I twisted the bayonet—the last living thing that poor bastard ever saw. Imprinted on those retinas.

What are we like? Eh? Us fucking Scots? A swirl of the tartan; a skirl of the pipes; here's your blade; we're off to war—Hooray!

The fucking Heart of Self-Lothian.

SCENE 12

PETROL STATION

MOTHER: I drove off, early that morning. Very early: I don't know two forty five? Three? After the identification I couldn't sleep at all.

I drove for miles and miles. Hours. Not knowing where I was going—in a kind of dream really. Trying to remember his face. He'd had so many faces—baby face, toddler face, twelve year old's, surly teenager face, young man's face with a bumfluff goatee. All him. But I couldn't work out which one was him. Which one I'd lost most.

God knows how I didn't hit anything because when I pulled in to the petrol station I realised I had no memory of how I got there. I had to ask the young man on the till where I was. I didn't quite hear what he said because I was thinking that he was probably five or six years older than James.

Turns out the garage was only four miles from where I live, but I'd been driving for nearly eight hours by then.

And then I asked the lad on the till where neds live.

He didn't understand, so I said. "You know, neds? Where do they live? What areas do they live in?"

He said there were areas all over Glasgow, but thinking about it, wouldn't it be a great idea if ned areas were labelled in the AA map?

I said yes it would.

I didn't realise he was joking.

And then he suddenly asked, very gently, if he could phone someone for me. My husband? A family member?

His kindness upset me, so I said yes. Yes. Would you call James? Can you do that?

POLICE OFFICER: We got a call from a petrol station attendant at ten to eleven that morning. The young lad said, and these are his words,
"She's lost and she's lost it."

SCENE 13

THE BURGER BAR

The MOTHER enters with a cup of coffee in a paper cup. All this is watched carefully by MACKIE.

MACKIE: Oh Fuck! I know exactly who she is:
His Ma. From that appeal on the TV.

She picks up the coffee and takes a sip, puts it back down on the table and looks around. In doing this she hits the table and the coffee spills. MACKIE who has been watching, jumps up and rescues the cup and quickly throws some serviettes in the path of the coffee to stop it reaching her.

MOTHER: Thank you, so clumsy, I...

MACKIE: Cool, cool. I got it.

MOTHER: Thank you.

MACKIE: (*to audience*) She's not like women that you see round here,
Who curse and wail, and screech aloud in angst
When, after sniffing cans, their kid's found dead.

(*To MOTHER*) D'you want another one? I'll get one out of them for you.

MOTHER: No, it's OK. You've been very kind. Thank you.

MACKIE: (*to audience*) She's full of grief and pain for her lost son—
Her sorrow makes her.. beautiful, to me.

(*to MOTHER*) You famous?

MOTHER: No. I'm not famous.

MACKIE: I seen you on the telly, but? On the news?

(Beat.)

That student that got stabbed, you're his ma, int ya?

MOTHER nods.

MACKIE: You greeting?

MOTHER shakes her head.

POLICE OFFICER: All her friends at home said not to come,
Or if she must, then not to go alone
To such a place as this where life is cheap.
Where "Drunks and addicts wait on every street!"
Her friends all begged her stay, with pleading cries,
And all the time in tears, as if they felt
That she, by setting foot in Housing Scheme,
Was facing certain injury or death.
They even hid her car keys, just in case.

MOTHER: I had a spare.

POLICE OFFICER: She will not be denied.
She has the strength of purpose of The Damned
Who have to follow what is in their heart

No matter what the consequences be.

MACKIE: Why the fuck don't I just run out fast
And get the hell away from her right now?
It's bad enough tae live from day tae day
Wi' guilty feat and puking in my guts.
Why make it worse by gazing at her here?

I slashed those lines of grief into her face—
As deep and evermore as Andy's scars.

MACKIE goes to the table and sits beside her.

POLICE OFFICER: You're playing a dangerous game

MACKIE: It's not a game.

POLICE OFFICER: Haven't you done enough to her?

MACKIE: I know what I done!

He puts down a handful of paper serviettes.

MACKIE: Here. They have them for the burgers.

She takes a serviette and wipes her nose. They sit at the table for a while without saying anything.

POLICE OFFICER: Go on then. Ask her. What's she doing here? Ask her.

MACKIE: You fucking ask her!

(Silence.)

MACKIE: Whit you doing here?

MOTHER: I came to see.

MACKIE: See whit?

MOTHER: I came to see what it's like in a place like this.

MACKIE: A place like this? You know this place?

MOTHER: No.

MACKIE: You reckon they come from here? D'wans who killed him?

MOTHER: Not here, no...

MACKIE: But a place like this?

MOTHER: I don't know.

MACKIE: Where do you live?

MOTHER: I don't want to....

MACKIE: It's not a place like this though, is it?

(Beat.)

MOTHER: No, I live... somewhere..

MACKIE: Better?

MOTHER: Else. I live somewhere else.

MACKIE: You've come here, tae a place like this and you're looking at people like us, because you're thinking it must be one of us that killed him.

Cos we come from a place like this.

MOTHER: That's not what I meant.

MACKIE: It fucking is.

(Beat.)

MOTHER: Yes. Maybe it is.

(Beat.)

(Long silence.)

MACKIE: *(to audience)* She's right, this is the very place indeed
Where you can find such murdering cunts as me.

This scummy, no-hope shit hole, left tae rot,
Where angry fuckers skulk around the place
Wi' desperation in their desperate minds,
In case a chance for something comes their way.
What kind of chance do we have growing up,
All couldn't-give-a-fuck, in wasteland place?

POLICE OFFICER: You had a chance, but chose to take a knife
And thrust it deep into a young lad's heart.
Don't whinge and say the fault all lies elsewhere
'Cos at the crunch, you didn't give a shit.

MACKIE: Well, no-one gives a shit about this place
And no-one gives a shit for people here,
So I don't give a fuck for what you think,
Or any other cunt, Fuck you. Fuck you.

POLICE OFFICER: So why are you all wound up by the deed
If what you say is true in your defence?

MACKIE: Why don't you get the fuck tae Portugal?
Go find that girl who matters tae you all
And leave the dross like us tae drown in filth.
Your papers are nae full of how we must
In destitution live in gulag schemes,
You're only interested when little girls
From caring homes of comfort come to grief.
See we are bred in need and poverty
So she can live in comfort in her place.

POLICE OFFICER: Well, come on then, explain to her right now
The Class War justice of your murdering deed.
Go on.

MACKIE: *(to MOTHER)* You drive here?

MOTHER: Yes.

MACKIE: Is that your Jeep? The BM?

MOTHER: Yes.

MACKIE: Did you look out of the windae of that when you drove here?

MOTHER: I was upset I.. I wasn't looking.

MACKIE: So you didnae see it get poorer and shittier and more fucked up as you drove here? You didnae see your nice big buildings and trees gradually turn intae fucking slums and shit holes?

MACKIE: *(to POLICE OFFICER)* I bet she's got insurance on that car.

I bet she'll have insurance on her home.
I bet she's got a dog and that's insured;
She's taken steps tae guard against all harm:
Except—for when her son would meet wi' me.
Why the fuck did she not think of that!
A few quid spent insuring that this place
Could never breed young fucked-up men like me.
But cheaper tae get strong-arm pricks like you
Tae lock the stable door when damage done.

POLICE OFFICER: You're not alone in coming from this place,
There's loads of lads like you who live round here
Who never get in trouble with the law,
So don't go making claims to be Rob Roy
Or any kind of hero for your class.
I'm from such a run-down place as this
And there's no way that you speak up for me.

MACKIE: I bet you don't live round here anymore!

POLICE OFFICER: That's not the point! Keep sight of what you did;
Which simply put is slaughter, cold as day.
And though your life's been tough up to this point
Not everyone from here goes out and kills.

MOTHER: Why is it that someone can simply take a knife and stick it in another person? Without any care for what will happen? What's going on when something like that can come about? I'd better go.

MACKIE: No! No. Don't. Don't go.

POLICE OFFICER: *(takes the small black book out of MACKIE's top)* A reading fro the Final Book of James.

MACKIE: You fucking bastard!

POLICE OFFICER: *(opens it and reads)* "There'll come a time...

MACKIE: No, don't!

POLICE OFFICER: ...when I will have to look
Upon my Mother's face when she is dead
It is the natural order of the world..."

He breaks off and puts the book back in MACKIE's top.

MACKIE: (*to MOTHER*) Everything's fucked up. It's all fucked up and can't be put right. I'm sorry.

MOTHER: Why are you sorry?

MACKIE: Because you're right. About us. The kind of people that live here. It will be somebody from a place like this has killed him. Won't it? It always is. It'll be some cunt my age. Any one of us. Look around. There, see? It could have been him that done it. Or him. Or him.

You can't even be sure that's not the hand that killed him.

MACKIE holds his hand out to show her.

MOTHER: I'm sorry, I'm really sorry. I'm sorry that things are the way they are. I'm sorry there's no justice in the way things are. And I'm sorry that I haven't given this a moment's thought til now.

(Beat.)

Can you help me?
I need to know ... what it was like, for him, to die, to die like that, on the street, alone.
Without friends or fam...
I just can't stop thinking...
I can't bear the...
It...
I need to know if he said anything. At the end.
He must have known he was going to die.
I know he wouldn't have been able to say much, because of all the blood in his lungs, the police told me that. They said he wouldn't have been able to speak at all.

But he might. He might have said something He might have. I need to know. I have to know.

MACKIE: You'd have tae ask the bloke that stabbed him.

MOTHER: Or maybe someone who was just there. Maybe not even in the gang, not meaning to do any harm.
I'm not here to get anyone.
My James is dead. That won't change.

But if I could find out what he said I'd give anything for that. Just another moment of contact. Before he fades into the past. I don't need someone to go to jail for it. Some young lad who never had a chance...
I just need to know..

(Beat.)

MACKIE: He was trying to save his pal wasn't he? When he got stabbed.

MOTHER: Yes. He was.

MACKIE: They said that on the news.
I couldn't have done what he done—stand up for a pal against someone wi' a knife. That takes real balls.
He was—brave.

MOTHER: Yes, he was brave.
Thank you.
Are you brave?

MACKIE: What d'ya mean?

MOTHER: How would your mum feel if you died like that?

MACKIE: My Maw? What would you know about my Maw? She's not a mum like you. Your face is all posh and my maw's is all boney. And even when she's no sucking on a ciggy her face's still all pulled in. You smell like soap, but she smells of fags. And you're clean, but my Maw will never get clean. When she was smashed she telt us tae get tae fuck, and when she was sober she telt us tae get tae fuck. It was only when she was greeting about some shit or other she'd say she loves us all. Ma sister had tae feed me and wash me and look out for me.

MOTHER: I just meant if your mum asked you for something to make her life bearable, you'd give it to her, wouldn't you?
Or your sister—if she was a mother to you.

MACKIE: What's so special about mothers, anyway? Mothers are just people and they're as fucked up as everybody else, and they can fuck their kids up or they treat them like fashion accessories or pets.

But kids do love their maws. No matter how fucked up or mean or selfish or posh they are. It's the kids who always love their maws.
Does that help you?

(Silence.)

I'm gonnae go.

MOTHER: No! Please. Don't go. Don't leave me. Please....

They look hard at each other.
After a little while MACKIE reaches into his top and takes out JAMES'
BLOODSTAINED BLACK NOTEBOOK and puts it on the table in front of her. She recognises it at once.

SCENE 14

FUNERAL PYRE

POLICE OFFICER appears in light on one part of the stage.

POLICE OFFICER: Days later, in the Glasgow mournful air,
The people gathered round the funeral pyre
Of our sad city's latest fallen son.
They quenched the fun'ral flames with tears of grief,
Then took away his ashes in an urn
And placed them in a grave upon the hill,
Which gates they locked..

The GANG reappears, silently, around the stage.

POLICE OFFICER: ...in hope to keep at bay
Such scum as them, who might deface the stones.
And so they left and gathered in her house,
To mourn, in sad remembrance of a son.
Then closed her door and headed, all, away.

BLACKOUT

One Day in Spring

Odis

by Alaedinne Chouiref, Soumer Daghastani,
Arzé Khodr, Omar Madkour, Zainab Magdy
and Alia Mossallam

NTRODUCTION

David MacLennan and I programmed five international seasons at A Play, A Pie and A Pint in partnership with the National Theatre of Scotland and the British Council. These ambitious and collaborative seasons provided a rare opportunity for Scottish audiences to experience diverse international voices on our stage. We were proud to platform writers celebrated in their own country and writers whose works were marginalised or outright banned in their homeland. *One Day in Spring*, curated by playwright David Greig, encapsulates the spirit of internationalism, political awareness and enquiry, and a 'fuck it, let's do it' ambition that sums up the spirit of A Play, A Pie and A Pint.

Susannah Armitage
Senior Producer, Eden Court

One Day in Spring first performed in May 2012 at Òran Mór.

ONE DAY IN SPRING

MUSIC: 'Rock el Casbah'

SARA and SEIF enter with scarves over their faces.

They graffiti a map of the Arab world.

Sirens.

They act innocent, hide.

The sirens pass.

They return to graffiti.

Check for police.

Sara clicks.

SEIF: One day in spring.

SARA: 24 hours in the Middle East.

Seif: Or How to be a revolutionary in 18 easy lessons.

SARA: I'm Sara.

SEIF: I'm Seif.

SARA: Those aren't our real names.

SEIF: They are our real names.

SARA: OK, well pretend they're not our real names.

SEIF: Don't tell anyone.

SARA: Especially your border people—they're a nightmare—trying to get a visa. Have you seen Heathrow? The queues! I was there for eight fucking hours.

SEIF: (*in Arabic*) Sara! What the fuck are you saying?

SARA: Sorry.

SEIF: Ladies and gentlemen, I am so sorry but I will be performing today's lunchtime in a wheel chair. Well, it was actually quite stupid, I had attempted to jump off the stage and..

SARA: *(in Arabic)* Seif! You can't tell them that!

SEIF: Oh right! Sorry! Ladies and gentlemen I will performing this lunchtime in a wheelchair because I have been run over by a tank in Tahrir square.

SEIF: Welcome to the Middle East.

SARA: We're going to take you a trip.

SEIF: A day trip through the Arab Spring.

SARA: Which isn't so much spring as... late winter by the way. Kind of like the Scottish spring, fucking freezing!

SEIF: Stick with us.

SARA: And we'll teach you how to be a revolutionary.

SEIF: In 18 easy lessons.

SARA: But first—you need three things—a scarf, half an onion and a tennis ball. Do you all have a scarf?

Audience unsure, SARA goes into the audience.

SARA: You can just use something to put over your mouth. Jumpers, jackets, anything. You just need anything to cover your faces just in case they attack us with tear gas.

Next you need half an onion.

Have you got onions?

Audience is unsure.

They don't have onions?

SEIF: What is this... a pie? What's a pie?

SARA: I think it's some kind of Scottish Shawarma?

SEIF: Has it got onion in it?

Audience is unsure.

SARA: It's quite tasty.

OK, I guess you can use these. You just have to pretend they're onions. You need the onions to breathe in when they attack with tear gas so you don't choke to death. I have an onion. You can use that one, just pass it around if you need to.

And last of all, you need a tennis ball. Do you have tennis balls?

Audience is unsure.

OK, fine. I need someone to volunteer to hold this ball for me throughout the show.

(*to the person*) At some point in the show I might ask you to throw it so pay close attention.

Lesson number 1 for a revolutionary—know how to improvise.

Are you all ready to be revolutionary?

Audience is unsure.

'Yes.'

Really? You guys really think you're gaining independence with that attitude?

Let's try it again! Are we all ready to be revolutionary?

AUDIENCE: YES!!!!

SARA: Right! Let's go to Tahrir square! Where the revolution first broke out on the 25th of January 2011.

OK—It's busy... people are gathering... stay close—

What we need to do is join the demonstration and start chanting. Do you know the chant? Why am I even asking, of course you don't know the chant. It's alright, I'll teach it to you quickly, it's very easy.

SARA begins to teach the audience the chant

The People Want The Fall of the Regime.

SEIF writes down the chant phonetically, then in Arabic and the English translation on the back wall.

The crowd starts to chant.

SARA: Faster! (*chant*) Angrier! (*chant*) Throw your fists in the air! Start marching!

Shit! They're attacking us with tear gas! Cover your faces quickly! And pass the onion around to breathe in. Keep chanting! And those of you who are fit enough, throw the tear canisters back!

Shot

Shit! I'm so sorry everyone! I have no idea what's happening, is everyone alright? Be careful, there might be snipers on the roof, you never know. Let's keep chanting, we can't show them that we're weak! (*chant*) Now insult the police! Fuck you!

Shot

I'm really sorry.

Jumps off chair, looks around in disbelief, walks to edge on the stage.

SEIF is drawing angel wings, gets his crutch and wheels himself back so that he's positioned himself in between the wings.

SARA: I'm not really sure what happened. But I think I've been shot.

SEIF bangs on the ground twice with his crutch.

SEIF: Heaven.

GIRL: This is heaven?

PRIVATE: This is paradise, Yes.

GIRL: Oh... well... can I come in?

PRIVATE: ID.

GIRL: Sorry, it's a bit sticky... it's got blood on it...

He looks it.

PRIVATE: Visa.

GIRL: I just arrived.

PRIVATE: You need a visa, an official stamp of martyrdom, three forms of ID. And a recent photograph signed by a doctor or a lawyer.

GIRL: But I don't have any of those things.

PRIVATE: If you don't like it you can go over there.

GIRL: What's over there?

PRIVATE: That's Tunisian Heaven.

GIRL: I don't want to go to Tunisian heaven!

PRIVATE: Maybe you should go back then.

GIRL: Go back to earth?

PRIVATE: Yes.

GIRL: You mean I can be alive again?

PRIVATE: Not exactly.

GIRL: What then?

PRIVATE: Zombie.

GIRL: Zombie?

PRIVATE: That's it. That's what Zombies are. People who die without the relevant paperwork.

GIRL: NO! Look I'm Egyptian. I'm a martyr. I died in Tahrir. I belong here.

PRIVATE: I'm sorry, but I can't let you in.

GIRL: How long have you been here?

PRIVATE: 38 years

GIRL: 1973?

PRIVATE: Yes.

GIRL: You guys did a great job back then. Defending the nation.

PRIVATE: Thanks. (*whispers*) By the way, I think you guys are doing a great job too.

GIRL: You do?

Private: Yes.

Girl: You follow the news up here?

PRIVATE: Of course—we see everything down there

He shows her how they can see down through the clouds.

GIRL feels flattered and smiles.

PRIVATE: Actually ever since the 25th of January we've had a lot of you youngsters coming up here.

GIRL: Why can't you let us in then?

PRIVATE: I wish I could but I'm just following the rules. I would get in trouble if I don't.

GIRL: Get in trouble?

PRIVATE: Shhh—not so loud.

GIRL: Get in trouble with who?

PRIVATE: The military government.

GIRL: Egyptian paradise is under military rule?

PRIVATE: Transitional government. Once things calm down we'll go back to democracy.

GIRL: So where are the protestors who died on the 25th and 26th of January?

PRIVATE: Can't you hear them? Listen.

Chanting.

PRIVATE: They're in Tunisian Paradise... they're in front of the Egyptian consulate there—protesting

The sound of chanting—THE PEOPLE WANT THE FALL OF THE REGIME.

SARA gets up and writes 'Damascus' on the back wall.

SARA: Damascus

SEIF: Mt. Quaysoon

SARA: It's cold.

SEIF: We're up a mountain—

SARA: A mountain in the middle of Damascus.

SEIF: We're on a protest.

SARA: Welcome to Syria.

SEIF: Syria's different—

SARA: There's no Tahrir Square in Syria.

SEIF: The government don't use tear gas.

SARA: They use snipers.

SEIF: The internet's monitored.

SARA: You can't just organise a demo on Facebook—

SEIF: Here's how you start a demonstration in Syria.

SARA: You and a friend

SEIF: Someone who you can totally and completely trust—

SARA: Print some flyers on your computer.

SEIF: Then you go to a suburb where you think there might be support.

SARA: And you sit in a café, separately, getting up your courage.

SEIF: And then you nod.

SARA: And then you walk out into the middle of the street.

SEIF: And you start—

SARA: (*Bashar Chant*) Yallah Erhal Ya Bashar!

SEIF: Yallah Erhal Ya Bashar!

SARA: And you hope—you just hope that other people join you. (*Bashar chant again*)

SEIF: Everywhere you go in Syria there's pictures of Bashar Al Assad.

SARA: Looking like a 1970's gay accountant.

SARA draws Bashar Al Assad.

SEIF: With his little moustache.

SARA: And his tight jeans.

SEIF: Underneath his picture the slogan reads—

SARA: 'We love you Bashar'.

She writes 'We love you Bashar' under the drawing.

SEIF: So in Syria—all you have to do to be a revolutionary is to say—we don't love you. Write it on a wall. On your jotter in school.

SARA: They hate that.

SEIF: We don't love you.

SARA: So, one night some guys decided on an action.

SEIF: They wrote 'we don't love you' on hundreds and hundreds of tennis balls.

SARA: And then they drove up Mt Quaysoon.

SEIF: All Damascus laid out below them—a dazzle of lights.

SARA: With Bashar's palace sitting proudly at the bottom of the hill.

SEIF: The guys got the tennis balls—

SARA: And they started throwing them.

SEIF throws a tennis ball at SARA, they start throwing it back and forth as they speak.

SEIF: Down the hill—

SARA: Hundreds and hundred of bouncing balls.

SEIF: Bouncing down into the city.

SARA: Bouncing into the presidential palace.

SEIF: Each one saying.

SARA: We don't love you we don't love you we don't love you.

SEIF: And at the bottom of the hill—the presidential guards.

SARA: Big men—with big muscles—and big fat fists.

SEIF: Desperately trying to catch them before they bounced into the presidential garden.

SARA: It's a great way to promote revolution.

SEIF: We don't love you we don't love you we don't love you.

SARA: It's also a good way to break up with your boyfriend—
You still have that tennis ball—right? You need to be ready. Keep alert.

SEIF: Don't sleep.

SARA: Seif, look over there!

SARA throws the ball at SEIF.

SARA: Lesson 2: Revolutionaries always have to stay alert.

SOUND: the call to prayer.

SARA: The call to prayer (*she sits on her knees*).

SEIF: You don't have to pray to be a protestor.

SARA: Some do.

SEIF: We don't.

SARA: You can if you want to.

SEIF: But it doesn't matter if you pray or if you don't... at dawn there's a pause...

SARA: In Homs they pause from fighting...

SEIF: in Cairo they pause from beating up detainees...

SARA: in Gaza they pause from hunger striking...

SEIF: In Tunis they pause from being super smug about their new democracy...

SARA: In Beirut they pause from pausing...

SEIF: all across the Middle East...

SARA: the same sound...

SEIF: rising into the morning like a chord...

SARA: ...peace.

SEIF: Doesn't last though!

SARA: Lesson 3: Life goes on!

SARA writes @NazeehaSaid as SEIF speaks.

SEIF: Nazeeha Said—17th February 2011.

Nazeeha's a Bahraini journalist, 30 years old, she's been covering demonstrations for days—she's got papers, microphones, pens, harassed and tired she's on her way to Pearl Square where people from the shia majority are protesting about the unelected Sunni Royal Family.

SARA: I'm on the street 6:15.

SEIF: She's been live tweeting the events of night.

SARA: Just come from the hospital. Getting interviews from the wounded after the army attacked protestors last night.

SEIF: She's quickly picked up a worldwide following.

SARA: It was horrible.. crying and screaming, many wounded, two killed, dozens of missing...

SEIF: The Bahraini authorities have realized this and tomorrow they're going to arrest her.

SARA: I can't bear what's happening to Bahrain. I've never seen anything like this.

SEIF: She'll be detained and interrogated—she'll be blindfolded and abused. Her twitter account will be deleted. But for now—she doesn't know any of that. For now she's just trying to get home.

SARA: Pearl square. Traffic jammed. The army's closed the streets.

SEIF: She's just trying to get some rest.

SARA: Shit—wait—something's happening... 6:32. The protestors are heading towards the square again... 6:34. They're throwing stones at police.

SEIF: Come on, Nazeeha, you need stay alert to be a revolutionary. #pro-plus

SARA: I'm fine—I'm fine—the police are firing at us. Shit.

SEIF: Go home Nazeeha. #staysafe.

SARA: I can't! The demonstrators are being attacked. Oh God!

SEIF: Watch out Nazeeha!

He mimes shooting.

SARA: They shot the car in front of me. The demonstrators are running at the cops. The kids have sticks. The cops are charging—

SEIF mimes shooting a demonstrator.

One of the demonstrators They shot him He's fallen on the ground... he is still moving.

SEIF: Why are you surprised Nazeeha? You think the regimes didn't learn from Tunisia? Lesson 4: there is only one way to stay in power.

SEIF has bunched up his scarf to form a head.

#Absolute, uncompromising violence.

SEIF shoots the scarf.

SARA and SEIF start to sing Salma Ya Salama, as they prepare for the next scene. SARA sets up the sail and goes to sit on the floor next to SEIF's chair.

SARA: Tunisia. On a felucca.

SEIF: What are you thinking about?

SARA: Elections.

SEIF: Still?

SARA: I'm worried about the Islamists winning.

SEIF: Come on, have a beer. Relax.

SARA: You're saying we should drink our last drink before they make it illegal.

SEIF: We're not scared of God so why should we be scared of them?

SARA: How can you be so complacent.

SEIF: How can you be so cynical? We have to give things a chance we're fighting for democracy.

SARA: Don't be so touchy.

SEIF: It's already cold out here and now I'm feeling colder thanks to you.

SARA: They're using democracy so they can defeat us on our own ground. The freedom we've dreamt of all these years, will turn into a nightmare that we'll never wake from.

SEIF: The poor just want to feed their children. They don't care about "Islamist" or "secularist". It's up to the revolution to serve them. They don't care about Islamic identity, or women's rights, or single mothers—she just wants someone to help. If the Islamists help, they win, if we help, we win.

SARA: Do you know what I love about you?

SEIF: What?

SARA: You're an optimist.

SEIF: Look at that sunrise. How can you not be optimistic? Any country where the sunrise is this beautiful is going to be all right.

Sunrise.

SARA: See—I told you Tunisians were smug!

SEIF: Lesson 5. Revolutionaries must always trust the sunrise.

SARA: Revolutionaries also need good cold beer. So let's go to the supermarket in Cairo!

SARA continues speaking as she gets rid of the sail.

SARA: And onions—we're running out of onions. Also painkillers, bread, bananas, oh and milk, milk for the tear gas.

SEIF: I'm tired I want to go home.

SARA: You can't go home.

SEIF: Please—just for a little snooze.

SARA: Seif focus! We also need beans, gauze, alcohol, not for drinking for cleaning wounds, tuna and coke bottles for the Molotov cocktails.

SEIF is drawing the grocery list items on the wall.

SARA: Of course not everyone in Cairo supports the protestors. Some people just think we're lazy and dirty. Check out these woman.

SARA wraps the scarf around her head.

WOMAN 1: Oh my God! Those lazy bums in Tahrir!

WOMAN 2: I know! They're ruining the country, not to mention the economy, the tourism..

WOMAN 1: And you know what else I heard?

WOMAN 2: No, what?

WOMAN 1:: I heard they have sex!

WOMAN 2: (*gasps*) You're joking?!

WOMAN 1: No, no, no. I heard it from my sister's cousin!

WOMAN 2: Your sister's cousin? Isn't that your cousin?

WOMAN 1: Madeeha please! You can't just interrupt me in the middle of the story like this! Not only do they have sex, I heard they have... orgies!

WOMAN 2: Orgies??

SARA takes the scarf off.

SEIF: OK, got the coke bottles, do we need anything else?

SARA: Wet wipes! Don't forget the wet wipes!

SARA puts the scarf back on.

WOMAN 2: I also heard they were thieves!

WOMAN 1: Of course they are! Did you see all the raids on the malls?

WOMAN 2: : Yes! I don't know where to buy my shoes anymore!

WOMAN 1: I know exactly what you mean!

SARA takes the scarf off.

SEIF: OK, so we have the onions, painkillers, bread, bananas, milk, beans, gauze, alcohol not the drinking type, tuna, coke bottles and wet wipes. Do you think that's enough?

SARA: It depends how much longer we're going to stay in Tahrir.

SEIF: How long do we have to stay in Tahrir?

SARA: As long as it takes.

SEIF: Lesson 6: The revolution takes as long as it takes. *(big sigh)*

SARA: Let's go to the beach.

SARA clicks her fingers, music starts.

Music – Serbi Serbi.

SARA and SEIF put on sunglasses. SEIF takes out a beer, SARA spreads the scarf on the floor as if it's a beach towel.

SEIF: To Sinai. Where we can relax.

SARA: Because it's out of the jurisdiction of the Egyptian government, and under the control of the Bedouins.

SEIF: Where you can have a beer.

SARA: Where you can wear what you like.

SEIF: Where you can wear nothing if you like.

SARA: Where you can share a beach hut with a member of the opposite sex.

SEIF: And you don't even have to show a marriage certificate.

SARA: Where you can smoke hashish.

SEIF: Where you can smoke what you like.

SARA: You can do whatever you want as long as your money is good.

SEIF: In fact, take five. Relax.

SARA: Lesson 7: even revolutionaries need a break.

They both sleep with the music playing.

Phone alarm starts to ring.

SARA: Come on—wakey wakey—time to fly. Revolutions don't stop just because we're sleeping!

SARA runs backstage to get placards.

SEIF: Do you all have phones? Do the phones have cameras? Alright great. We need you to take them out, what we're gonna need you all to do is take pictures of protestors holding up placards from all over the Arab world. After that, upload it on Facebook, Twitter, make it go viral.

SARA comes back onstage holding a bunch of placards.

SARA: This is our strangest weapon, because it's how we spread the message of revolution. You guys all ready? Great! The first place we'll go to is Cairo, Egypt:

SEIF: *(holding picture that reads...)* **Leave already, I'm tired of holding this sign**.

SARA: He had to hold that sign up for over two weeks before President Mubarak actually stepped down. Next! Palestine:

SEIF: *(holding picture that reads...)* **Syria: World where are you? Palestine: LOL**

SARA: That's a really good one for Facebook! Next! Lebanon:

SEIF: *(holding picture that reads...)* **Lebanon is the football field where everyone else comes to fight.**

SARA: Upload it, it will go viral, trust me! Next!

SEIF: *(holding picture that reads...)* **Don't worry, baby, their own tough hearts haven't been scratched by love yet.**

SARA: I have no idea where that one comes from, but I really liked it so I put it in there! Next Syria!

SEIF: *(holding picture that reads...)* **I'm sorry my love – I mentioned your name in the interrogation.**

SARA: You can take a picture of that if you want. I don't know the story behind that one, but I really did see it. Lesson 8: If there's one single act that makes you a revolutionary today—

SEIF: It's speaking.

SARA: Just that.

SEIF: Saying what you really think.
Now let's go to Zamalek. That lovely cool island in the middle of the Nile.

SARA: Let's land on a windowsill of an apartment, where Zeinab, a student, is choosing what to wear to the demonstration.

SEIF: She opens the small brown jewellery box and looks inside. Trying to find the earings to match her mission.

SARA: Whose gift, whose love, do I want singing in my ears if I die today?
Grandmother's old silver earrings that were a twelfth birthday present? The Yemeni jade ones that Khaltoo Mona gave me before she left? Mama's little sterling heart—rose quartz so soft. Or the earings my boyfriend bought me—

SEIF: The first time she went to Tahrir Square she didn't leave her boyfriend's side. Now she tells him, "Don't worry. I will call you when I'm there."

SARA: Never go out without earrings. That's what my mother says.

SEIF: Her mother believes in standards.

SARA: So I choose my bird earrings. (*she puts on the earrings*)
Bye Mama.

SEIF: (*puts on headscarf*) You look pretty. Where are you going?

SARA: To Alaa's house.

SEIF: As soon as Zeinab leaves the house. She's going to take those earings out of her ears and put them in her pocket.

She takes earrings of.

SARA: Advice for female revolutionaries... do not wear any kind of jewelry: necklaces, pendants, earrings, etc. anything they can pull from you.

SEIF: She doesn't want her mother to worry, so she lies. She puts up pretences. She wears her earrings til' she leaves the house. Then she's going to take those earrings out of her ears and put them in her pocket.

She puts earrings in her pocket.

SARA: Bye mama.

SEIF: Bye love.

SARA: It was my friend Alaa was the first to say it. Lesson 9: We fear our mothers more than bullets.

And now let's go to Damascus!

SEIF: The presidential palace.

SARA: On the 14th of March 2012 The Guardian published details hacked from President Bashar's Al Assad's email account.

SEIF: In one bizarre message, he sent his wife the lyrics of a country and western song by the US singer Blake Shelton, and the file downloaded from iTunes.

Music comes on.

I've been a walking heartache / I've made a mess of me / The person that I've been lately/ Ain't who I wanna be/ you stay here right beside me/ watch as the storm goes through/ I need you.

SARA: His wife, meanwhile, spent entire evenings online wondering which pair of designer shoes to buy.
Oh, Bashar—link to shoes—I love these. But I don't think they're not going 2 b useful anytime soon because of these silly protestors! Sad face!
What is it with dictators and shoes?

SEIF: Oh Salma – isn't it lucky that we love each other and that the people love us?

SARA: (*to audience member*) Do you still have that ball I gave you? I think this is a great time to throw it.

Audience member throws ball at BASHAR.

SEIF: 'We don't love you', what does that even mean?

SARA: Lesson 10: Dictators are stupid.

MUSIC – BLAKE SHELTON, GOD GAVE ME YOU.

SARA writes Beirut and draws a big heart around it, as SEIF brings out joint, sunglasses and the umbrella.

SARA clicks to stop music.

SARA: Beirut.

SEIF: Revolutionaries, we may not love our presidents—but that doesn't mean we neglect love entirely.

SARA: Life goes on.

SEIF: Love conquers all.

SARA: And where better to see the true power of love than here in the beautiful city of Beirut? On the Zalka highway.

SEIF: Where a tender-hearted young woman...

SARA poses as the woman.

...from one side of the sectarian divide... is waiting for her lover... from the other side... it's a kind of Romeo and Juliet situation... listen to her as she cries... Romeo Romeo wherefore art thou Romeo?...

THE GIRL: Romeo! Where the fuck are you?!

BIG RANT IN ARABIC

THE GIRL: Romeo? So where are you?...

SEIF: Beirut is a beautiful city but, alas, Romeo is caught in traffic.

THE GIRL: Excuse me, I would like to sit down for a while. The sun is too strong and I can't take it anymore.

THE OLD MAN: You're most welcome.

THE GIRL: Bloody traffic.

THE OLD MAN: It's like this every day.

THE GIRL: It's worse today, there's a demonstration.

THE OLD MAN: What demonstration?

THE GIRL: A workers' demonstration.

THE OLD MAN: There are people in jobs?

THE GIRL: Electricity workers.

THE OLD MAN: Do we have electricity? It thought it was always cut off.

THE GIRL: Maybe that's what they're demonstrating about.

THE OLD MAN: Good for them.

THE GIRL: What a country.

THE OLD MAN: Maybe they are demonstrating in solidarity with the Syrian people against their brutal regime.

THE GIRL: Maybe.

THE OLD MAN: Or maybe they're demonstrating in support of the Syrian regime against the western-backed terrorist agitators.

THE GIRL: Whatever it is, the traffic is still jammed.

THE OLD MAN: Or maybe—maybe it's a demonstration calling for a secular, free democratic state in Lebanon.

THE GIRL: It can't be them.

THE OLD MAN: Why not?

THE GIRL: Not enough of them to cause a traffic jam.

THE OLD MAN: Are you waiting for something?

THE GIRL: I'm waiting for... love.

THE OLD MAN: Ah, Love!

THE GIRL: But it seems I'll be waiting for a long time.

THE OLD MAN: What can you do about it? You have to be patient.

GIRL goes on a big rant in Arabic.

THE OLD MAN: Maybe your blood sugar is low. Why don't you eat one of these pies? Then we can wait in the shade 'til God clears a path in the world for love.

THE GIRL: I'm not hungry.

THE OLD MAN: Then have a smoke.

She takes joint, SEIF gets a lighter.

SARA: Seif! Wait a minute—you can't smoke in Scotland.

SEIF: What?

SARA: No really—not inside.

SEIF: But we're in a play.

SARA: Not even in a play!

SEIF: (*to audience*): Is this true?

Audience say yes.

But that's censorship... do you only do plays about nice people here?

SARA: Seif—come on—this play is only 50 minutes long—we have to hurry. (*to audience*) Can you all imagine that we're smoking?

SEIF: And we'll imagine that we're smoking too.

SARA: (*takes a puff*) And we'll imagine that God is clearing a path in the world for love.

SEIF: (*takes a puff*) Lesson 11: Be patient.

Both exhale and music starts.

Music: Mashrou Leila – Fasateen

They dance.

Explosion.

SEIF: Homs.

SARA: When all else fails—try Skype.

Sound: Skype connecting.

KINAN: Finally!

OMAR: Sorry the Internet's been down for two days.

KINAN: I was so worried. How are you?

OMAR: Still alive, you?

KINAN: There's something important I have to tell you.

Bomb.

OMAR: Do you hear me?

KINAN: What?

OMAR: Fucking Internet... fucking Skype... fucking city.

KINAN: I can hear you again.

OMAR: What is it you want to tell me?

KINAN: I'm gay.

OMAR: What?

KINAN: You heard me.

Short silence

OMAR: I thought this was a show about revolution and shit—not 'gay'. Sorry... I mean... I'm just like... surprised...

KINAN: I've been scared. Scared of dying without telling anyone... Have you ever thought of how it might feel to be free? You know, just to be able to say the things that you want to say without pretending... without fear?

OMAR: I still remember the first time I was in a protest... I was chanting "yallah erhal ya bashar"... I felt like I was soaring... you know what I mean... the kind of feeling druggies say they get when they're on E.

KINAN: Drugs and freedom. You haven't changed.

OMAR: You gotta be careful telling people though... you know... gayness is like Islam, once you're converted, you can't go back.

KINAN: Well, I'm not quite a Muslim.

OMAR: I suppose it's just as well. If you died now I don't think you'd be interested in the forty virgins.

KINAN: Maybe God'll give me forty studs.

OMAR: Are you coming out as a slut now, as well?

Confusion 'hellos', 'can hear mes' in Arabic.

KINAN & OMAR: ya'b dan.

SEIF: Lesson 12—keep the channels of communication open.

Gunfire, SARA pulls SEIF back towards the wall.

SARA: Lesson for female revolutionaries—part two—

SARA stands against the wall as SEIF traces her figure and begins to draw a naked woman.

Egyptian blogger, Alia Mahdy wanted to cause a social revolution as well as a political one. She particularly angered by the fact that art universities in Cairo no longer used nude models like they did in the sixties. So what she did in protest was take naked pictures of herself, and post them on her blog. This caused a huge controversy. Some people called her indecent and immoral, some praised her, some men said they masturbated to these pictures and most, they just called her a whore.

SARA writes the word WHORE on top of the drawn naked figure.

SEIF: Some people said that peole should stop caring about Alia, and focus on the fact that women protestors were being forced to undergo so called "virginity tests".

SARA: What we know from a testimony given by Samira Ibrahim, is that these women protestors were electrocuted, beaten and abused before forced to take off their clothes and spread their legs. Where then a doctor would check to see if their hymen was intact, if it was intact they were sent home. But those who weren't so lucky were then threatened to be taken to court and be put on trial, accused of being prostitutes.

SARA gets up and draws a niqab over the naked figure during SEIF's monologue, she draws a blue bra as well.

THE STORY OF THE BLUE BRA WOMAN

SEIF: In the events known as the Mohammed Mahmoud Riots there was a great deal of brutality used against protestors. In one incident that was captured on a mobile phone, a woman wearing a full niqab is pushed to the ground and her clothes torn open. As she is dragged along the ground her blouse tears revealing her underwear. She is wearing a blue bra. A soldier stomps repeatedly on her breast. These events was uploaded to YouTube where it caused a sensation. It became known as the Blue Bra Day. Some people were horrified that the army was attacking women in Tahrir Square. Other people were shocked that a devout woman was a protestor. The official position of the Islamist parties was that any woman who was wearing a blue bra was probably a whore.

SARA: It just goes to show if you're a revolutionary, it doesn't matter what you wear, there's always someone who's going to call you a whore.
You bastards! You fucking assholes!
I'm sorry for swearing this stuff just really gets to me.

SARA starts to rant in Arabic—genuinely expressing her anger, her fury, her despair.

Becomes tired.

She collapses to the ground, music begins.

SEIF: Lesson 14. You will become tired.

SARA: You will experience defeat.

SARA begins to draw a placard.

SEIF: I never was very brave, was I?
That day on the rollercoaster?
When I told you I was scared of heights,

'I'm really not comfortable with this', I said,
Pale as milk. 'I'm not joking,' I said, 'I'm scared'
And you took my hand and told me
'Don't worry, you're safe with me." Remember?

We screamed.

Both scream.

SEIF: Do you remember.
We screamed at the drop.

Both scream.

The freefall we took towards the crowds below
The kids with candyfloss and the people shooting guns at ducks?
And then the unbelievable relief
As we were caught in the upward run
And the car slowed up again.

You were laughing
I was embarrassed
Because I'd gripped your arm so hard I'd bruised it
Black and blue, you had the mark of my nails on you.

SARA hands give the placard written in Arabic.

Forgive me my love, I mentioned your name in the interrogation.

SARA: Lesson 15...

BOTH: Riot!

Music: Take me back to Cairo

Throw rocks.

Tear gas.

Get beaten.

Attack.

Petrol bombs.

Swear at the police.

Tank.

SEIF: *(clicks to stop music)* Lesson 16: When you see a tank, fucking run.

Alexandria
University Hospital's Morgue.

SEIF lays his scarf on the floor.

SARA: The first thing I notice is their feet.

The white sheets cover all but their feet.

In an attempt to hold it all in; all the emotion; I focus on their feet.

How are they so white? Ibrahim, the young man who dragged us in here, pulls at my arm to get my attention.

SEIF: "Laazem teshuf benafsaha..."
"Laazem teshuf!"

SARA: That's what Ibrahim says:

SEIF: "You have to see!... to see for yourself so you can tell the world... numbers are not enough... we need stories... you has to see!"

SARA: Ibrahim lifts the first white sheet.

SEIF lifts scarf.

SEIF: : "Mostafa Mohammed 26 years old... my friend"

SARA: Mostafa's face is bruised. His lips are parted, his hair messed up. Mostafa looks so much like my brother. I look up at Ibrahim and nod.

I'm ready.

SEIF: "Mohammed Mahmoud, 23 years old..."

SARA: This one too, looks like my brother. Do they all look like my brother? I keep nodding. "Ana shayfa..." (I can see....I can see...)

Suddenly someone else yanks at my arm. I turn and find a woman I had spoken to earlier, outside the morgue.

SEIF picks up his scarf from the floor, SARA puts headscarf on.

"ta'aley...come..." she says, "Remember I told you about my son? Come, come and you'll see him yourself."

We arrive at a cold steel bed, she peels the blanket away from a young man's face, and she looks back at me smiling,

"Isn't he beautiful?"

She pulls the blanket off him, she holds his hand in hers.

"Mohammed...get up darling, wake up..." Wake up habibi...let her see how beautiful you are... get up... let him hear your voice... I'm mama... don't you love your mama? Don't you? Get up then and let him see how beautiful you are..."

SEIF: "Your son is a martyr... A martyr, Shahid...his blood will not go in vain...

SARA: "Shahid..."

SEIF: Why did I say that?

SARA: "Shahid..." (*she repeats it over and over again*)

SEIF: Is he a martyr? Who decides who is a martyr and who is just dead? What if they arrest us all? Or kill us all? How do I know his blood hasn't been spilled in vain? I want to put my hand on her mouth... stop her from saying it.

From outside I hear the chant.

Al sha'ab yurid esqat al nidham!

SARA: Lesson 17: Chanting gives people hope.
For this next lesson, we're going to Glasgow/Edinburgh.

SARA writes Glasgow on wall.

SEIF: How do we get to Glasgow?

SARA: We fly.

SEIF: Fly? How?

SARA: The magic of theatre.

She sits as British airways music comes in.

SEIF: How long is the flight?

SARA: Five hours.

Take off.

BOTH: 8pm. (*look outside window*) Oh, I can see my house from here!
9pm. (*eating*) Haggis, disgusting!
10pm. (*sleeping*) zzzzzzzz...
11pm. (*watching film and crying*) Sleepless in Seattle!
Midnight. (*looking out from window*) Oh, Glasgow is so pretty/ Oh Edinburgh is so much prettier than Glasgow.

Applause.

We're here!

SARA: Now we've taught you how to be revolutionaries—now is the time to start a revolution yourselves.

Meet Abdelrahim Alwaj he's Lebanese—he's the writer of this scene. You might remember him from last week's play? He wrote that?

SEIF: Thank you—thank you.

SARA: After what happened in the Arab world, Abed thinks that Glasgow also needs its own revolution. But because nobody cares about what he thinks, he's decided to take some action. So, for starting a revolution we need: a public place and where better than Oran Mor/Traverse.

SEIF: I hope you don't mind.

SARA: We are going to need a bottle of gasoline, a lighter, and someone willing to burn himself. (*looking for volunteers in the audience*). Like Abo Azizi in Tunisia! Anyone? (*improv with audience, trying to convince them to do it*). Alright we'll show you how it's done and maybe you guys will change your mind. Yallah Abed?

SEIF: Me?

SARA: Who better?

SEIF: But!

SARA: You wrote a hit play. You'll get publicity.

SEIF: It wasn't that big a hit, did you see what The Herald said about it?

SARA: Quiet! First we pour the gasoline over the jacket, then we take the lighter.

SEIF: Wait!

SARA: What?

SEIF: You can't burn my jacket., it's Massimo Dutti.

SARA: Okay, take it off. Come on quickly! (*Abeds protests*) Stop being so fucking Lebanese!

ABED takes off his jacket.

Alright, now burn yourself.

SEIF: I can't.

SARA: Why?

SEIF: Well, my jacket's covered in petrol but not my body! We need more petrol.

SARA: Okay, wait—does anybody know where the nearest petrol station is?

Audience tells her.

OK. hurry up. Go to the petrol station and bring some back here.

Abed protests.

SARA: Go! Look, people did not pay money just to watch you sitting in a wheelchair!

SEIF goes backstage.

He won't be long. He's a very fast runner. It's going to be spectacular. Well worth the wait. Does anybody have any medical conditions we need to worry about? Anybody allergic to fumes. ABED! Where are you?

SEIF: I'm sorry. Well, petrol is fucking expensive in Glasgow! I can't afford it.

SARA: The show has a budget.

SEIF: An Oran Mor show? Have you any idea how low the budget is?

SARA: OK. OK. Hold on. Does anyone have a phone I could borrow? (*takes a phone from audience member*) Hey! Listen, Mr. Esso Petroleum. We are trying to start a revolution and bring democracy to Glasgow. If you don't give us petrol at reasonable prices we will send troops and planes to kill you and to teach you how to be democratic! For goodness sake—didn't you see what happened in Libya?
Good. Now we have petrol.

SEIF: Wait! I thought you said you can't smoke on stage in Scotland?

SARA: The magic of theatre.

ABED starts to burn. While he is shouting, SARA draws flames on wall/

ABED dies.

SARA clicks fingers to stop music.

MUSIC: Im Jacket

SARA: Oh my God—we're nearly finished—and there's so many places we haven't taken you.

SEIF: We wanted to show Yemen where protestors have overthrown President Saleh.

SARA: Or to Morrocco where they're boycotting elections.

SEIF: Or to Libya where—Jesus! It just went fucking crazy there!

SARA: Or to Palestine where the biggest hunger strike is currently taking place.
But if you want to know what's happening just add us on Facebook.

SEIF: Or follow us on Twitter.

SARA: You're real revolutionaries now.

SEIF: You've got your tennis balls! Scarves! Onions! You'll be alright.

SARA: You know exactly what to do. But before you all leave there's just one last lesson to show you.

SEIF bangs ground twice with his crutch.

SEIF: Heaven.

PRIVATE: What's happening down there?

GIRL: They're still protesting.

PRIVATE: You know, I think if I were still alive, I would have been down in that square right now.

GIRL: What makes you think that?

PRIVATE: My son is there.

GIRL: Can you see him?

PRIVATE: There—He is the one wearing a white jacket with a black scarf and jeans.

GIRL: I can't see him, it's very crowded. But I can see my boyfriend Nader. See—he's in front of the Cairo Opera House. Wait, oh my God, my mother is there. With Nader.

PRIVATE: She must have gone down after they received your body.

GIRL:: The police are attacking. An old man's gone down.

PRIVATE: My son's giving the people around him onions and vinegar to smell. Did I tell you he was a doctor?

GIRL:: No way. Let's hope he runs into this poor old man.

PRIVATE: I wish he would come and live with me here... for good.

GIRL: Not soon.

By now the sound of the chants is clearly audible but we can still hear the actors.

GIRL: Can you hear them?

PRIVATE: Yes. They are chanting.

GIRL: In heaven or in the square.

PRIVATE: Both.

SARA: Last lesson: The revolution still goes on.

SARA draws a door. They open the door. They leave.

Lights down to spot on the door.

A hand reaches back around. A victory V through the door.

THE END

Daividh Aeonderson

Tír na nÓg

or

ADRIFT

(Tall Tales from the High Seas)

Board Choice

The current Board of A Play, A Pie, and A Pint nominated Tír na nÓg collectively, celebrating Dave Anderson's enormous contribution to the last 20 years.

Dave Anderson has been writing shows for A Play, a Pie and a Pint since Season One, in 2004, when his solo show, *Mobile*, about a man who lives in a wheelie-bin was produced. He has since written, performed or directed (or a combination of all three) for two decades. Dave was David MacLennan's partner-in-crime with Wildcat Stage Productions through the 1980s and '90s, and collaborated on multiple Òran Mór Pantos.

If you're old enough, you might remember Dave from BBC's *City Lights*, or various TV and film roles, like Gregory's Dad in *Gregory's Girl*.

Tír na nÓg was first performed in August 2006, with Myra McFadyen in the role of The Poet, and later, in 2007, winning Music Theatre Network's Best New Musical at the Edinburgh Fringe, with Pauline Knowles in the lead role. It was revived recently with Dave Anderson as the Poet, but Dave prefers the part to be played by a woman...

The story is told in song—if you fancy performing the piece, chord charts and recordings are available on request.

CHARACTERS

VERSE:
Our Heroine

CHORUS 1:
Bird, Spouse, Boy, Tourist, Siren, Baby, Pebble on Beach, etc.

CHORUS 2:
Old Guy, Tourist, Black Dog, etc

OVERTURE: SEA SHANTY

"BIRD" INTRO

CHORUS 1: Please, take my word for it, I'm a wee bird
And this that you're on, Is the wide, wild sea
And here comes a craft With ocean fore and aft
And balmy breezes waft.... No, that's daft.
Who's on board it? And how did this come to be?
Well, listen, youse all, here to me.

There was a et ho took to sailing
'Cross the North Sea in the Winter
So was she crazy, with the North Wind wailin'?
Or was she searchin'; or was she runnin'?

And TirNan Og is far across the sea
Out of reach of the livin'
There once were Giants who sailed across the sea
To a Beach close to Heaven.

VERSE: Frantic bird off the starboard bow
By the upside-down Moroccan moonlight
Are you lost? You look so pale—
And romantic, Bird, Will you land on deck?
Gie your wings a break? Before you weary me?

CHORUS 1: Too late now, We must tell the tale...

SC/S 2:

"CROSSING OVER"

VERSE: The month is September Or maybe October
And maybe I'm sober But I don't remember
I stand in my loft As I'm wont tae,
Long and oft And the nights are fair drawing in
On my soul The nights are fair drawing in

A cold Autumn breeze Blows the leaves from the trees
And carpets the ground Leaving branches blue
Thinking, I'm like a tree Leaves are falling off of me
And soon, I'll be naked and barren too
The nights are fair drawing in.

It's not enough that I'm old and disillusioned
I'm a boozer and a loser I've got failures in profusion
I'll be naked and barren soon. It's not enough.

It's not enough that my lover doesn't love me
And I'm cold and disaffected And my Mojo's disconnected
And it's a long, long time till the month of June
But that's not enough

POET: There's a guy next door
On the attic floor
Bangin' a piano
Drivin' me bananas, going...

VOICE: Crossin' over some day...

POET: Something about a river...

VOICE: That Jordan river some day...

POET: Sometimes, it's the sea...

VOCE: That stormy ocean some day...

POET: Sometimes, Jesus will help him...

VOICE: Jesus! Jesus help me across...

POET: Sometimes, it's just - other folk...

VOICE: Brothers and Sisters! Gonna help me cross that river some day...

POET: Sometimes , there's Glory on the other side...

VOICE: Bound for Glory! Bound for Glory some day...

POET: Sometimes he just wants to lie down and die...

VOICE: Gonna lay me down some day...

POET: Sometimes I like it; sometimes I don't
Sometimes I'm glad he does it

Sometimes I hope he won't
Sometimes it's wonderful:
Sometimes it's pish
Either way I want to scream,
"Neighbour, I wish you'ld
Please, please, please, Gi' es peace
Please, please, please, Gi' es peace"

(V. & GND continue under)

SPOUSE: Just to let you know There's nobody there
We don't have a neighbour At the top of the stair
Either she's hallucinating
Or just avoiding communicating

Talk to me

Talk to me

VERSE: Love of my Life, I will die Driven crazy by this guy
And I can't pay the rent And I'm bent down low
And if I hang around I will only bring you down
I'm drawn; where I'm gone, I don't really know
I only know that I must go.

CHORUS/SPOUSE: In a civilised society Everyone's an artist
Everyone's a Star, Nobody's the Chorus.

THE NEXT TWO VERSES ARE SIMULTANEOUS

VERSE: Love of my Life, I must pack
In a month, I will be back
I've landed a gig And I can't say no And maybe I'll find—
Whatever, in my mind
I'm packed, and I'm ready to go
So...
That's me away,
Cheerio.

CHORUS/SPOUSE: Please don't think I don't know what's gone on
It's a smokescreen for the things she's done
That affair with you know who I mean
Her I call the Karaoke Queen
The way she carries on, for Goodness sake

Maybe it's high time I got a break
I know what I know
But I'll go with the flow
Is that you away?
Cheerio

CHORUS 1/ SPOUSE: And a lover who can leave you
Is no great loss
Let her "Go Across"
Anyway,
I'm shagging the boss.

("HORN-PIPE" STING - INTO:-)

SC/S 3:

"MAL DE MER"

VERSE: Oh, The Pride of Venezuala is an Empress of a ship

CHORUS: Oh, sling yer hook to starboard, lads,
And sling yer hook to port

VERSE: She's the length of twenty buses
from her anchor to her tip.

CHORUS: Keel-haul yer Granny, get it up ye

VERSE: She's a dozen storeys high, and she's at least a fathom wide..

(Sling etc)

There's a Shopping Mall, and a choice of Bars and Restaurants inside.

CHORUS: Keel-haul, etc.

("HORN-PIPE" STING)

VERSE: With a Ballroom, and a theatre, and a Creehe, and Cabaret...

CHORUS: Sling yer hook etc...

VERSE: A Casino, Beauty Parlour, and an Internet Cafe.

HORUS: Keel-haut etc.

VERSE: She's an Ocean-Going City, she's a Miracle Afloat...

CHORUS: Sling yer hook, etc..

VERSE: She's magnificent, she's so much more than just a fuckin' boat.

CHORUS: God Bless the Pride of Venezuala!

VERSE: Sadly, the vessel I was sailing was the Duchess of Arbroath.
Which was a tub, a rusting bucket from the Boer War
Stuffed to the gills wi' drunken Geordies, ever ready with an oath

It was my gig to entertain them in the Piano Bar
And so it was we set sail on a dreich November morn
Steering a course across the North Sea, clear to Amsterdam
Fetching a cargo on the lookout for some ganja and some porn
And wi' the bar bein Duty-free, maybe a wee bit dram.

And on the very first night I was a sailor
I saw a thing I hope I'll never see—again
For as soon as the Night-time fell, the
Sea began to swell, and a
Storm came up, and tossed that tub, like a
Cork in a barrel, Like a duck in the bath.

Up went the Stem,	Down went the Prow
Up came the waves	Over the Bow
Up went the Starboard,	Up went the Larboard
Up came your lunch	Over the side
Down came the rain	Up came the deck
On came the pain	

Ever had the Mal de Mer?

CHORUS: Mal de Mer?   Mal de Mer?

VERSE: And when the storm abated, and the rolling settled down,
The Bar was devastated, and the people lay around
Suffering Mal de Mer

CHORUS: Mal de Mer
The Passengers had it—   The Crew had it

The Captain had it—   The Cook had it
The bosun had it
The Croupiers in the Casino had it
Even the Phillipinos had it
Everybody had it
But me.

Mal de Mer, etc

I saw a Malevolent Mist Amongst the people lying Stealing their
Will to Resist Soon they gave up trying

Mal de Mer, etc

The Mist became a Wild Pack Of Dogs with Vicious Teeth
Who chewed, not at the bodies, But the Spirit underneath

Mal de Mer, etc

They laid where they had fallen
Their groans grew long and loud
God help me, I stole their money—
They'd been an ugly crowd

Mal de Mer, etc

What a shame
Get it up ye

Mal de Mer...

("HORN-PIPE" STING)

The ship hove into harbour in the morning, just as planned,
(Sling yer hook to the Starboard, sling yer hook to the port)
And never was I happier to see a stretch of land
(Keel-haul yer Granny, get it up ye)
The Captain couldn't hear me, but I thanked him for the trip
(Sling yer hook... etc)
He lay there unresponsive as I jumped his fucking Ship
(Keel-haul yer Granny, get it up ye)

(SAX/FLUTE INTO)

SC/S 4

"AMSTERDAM"

VERSE: I never sold my soul to the Devil:
He just took it, and left me damned
I couldn't see no, hear no evil:
I couldn't see nothin' at all
For the alcohol—
That was quite a fall,
Back in old Amsterdam—

ALL: Wasted...

VERSE: Every single night—I had—

ALL: Tasted...

VERSE: Everything in sight. I got...

ALL : Pasted...

VERSE: I knew it wasn't right—when I was...

ALL: Hawkin' my bahookie
In the port of Amsterdam.

VERSE: Well, I know my old Ma would be shocked if
She had seen me in old Amsterdam
I didn't care: I took it up the octave—I was

ALL: Gross and base—

VERSE: I was out

ALL: My face—

VERSE: I'd go

ALL: Any place

VERSE: For another gram....

ALL: Degradation

VERSE: Was my middle name

ALL: Aberration

VERSE: And I knew no shame

ALL: Fornication

VERSE: But I never came—when I was...
Marketing my meat

ALL: In the port of Amsterdam

VERSE: Trading my toosh

ALL: In the port of Amsterdam

VERSE: Flogging my Fannie

ALL: In the port of Amsterdam

VERSE: Sitting in a window

ALL: In the port of Amsterdam

VERSE: I was the Hooker of Holland

ALL: In the port of a Amsterdam

VERSE: And it didn't matter how stoned I got—
Or how drunk I got—
Or how fucked I got—
I couldn't shake that...

VOICE: "Crossing over..."

VERSE: What is that?

VOICE: "...some day..."

ALL: Crossing over some day

VERSE: As I lay every night
In the gutter in my fluids
Passed by all the junkies,
Punks and drunks and druids,
There was somebody there looking over me—
I could barely see, but he was there,
Playing sweet music...
I'd my own Guardian Angel
Urchin boy from the ghetto

With his dark Latin eyes I would call
Senorito, standing guard, playing soft
On a little lute,
Which became a flute, then an oboe—
Playing sweet music...
I woke up in the gutter one morning
And I looked round my neighbourhood
And my angel had gone without warning
And a cold...

ALL: Wind blew—

VERSE: Chilled me through...

ALL: And through,

VERSE: And somehow I knew,
he was gone for good...

ALL: Hopeless

VERSE: Thinking I'd go on

ALL: Helpless

VERSE: With my angel gone

ALL: Loveless...

VERSE: Knew that I was done with

ALL: Hawkin' my bahookie
In the Port of Amsterdam (repeat...)

VERSE: I'll find a new ship
Take a new trip
But not on the North Sea -
Maybe the South Sea
Sun's gonna shine on me - I'm done with...

ALL: Hawking my bahookie in the port of
Amsterdam...
(uno, dos, tres, quatro!)

SC/S 5:

"SENORITO"

VERSE: What's goin'on now?—I'm in
Puertg De Las Tapas Tempranillo
In a cafe—Sippin' ob a wej al fresco carajillot
The birds on the windowsill Can't help but trill
This stupid song
The scabby wee cats And the dogs and the rats
Feel compelled somehow to sing along:-

CHORUS: You don't have to be unhappy
You don't have to be unhappy
You don't have to be unhappy
Lighten up, for Christ's sake

VERSE: Even the lizards Open their gizzards and sing
This stupid song
An army of ants In their Mariachi pants
Echo the geckos and sing right along:-

CHORUS: You don't have to be unhappy, etc

VERSE: And while the Plaza Has a Fiesta
I see before me Walking towards me
My Senorito From the ghetto
But now he's all grown up He's all grown up
And only yesterday He was a little boy
Where did that boy go?—Where did that boy go?
Senorito!—He doesn't know me
He's with a woman
His wife? His lover?

(RIFF IN)

CHORUS: You don't have to be unhappy, etc

VERSE: You don't have to... etc
And the ants dance
And the gulls chant
Give me another chance,

Senorito

> Please forgive me
> He walks on by me
> The woman turns
> And just becomes
> Like an old crone
> From sweet and young
> She spits these words to me
> She spits these words to me:

CHORUS 1: "This boy was born good

You stole his childhood He used to love you

And now he's done with you "Goodbye",

VERSE: ... She said
> And as she turned her head She was young again

ALL: Senorito!
> Senorito! Etc.

SC/S 6:

"FOREVER YOUNG" (ABOARD A CRUISE SHIP.)

CHORUS 2: My name is Sid - And this is Mabel
> We are not cyphers; -We're actual people
> We go abroad 'cos we are able:
> We've been to Cyprus; -We've been to Naples

CHORUS: But most of all, we cruise upon the sea
> Out of reach of the riff-raff
> We love the food; you can eat all day for free
> Entertainment; it's a right laugh

VERSE: I'm singin' my heart out on a ship-
> I'm barin' my soul I'm cryin' the Blues,
> and a little Celtic Rock'n'Roll
> I give it my all - I let it rip -
> Gospel in my heart - This is my Music:
> This is my Art

CHORUS 1: My name is Mabel - My husband Sidney
We love a cruise, We think it's all right
The Captain's table had steak and kidney
There'll be a buffet about midnight

(NEXT 2 VERSES SIMULTANEOUS)

CHORUS: Do you know "My Way"? Mack the Knife? Lady in Red?
You look Wonderful Tonight? Spanish Eyes? Barry Manilow?
Danny Boy? Do You Know the Way to Amarillo?

VERSE: I'm singing my heart out - Wailing the blues
Casting pearls before the swine out front
Night after night they want the same old shite
Neil Diamond is a cunt

CHORUS: Tír na nóg is Paradise...

VERSE: There's no such place as Tír na nóg.

CHORUS: What did you say?

VERSE: There's no such place as Tír na nóg.

CHORUS: Before that! Sacrilege! Heresy! Bastard!
Did you hear that?
She says Neil Diamond is a cunt!

I went the cry	The Infidel must die
id Sid & Mabel	The Infidel must die
The captain's Table	"
The whole Piano Bar	"
The cocktail Deck	Ballroom
Poolroom	The Beauty Parlour
Cybercafe	Dining Room
Casino	Even the Philipinos

The Infidel, the Infidel, the Infidel must die

VERSE: And they grabbed me by the ankles
And they grabbed me by the wrists

CHORUS: The Infidel must die; the Infidel must die

VERSE: They beat me with their canapes;
They beat me with their fists

CHORUS: The Infidel must die; the Infidel must die

VERSE: Shouting, "This is for Neil Diamond, And this is for the Lord"

CHORUS: Singing, take 'er to the side, me lads,
And make 'er walk the plank!

VERSE: But in the absence of a plank,
They simply threw me overboard

CHORUS: The Infidel must die, get it up ye

VERSE: And as I was sinking, realizing I was drowned
Some reason, I was thinking
That I still can hear that sound

(IT'S THE "GUY NEXT DOOR" THEME)

What is that?
Some day, I'll be crossing over,
I'll be crossing over some....day

SC/S 7:

"UNDEAD ON THE SEA-BED"

CHORUS: Corne and join the Mutants
Created by Pollutants
At the bottom of the Deep Blue Sea
There's a most attractive Fascinating shark-it
Carne from plastic Packets
⁻From your local Supermarket
Of a colour that you'll never see
Florescent, excrescent, & phosphorescent
Undead on the Sea Bed- We're the
Undead on the Sea Bed

Here comes a Serpent in Torment
Doomed to spend Eternity
With his Bucket and Spade

Tryin' to bio-degrade
"Neptune, have mercy on me!

Just a patch of soil
So my my mortal coil
Can shuffle off and set me free!"
Monsters of the Deep
Tryin' to get some sleep
Undead on the Sea Bed
Undead on the Sea Bed

(MINOR RIFF INTO)

SC/S 8:

"THE SIREN'S SONG"

VERSE: Languished at my lowest ebb; and I
Anguished, if my feet might web -
Apart from the fact that I was drowned
I was-
Barely aware of a human sound - Was it
There- could I hear a woman?

Did you ever hear the sound of Temptation
When you're down in the depths of the sea?
Promising instant gratification? -No
Strings attached - No catch-It's only
Natural, satisfaction guaranteed

CHORUS: C'mon

VERSE: (It seemed to say)

CHORUS: You know you want it- ifs Silkie

VERSE: (It seemed to say)

CHORUS: All for free- It's Milky

VERSE: (It seemed to say) - Was a
Lorelei
Brought me high - and I
Burst to the surface of the Tropic Sea

SC/S9:

"THE GHOST BOAT"

VERSE: The sun was beating down
And I could see the clear blue sky
And the voice that I'd been hearing
Now was clear to me
It was not a mermaid, friends, I heard a baby cry
From a little fishing boat

I scrambled up on deck
And all the passengers were dead
Their bodies lay around
And this is how they died
Their throats had all been slit
And all the deck was painted red
And somewhere down below the baby cried and cried

Down below I found her
She was such a lovely child
Blacker than the night
And whiter than the snow
And when she saw me coming,
She stopped crying and she smiled
And how she knew my language, I will never know

CHORUS: They promised us a new life
In a land called Tír na nÓg.
Where there is no unhappiness or poverty
Where people get respect
And they don't treat you like a dog
In what they call a civilized society

My father knew the Ferry-man
And took him at his word
Gave him everything we owned to find a better life
But when we were out at sea,
They started throwing us overboard
And those who tried to fight were treated to the knife

VERSE: And then the baby held her hand
Towards me and she said,

CHORUS: Help me,

VERSE: She said,

CHORUS: Help me-

VERSE: All I did was weep
And hold her in my arms, and then
The next thing, she was dead
And all I did was cry, until I fell asleep

The dawn would break, and I would wake
And there she was again
Saying, "Help me!" and again I didn't do a thing
And then she died, and then I cried
And then I slept again
And every day the same thing kept on happening

The dawn would break, and
I would wake - "Help Me", she'd cry- and
Then she'd die - And
Then I'd weep - And
Then I'd sleep - Till
One day-
Land Ahoy!

SC/S 10:

"THE MAGIC BEACH"

VERSE: See the pebbles on the Perfect Beach
Shimmering like spangles, gentle under-foot
Singing in the sunlight
Colours of the rainbow
Some as bright as diamonds
Some as dark as midnight

Every pebble has a song to sing
Every one a history,
How they came to be Stories of their travels
Giving up the mystery
When you hold a handful
You can only marvel

CHORUS: Amber, Jasper, Jet and Jade,
Marble Incas and Ancients laid
Stones like the Eggs of Exotic Birds
Burst yout heart with joy
Beyond words...

VERSE: Tho' I don't believe in Paradise
Never been so peaceful, this'll do for now
Leave me on my ownsome
I'm not going looking I'm expecting nothing
I can cope with lonesome

See the pebbles on the Perfect Beach...

Aship!

And what's the flag?

(VOICE OFF - MEGAPHONE)

SC/S 11:

"BLACK DOG"

CHORUS: My name is Black Dog,
And I own Tír na nóg.
The blood-thirstiest brigand ever sailed the sea
And you can't save your butt,
'Cos your throat's as good as cut
You're dead as a Poet can possibly be -
Say "Hello" to your Maker from me

The trouble I took;
Had to kill Captain Cook, who

Stole it from the Faeries, originally
And my beach won't pissed on by a wanky Fantasist
You're trespassing on Private Property
That's Death, by the Pirate's Decree!

VERSE: I ran from the beach
To be out of his reach
Through Forests and Swamps: And a whole lot more
I went through Death's Dark Vale -
But that's another tale
Exhausted, I came to another shore;
The one I was not on before

And the waves came crashing on the shore
Becoming wild horses,
One came up and spoke... said

CHORUS: I'nl on a mission
Mortal, saddle up, I'll take you out to sea
I have a proposition...

I come from the Queen of the Land of the Young
Her Erse name is Niam, as rm sure you knew
Tír na nóg is not here,
Tho' it's actually quite near
You're welcome, she says, as the morning dew-
She's taken a fancy to you

You can stay, every day of your life,
In a Heaven, where you'll never have to grow old
Where the leaves never fall from the trees, never leaving you
Naked, and barren, and cold-Or go back,
To your bleak, winter reverie, where you
Seemed to be so at home—
What will it be?

VERSE: And the Sea said:-

CHORUS: What will it be?

VERSE: And theWind sighed:

CHORUS: What will it be?

VERSE: And the Sky sang:

CHORUS: What will it be?

VERSE: And the Moon and the Stars came out, Just in order to shout.....

ALL: What will it be?

"ROLLING HOME"

VERSE: Frantic bird, what would I say to Eternal Youth?
Look at me, I'm eternally
Long in the tooth?

Rolling home, I'm going rolling home
Rolling, rolling
I'm going rolling home

I've sailed the seven oceans
I've done some scary shit
But if you're naked and barren too,
Just get used to it

Rolling, etc

No matter where I travel
Been with me all along

CHORUS: "Crossing over"

VERSE: Can't shake that song

ALL: Rolling, etc
Sailed the seven oceans—
Only learned two things;
Life is sad, with lots of jokes:
And everything sings

Rolling Home, etc

THE END

Oliver Emanuel

Storytelling

A Tribute to Oliver Emanuel

In loving memory of Oliver Emanuel, whose outstanding contributions and friendship to A Play, A Pie and a Pint are sorely missed.

Oliver Emanuel was an internationally award-winning playwright. He wrote over 30 plays for both stage and radio. Awards include: Tinniswood Award for Best Audio Drama Script (2019); Best Series at BBC Audio Drama Awards (2019); Herald Angel (2017); Best Adaptation at BBC Audio Drama Awards (2017); People's Choice Victor Award at IPAY, Philadelphia (2015); Best Show for Children and Young People at UK Theatre Awards (2015).

In 2020, *Tiger is Out*, an extract from *I Am Tiger*, directed by Lu Kemp and starring Ava Hickey, was broadcast on BBC as part of National Theatre of Scotland's *Scenes for Survival*.

Oliver was Reader of Playwriting at the University of St Andrews where he created the MLitt in Playwriting & Screenwriting with Zinnie Harris.

Storytelling was first produced in April 2023 at Òran Mór.

NOTE

I want you to play. Make a mess. I want you to tell this story using anything and everything you can to move the audience. Sing, dance, play guitars, jump up and down, draw a big picture of a tree or a crack in a man's chest on a whiteboard. Whatever works for you. But stay safe and remember that everything is there to serve the story and the audience. It's for two people of whatever age, race, gender you wish. One talks like this, the other talks like this. I'd like it if you could say hello to the audience before you begin and say goodbye at the end. I'd like it if you sang a song about halfway through. But this is your play now so the final decision is yours. Enjoy.

A dash (—) indicates an interruption.

An ellipsis (...) indicates a tailing away or a thought-pause.

A line marked... indicates an intention to speak.

(A word or phrase in parenthesis is thought but not uttered).

/ at the beginning of the line means the performers speak in unison.

Everything I'm about to say is false. I made it up.

This is a story.

Even though some of it feels like it's true.

That's what a story is.

Once upon a time there was a man, a nice man who lived in a nice house on the edge of the city. One day he woke up and decided to kill himself but in the end he didn't.

The end.

...

...

That's what happened.

Spoilers.

Once upon a time there was a man. He was nice.

He was... okay.

He was fine.

He was average.

His name was Robert and he was 44 years old. Robert had a wife and teenage twins and a fair number of friends. He was a moderately successful businessman with a moderately large house and a moderately large garden.

Everything was okay in Robert's world.

As okay as could reasonably be expected.

But then Robert woke up one morning and knew that today would be the last day of his life.

Once upon a time there was a man. His name was Robert and he was 44 years old. Robert had a wife and teenage twins and a fair number of friends. He was a moderately successful businessman with a moderately large house and a moderately large garden. Everything was okay in Robert's world. But then Robert woke up one morning and knew that today would be the last day of his life. He came down to the kitchen and embraced his wife. Robert said: 'I love you. I've loved you since the very first moment we met and every moment after. Our love has been the truest thing in my life. You have given me children, precious, darling twins who I love with all my heart, and more than that you have given me happiness greater than I ever imagined possible. I love you and I want you to know that none of what happens today is your fault. You cannot and should not hold yourself to blame. If I may borrow a cliché, it is not you, it's me. I love you. Thank you.' And so saying, Robert turned and left the house immediately and his wife never saw him again.

...

...

Except...

That's not what happened.

No.

No.

That's not what happened.

Once upon a time there was a man. His name was Robert and he was 44 years old. Robert had a wife and teenage twins and a fair number of friends. He was a moderately successful businessman with a moderately large house and a moderately large garden. Everything was okay in Robert's world. But then Robert woke up one morning and knew that today would be the last day of his life. He came down to the kitchen and embraced his wife. Robert said: 'Did you sleep okay?'

Not bad. You?

On and off.

You should take the pills the doctor gave you.

They make me feel drunk.

There are worse things than being drunk.

Tell that to a glass of water.

And his wife did that face she does when Robert makes one of his funny jokes, kissed him on the cheek, picked up her bag and was gone.

She never saw Robert again. ...

...

...

Except—

Except that's not what happened—

Nope.

That's not what happened.

Once upon a time there was a man. His name was Robert and he was 44 years old blah blah blah, you know the drill. He came down to the kitchen and embraced his wife. Here is what Robert actually said to his wife:

...

Nothing.

...

Robert didn't say anything.

She said goodbye, kissed him on the cheek and left. And that was the last time she saw him.

...

But if he'd been able to find the words, Robert would have liked to have said the things about love and happiness and blame.

But he didn't because he couldn't.

What had happened to Robert? From where had this feeling of ending things originated? Was there a moment when things changed?

We want to tell the truth.

Yes.

Even though this is a story, we want to tell the truth, the whole truth, nothing but etcetera.

It's important to tell the truth.

Despite the fact that the truth is sometimes a hard, slippery, painful, impossible bastard.

/For the last year or so Robert had found there were two different voices running in his brain at the same time—

/There were two different voices speaking in Robert's brain at the same time, it had been happening for a year ot more—

/It was like there were two radios playing at the same time—

/It was like there was one person talking in one ear and another person talking in the other ear—

/One voice was Robert living his life as others perceived it. That is, as a 44-year-old man who had a wife, teenage twins, friends, a moderately successful business, a moderately large house with a moderately large garden—

/The first voice was Robert as he was in real life. Man, wife, kids, mates, job, house, garden yada yada yada yada yada—

/While the other voice told a story that involved a deep sense of worthlessness, a feeling that nothing Robert did or had ever done had any value whatsoever and that whatever he did in the future it would probably make the world a worse place than it already was—

/The second voice was telling Robert that he was the worst human in the world or not even the worst but the worst person in the world's second cousin, someone you wouldn't invite to Christmas or even a funeral or 5-a-side football match they were so utterly shit and pointless—

/And it was hard to tell which of the voices he should listen to—

/He didn't know which voice to listen to from one moment to the next—

/Or if he should listen at all—

/Or if he should listen at all.

*

Robert had tried to manage the two voices in many different ways.

He had tried to listen to one not the other.

He had tried listening to neither, blocking them out.

Playing very loud music.

Reading books.

Energetic running.

Weeping in his car to mildly embarrassing rock music.

Brackets Phil Collins close brackets.

Bunking off work, hiring a hotel room and watching Korean action movies until it was time to go home.

Some of these things helped.

A bit.

For a time.

Some of these things helped a bit for a time.

He could have gone to the doctor, spoken to a friend but he☐well, he. Um.

He struggled to find the words.

Yes.

He struggled to find the words.

But it was getting harder for Robert to quieten the voices.

Harder and harder.

The voices were getting louder and louder.

Louder and louder.

So loud that Robert felt he couldn't take it anymore.

*

Once upon a time there was a man. His name was Robert and he was 44 years old. Robert had a wife and teenage twins and a fair number of friends. He was a moderately successful businessman with a moderately large house and a moderately large garden. Everything was okay in Robert's world. But then Robert woke up one morning and knew that today would be the last day of his life. Before they headed off to school, Robert stopped his teenage son and daughter at the front door. Robert held them as delicately as he had held them on the day of their births, thirteen years previously. Into this embrace Robert tried to communicate the love he felt, the pride, the wish for forgiveness, everything, everything he could into that single moment. Too soon, his kids broke off the embrace, gave Robert a look and said:

/Are you alright, Dad?

/*Are you alright, Dad?*

Are you alright?

Are you alright?

Are you alright? Are you alright?

Alright equals okay equals fine equals not bad equals on an even keel.

Does anyone really want to know the answer when they ask: are you alright?

Or is it one of those questions that is automatic?

In his life, Robert had been asked if he was alright approximately twenty-seven thousand times.

But now he came to think about it, Robert doubted he'd ever been alright.

In terms of storytelling, 'are you alright?' is a turning point.

A turning point is where several outcomes are possible.

For example, Robert could reply to his twins: yes, my loves, I'm fine.

Which would be a lie but it would ease any fear or concern his son and daughter may have and send them happily on their way to school.

Or Robert could reply: well kids, if I'm being honest, I'm not 100 percent.

Which is only a shade more complex than the previous reply but still gives the children the option of patting their Dad on the back and making tracks to Double Biology.

Or Robert could tell his teenage children the truth: I'm not alright, I'm actually very far from alright. In fact I wasn't going to mention it but since you asked I'm seriously considering ending my life today.

That would be the truthful answer to the question 'are you alright?'

And the truthful answer might have elicited a strong and decisive reaction.

But the problem with the truth is that sometimes it's too heavy a burden to pass to your loved ones.

So when Robert's twins asks him: are you alright, Dad?

Robert says: aye... aye, kids, I'm fine.

A quick note about Robert's wife and children.

Up to this point we have not given them names or suggested they are characters in their own right.

Which they most certainly are.

Yes.

This is not because we're trying to hide the truth.

Far from it.

This is not because we're trying to hide the truth but because we're trying to focus the story on its main protagonist, Robert.

Sometimes in order to tell a story in the most straightforward and clear-cut way it's necessary to make certain omissions.

The name and personality of Robert's family is one such example.

Yes.

But now is a moment where we might divulge this information to further illuminate Robert's narrative.

His wife's name was Michelle and their twins were called Adam and Ava.

Michelle worked at an ethical online bank, enjoyed water sports and Japanese literature.

Adam and Ava were in their third year of High School, played doubles in the local badminton team, and both fancied a boy called Daminola in the year above.

Michelle's favourite food was grilled oysters.

Adam and Ava liked Four Season Pizza.

Michelle was an honest and open person who struggled with confrontation.

Adam and Ava were fun, generous and boisterous but tended to deal with challenges by keeping quiet about them.

Michelle just wanted everyone to be okay.

Adam and Ava just wanted everyone to be okay.

Adam and Ava were like their Mum.

They looked more like their Dad but they were more like their Mum.

Flashback to last night.

This was a discussion that Michelle, Adam and Ava had last night after Robert had gone up to have a bath.

Do you notice anything off about Dad recently?

What do you mean by off?

I don't know. Like... he doesn't seem to be himself. He seems distracted, absent.

I guess.

Does that mean you haven't noticed anything?

No, we have... we have... but hasn't it been going on a while now? I mean, Dad hasn't been the same since he found out about Granddad.

This is the story of Robert's Dad. When Robert was 8 years old, his Dad left the childhood home and never came back. He never went to work. His boss said he had had a message from Robert's Dad saying that he had an appointment. With whom and where that appointment was, was never confirmed. After 24 hours, Robert's Mum called all Robert's Dad's brothers and sisters, his friends, work colleagues. After 48 hours, Robert's Mum called the police and Robert's Dad became an official Missing Person. The whole family, Robert included, was asked whether his Dad had displayed any behaviour that might suggest a reason for his surprise disappearance. Robert doesn't remember what he replied to this question but he has a keen memory of the policeman's watch which the policeman wore with the face facing down. Robert had never seen anyone wear a watch like that. Weeks passed. Months. A year. No news of Robert's Dad. His car was discovered at the train station but this was many years before CCTV and there were no further sightings. Robert's Dad had done an amazingly thorough job at disappearing from his life. Robert's Mum got a prescription from the doctor to help her sleep but Robert and his wee sister were kids so just sort of got on with it. When his Dad came up in conversation, Robert changed the subject. He never missed a day of school. He never cried. After 7 years, Robert's Dad was officially declared dead. Robert's Mum married a man named Geoff who had a Triumph motorcycle and called Robert 'Big Man' which was annoying but at least Geoff came back at the end of the day. And, as Robert got older, met Michelle, became a father to the twins, he almost completely forgot about the man who had been his father for the first 8 years of his life. It was the end of the story as far as Robert was concerned.

Except it wasn't.

No.

It wasn't the end of the story.

It wasn't the end of the story because the previous year, almost to the day that our story takes place, Robert received a phone call from the British Consulate in Helsinki to inform him that his father had recently died. At first Robert thought the call must be a hoax. Geoff was alive and well and living in Oban with his Mum. But when the consulate official repeated the information, the penny finally dropped. So began a strange, almost hallucinatory, few days. Robert flew to Finland to formally identify his twice dead progenitor before going on to the coastal village where Robert's Dad had lived for the last 36 years. Robert wandered around the small, wooden cabin that had no pictures, no personal items of any kind and asked—for the first time in his life—who on earth had this man been? What had made him run away? And what had made him want to live a life like this? Despite the fact that his Dad had named Robert as his next of kin, there was no note or letter to his son. Neither the neighbours nor the British Consul had any further information to pass on. For the second time in his life, Robert felt as if his Dad had vanished without explanation. And while the first time, Robert had been able to brush it off, return to school, play with his mates, act normal, this time… this time something broke. Robert felt as if a small crack had opened up inside him—just here—so small that you could barely notice it on first glance but if you came close you could see the sky on the other side.

*

Once upon a time there was a man. His name was Robert and he was 44 years old. Robert had a wife and teenage twins and a fair number of friends. He was a moderately successful businessman with a moderately large house and a moderately large garden. Everything was okay in Robert's world. But then Robert woke up one morning and knew that today would be the last day of his life.

He showered as normal.

He got dressed as normal.

He ate his breakfast as normal.

He said goodbye to his wife and children as normal.

He sent a quick email to his colleagues to say that he would work from home today which wasn't exactly normal but wasn't wildly unusual either.

He left the house as normal.

He decided to walk rather than drive but instead of turning left to head into the city, Robert turned right.

This is another turning point.

No pun intended.

No pun intended.

The whole story might have turned out differently if Robert had gone the other way.

By the way, the thing I just said, the thing about the crack that opened up in Robert's chest. You're probably assuming that this is a metaphor of some kind, an exaggeration or even a lie. It isn't. It's real. It was about the size of a one-pound coin. Just here.

...

If you stood close, you could hear the wind whistling through it.

...

...

The city in which Robert lived is the city in which you and I are currently sat together. Robert and Michelle and the twins lived in one of the northern suburbs. Once upon a time it had been a village but was now part of the greater metropolitan area. It retained some of its village-ness but there were direct links to the city centre and all the usual shops and amenities. The thing that first attracted Robert and Michelle to the area was the proximity to the country, the woods and the fields, the lochs and glens. They weren't country people. They had lived their entire lives in cities.

The country was somewhere you went on holiday, a weekend picnic or a slow hike with mates up a hill. Still it was nice to live in the vicinity of greenness while at the same time having direct links to the city centre and all the usual shops and amenities. But once they moved to their house, Robert and Michelle found that they rarely—in truth, never—went to the country. The country was there, tantalisingly within their grasp, but they never went. Not once. Every plan for a walk or spontaneous barbeque in the woods was, for one reason or another, abandoned.

Robert and Michelle had always turned left, towards the city.

Except that day.

That day, Robert turned right and headed out into unknown country.

Sometimes in a story, as in life, to get to the truth of a thing, it's necessary to take a diversion, to go around the houses.

Put it another way: you have to take the scenic route.

What follows is one such scenic route.

Once upon a time there was a young man. His name was Robert and he was 19 years old. Robert was a second year architecture student at university. He lived with five other young men in a three-bedroom flat, surviving on a diet of poorly made pasta dishes. One evening, Robert and his five flatmates were invited to a house party at a nearby flat of three young women by whom all were deeply enthralled. At around midnight, one of the three enthralling young women passed Robert an interesting looking cigarette. Despite his metropolitan upbringing, Robert had never taken drugs. His wee sister went out with a boy whose cousin was a cocaine dealer but that was as close as Robert had ever got. Not wishing to reject an offer from the enthralling young woman, Robert took the proffered intoxicant. It was delicious. Robert had never experienced anything quite as wonderful. He said as much to the enthralling young woman who smiled at Robert and rubbed her fingers around his left earlobe. Shortly afterwards, Robert blacked out and had to be carried home by two of his flatmates.

Once upon a time there was a young man. His name was Robert and he was 27 years old. Robert was an Apprentice Architect, living in rented accommodation in the capital city. He had never touched marijuana or any other drug since that infamous night at university. But then Robert was invited to his best friend, Kevin's stag night. Incidentally, Kevin was marrying the same enthralling young woman who had once rubbed her fingers around Robert's left earlobe but that had never been mentioned. The stags were in a private room at a casino playing very bad poker. As the evening wore on, Kevin produced a small plastic bag from which some small square pieces of paper were drawn. Put it on your tongue, commanded Kevin. Again, not wishing to be antisocial, Robert did as he was told. What followed was an evening of electrifying clarity, a sensory explosion that was as close to orgasm as can be imagined without the need for extensive clean-up. After they were kicked out of the casino, Robert stepped into a changed universe. Both sides of his brain were fully alive. He felt the light from distant stars. He touched the ground and sensed history, the primordial chaos beneath his feet. He breathed and communicated with the gods. It took three days to fully come down from this high. Forever afterwards Robert believed that that night was the night when he was most fully human.

Back in the here and now, Robert passed through a metal gate a few miles from his house. He found himself in a wide meadow. It was astonishingly beautiful. Robert did not know the name of wildflowers but there were red ones and purple ones and yellow ones. The grass was yellow and tall, almost up to his chest. There were late season butterflies, swifts and swallows skipping through the air. Robert hadn't experienced such pure beauty since the night of his LSD trip seventeen years previously. Why had the family not come this way before? They spent so much of their lives in the hustle and bustle of the city, being busy and achieving things, when there was all this⎵all this beauty was within easy reach.

And it was at exactly this moment—this moment of euphoric clarity—that Robert fell in a ditch.

FUCK YOU, WORLD!

That's how life works, right? At our highest moments someone or something to comes along to knock us (down)—

STOP!

What? What are you doing?

Stop. Let's just... can we just.., take a moment?

...?

You didn't have to do that.

I didn't do anything, I was (just telling the story)—

You didn't have to have that happen. Robert didn't have to fall into the ditch.

But he did fall into a ditch...

Why? Why couldn't he have jumped over it? Why did you have to ruin a perfectly wonderful moment?

That's... what happened.

You could have had something else happened.

It's not up to me.

Of course it is. We're making it up.

No.

Yes. It's a story. In a story anything is possible.

That's true but—

If anything is possible then while it's possible that Robert falls in the ditch it's equally possible that Robert did not fall into the ditch—

No but—

Why can't we have something positive happen? Why does it have to all be terrible?

That's not how stories work.

Isn't it?

In stories, people need to change, they need to face adversity—

Why?

Why ?

Why do they need to face adversity? Why can't they just have good things happen to them?

'Good things'?

Why do we always have to change because terrible things happen? What about a story in which a person is changed not by adversity but by success?

Well, I... I, mean... No, that's not—

Why?

...

Why?

...

Why? Why? Why? Why?

Because... that wouldn't be the truth.

*

Back in the here and now, Robert passed through a metal gate a few miles from his house. He found himself in a wide meadow. It was astonishingly beautiful.

It was.

Robert did not know the name of wildflowers but there were red ones and purple ones and yellow ones. The grass was yellow and tall, almost up to the hole in his chest. There were late season butterflies, swifts and swallows skipping through the air. Robert hadn't experienced such pure beauty since the night of his LSD trip seventeen years previously. Why had the family not come this way before? They had spent so much of their lives in the hustle and bustle of the city, being busy and achieving things, when there was all this—all this beauty was within easy reach.

And it was at exactly this moment—this moment of euphoric clarity—that Robert fell in a ditch.

FUCK YOU, WORLD!

That's how life works right?

Apparently.

At our highest moments someone or something comes along to knock us down.

Robert fell headfirst into a ditch.

Robert fell headfirst into a ditch that was full to the brim of slick brown, stinking effluent. A heady cocktail of rainwater and cow shit.

There were cows in the nearby field.

And, as the fetid liquid seeped through his clothes, it was impossible to feel anything other than that this was deserved, that this was his fault, Robert's fault, that nothing like this would have happened to anyone except him.

He *was the problem.*

Despair—

Anxiety—

Loss—

Sorrow—

Shame—

Self-loathing—

Robert lay in the ditch and cursed not the world or the weather or the cows but only himself.

And rather than call for help or pull himself out of the ditch, stagger to his feet, wipe himself using the pocket tissues he always carried, Robert let himself sink further into the ditch—

Deeper and deeper—

Until Robert's whole body was under—

Robert let out a deep sigh before finally lowering his head, sinking entirely into the ditch. His mouth. His nose. His ears. Everything was submerged in filth.

Robert vanished from this world.

And found himself in another.

Robert tramps home, the mud and the shit slick on his clothes and skin. Flies buzz. He can hardly see through the scum. Everything has a layer of brown.

There is a For Sale sign bolted to the garden fence.

Who the hell put that there?

Robert spends five minutes unsuccessfully trying to take the sign down. He can't get a firm hold with all the shit on his hands.

Robert enters the house where he's surprised to see a large number of cardboard boxes lining the hall. What is going on?

Robert shakes his head. First things first. He needs to get clean.

Only when Robert emerges from the shower, drying his hair on the bathmat—who took all the towels away?—does he stops to consider.

Something is seriously amiss.

The bedroom is stripped of all but the major furniture. The pictures on the wall, personal items, the flowers that were in a vase on the windowsill when he left this morning, all gone. None of his clothes are in the drawers. Robert finds everything he owns in plastic bags in his son's room.

If Robert wasn't concerned before, he is now.

Michelle? Adam? Ava? What's going on?

His wife is on the phone in the kitchen. Her eyes are red. Her face is pale. It looks like she hasn't slept for a month.

Hey love, what's with all the stuff in boxes? Are you leaving me and haven't mentioned it?

Michelle ignores him, listening intently to the person on the other end of the line.

Robert waits for another minute but Michelle does not end the call.

He finds the twins sharing a cigarette in the garden.

Since when did you lot smoke?

Adam and Ava glance at one another but don't reply.

Robert used to smoke 20 a day so isn't going to lecture his kids. In fact, Robert suddenly feels an ancient, overwhelming urge: do you mind if I have one of those?

...

Adam? Ava?

...

Hey are you hearing me? Can I have one of your cigarettes, please?

...

Hello?

...

And it's at this point that Robert realises that this isn't where he's supposed to be.

He isn't where he's supposed to be.

This is not right.

That this was not how the story was supposed to go.

For a while before these events, Robert had had the sense that he was not in control of his own story. That rather than being the main character in the story of his life, he was a bit part, a cameo, an extra. Perhaps not even that. He was simply one of the crowd, passively observing as events unfolded around him. Life happened to Robert rather life happening because of Robert. Robert had little or no control over the outcome of events.

The ditch was a case in point.

As Robert staggered to his feet, wiped himself down as best he could with the pocket tissues that he always kept in his left trouser pocket, Robert considered the ditch.

The ditch was a case in point.

Robert had not chosen to fall into the ditch. The ditch had happened to Robert.

He was subject to the ditch rather than the ditch subject to him.

But this... this was the end.

He'd had enough.

This was the end.

He knew there was an abandoned quarry nearby, as well as a deep lochan on the side of the hill.

Each offered possibilities.

Yes.

He would make a choice.

Robert took a deep breath and set off, determined to take control of his story.

/*Meanwhile...*

/Meanwhile

Once upon a time, there was a boy and a girl. His name was Adam, her name was Ava and they were 13 years old. They had a Mum and a Dad and a fair number of friends. There were moderately good students and excellent badminton players. Both were fun, generous and boisterous kids but tended to deal with challenges by keeping quiet about them. They just wanted everyone to be okay. But just before he reached the school gates, Adam looked at Ava and Ava looked at Adam.

They always knew what the other was thinking even without saying it.

So they texted their mum:

Something wrong with Dad. We're worried.

Once upon a time there was a woman. Her name was Michelle and she was 39 years old. She had a husband, a son and lots of friends. She enjoyed her job as a Human Resources Manager at an ethical bank and lived in a moderately large house with a moderately large garden. Michelle was an honest and open person who struggled with confrontation. Nevertheless when Michelle received this text from her 13 year old twins:

Something wrong with Dad. We're worried.

Michelle knew she couldn't ignore it.

Michelle called Robert's mobile but got no response.

Michelle called home but got no response.

Michelle called Robert's work and was told he was working at home.

Michelle told her colleagues that there was a problem and she'd be back later.

This being an ethical bank, her colleagues were 100 percent supportive.

Michelle drove home to discover her husband's car but no husband.

Michelle texted Robert's sister, his friends and the neighbours.

Angela who lived at number 7 said that she thought she had seen Robert heading down the road an hour or so ago but she couldn't be certain as she didn't have her glasses on at the time.

They lived at number 3 so if Robert had passed number 7 then it meant that he had turned right and was heading out of the city towards the country.

Where was he going?

Michelle called Robert's mobile again.

And again.

And again.

No answer.

What was Robert doing? Why had he not gone to work? Why was he not picking up?

Michelle felt a chasm form in front of her, in the carpet of the hall, where everything she didn't know about Robert was suddenly revealed.

This is a metaphor FYI. There wasn't a real chasm in the carpet. The carpet was totally fine.

The chasm was a metaphor but it was also true.

It represented what Michelle did not know about Robert's inner life.

It turns out that you can live with someone your entire life and still not understand everything about them.

Robert had been acting differently for weeks.

Months.

A year, if she were honest with herself.

But rather than ask him about it, rather than interrogate the things that had been troubling him, Michelle had said nothing.

She avoided confrontation.

And yet the quality in Michelle possessed was that when confronted, Michelle would act.

Michelle acted.

Michelle composed a text to send to all of her contacts and all of her social media accounts.

This is my husband, Robert. We love him and we are very worried about him. Please if you see him, call this number.

She pressed send.

There's a rule in storytelling that you shouldn't introduce a major character at the end of a story. Especially a major character who has a significant effect on the outcome of the story.

It feels like a lie.

Like the US army turning up at exactly the moment when the hero's back is against the wall.

Or the rich Uncle dying just as the Bailiffs are hammering at the front door.

It feels like a lie.

But then the truth is complicated and does not always follow the strict rules of storytelling.

Call it Deus Ex Machina.

Call it coincidence.

Whatever.

Sometimes a story does not behave as it should.

Once upon a time there was a man. His name was—coincidentally—Robert, although everyone called him Robbie. Robbie was 67 years old and recently retired. He had spent his whole career as an official in the civil service, mainly dealing with road signs.

Robbie was actually the person in charge of all road signs across the whole of Scotland.

If there was a road sign somewhere in Scotland, Robbie had put it there. Stop. Give Way. Dual Carriageway 2 Miles. It was dull, fiddly work but Robbie had been ideally suited to it.

He was a meticulous and thorough man.

Now Robbie had set off on foot to meet his creations in real life, to find and photograph as many road signs as he possibly could.

It was a little before noon. The sun was high. The clouds rolled across the sky like they had somewhere important to be.

Robbie had just taken a selfie of a slightly off-centre Passing Places sign on a country road north of the city when he received a text message from his cousin.

His cousin was one of those people who were always sending joke messages, pictures of kittens or terrifying articles from The Guardian, and other unnecessary junk.

His cousin was also the sister of a friend of a school mate of an old boyfriend of Michelle's.

There was a text message with an accompanying photo.

This is my husband, Robert. We love him and we are very worried about him. Please if you see him, call this number.

Normally, Robbie would have ignored this text from his cousin.

As he ignored almost all texts from his cousin.

But there was something about the fact that the man's name was the same as his that caught Robbie unexpectedly.

Robbie stared at the picture for a long moment.

And then he looked up to see a man passing close by the edge of the field.

Hello.

Hello.

Lovely day.

Yes.

Where are you off to?

I'm... well, I. I. I'm just walking.

I hope you don't mind me saying but you appear to be covered in shit.

Ah. Yes. I fell in a ditch.

Bugger.

You can say that again. I was planning on trying to wash myself in the lochan on the hill.

Good plan.

Although I seem to be a bit lost.

Would you like a cup of coffee? I have a thermos in my bag.

Well, that's erm... yes. That's very kind.

My name's Robert, by the way.

Oh. That's funny. Mine too.

I wonder, Robert. Are you alright?

...

...

Do you know what, Robert, I don't think I am.

*

We are the stories we tell ourselves.

Yes.

But sometimes those stories are a lie.

Yes.

Sometimes those stories can feel out of control.

Or do us more harm than good.

Like the story Robert had told himself that he was not the sort of man to feel despair, anxiety, loss, sorrow, shame, self-loathing.

That if he felt these things that he was in some way broken, unfixable, worthless.

This story was a lie.

And frankly tedious.

There are better stories.

There are much better stories.

Like the story of Robert turning right out of his house instead of left, discovering a rolling countryside that he had never before entered where he could breathe and get lost and, yes, get covered in shit but also meet a man with the same name as him who would sit and listen to him talk and at the end of talking there would be a silence then the other man would say, 'yes I know what you mean' and it was like something heavy shifted from Robert's shoulders.

Or a hole had been filled in somewhere inside him.

Nice.

And that wasn't even the end of the story—

No—

There was more to come, much more in terms of talk and tears and overcoming—

But also—

But also because Robert had left his phone on.

Robert had had his phone on him the whole time.

It was on silent in his right trouser pocket.

Once upon a time there was a man, a nice man who lived in a nice house on the edge of the city. One day he woke up and decided to kill himself but in the end he didn't.

No he didn't.

But he did die.

Eventually.

Yes.

It's what happens to us all.

This is the story of Robert's death. He was eighty-seven years old. He had been picked up by his grand-daughter Emily from a hospital appointment. Robert had long suffered issues with his heart but the medication seemed to be working. His heart was in a good way. Emily picked him up in her Mini and drove him home. Emily and Robert adored one another. They shared many things in common: she had his eyes, his sense of humour as well as his enthusiasm for the outdoors. The other thing they shared was a love of sweet things. Technically Robert wasn't allowed sugar because of his medication but what was life without sweets? So when Emily dropped Robert at the house she slipped him a packet of Skittles. But it wasn't until later that evening when Robert was sat in his chair, facing the fading sun, the silver birch and cherry trees that lined the garden, that Robert choked on a strawberry Skittle and expired.

At Robert's funeral, everyone agrees it's how he would have wanted to go.

And that is the story of Robert's death.

Spoilers.

What else is there to say?

Not much.

Except to pick up a few random threads.

The watch worn with the face down. A rubbed earlobe. Tissues kept in a left-hand pocket. A small hole in the centre of a man's chest the size of a pound coin.

These are small things.

Details.

But details are what give a story life and the things we remember when we tell the story of our lives.

The details are what count.

The details are the good bit.

Robert was born. Robert will die.

Yes.

But not today.

No, not today.

And that's the end of the story.

Yes.

END OF PLAY

Uma Nada-Rajah

The Great Replacement

Previous Artistic Director's Choice

Jemima Levick, Artistic Director from 2021-2024, nominated Uma's play for the collection.

Uma is a playwright based in Kirknewton, Scotland. She is one of the BBC's Scottish Voices 2020 and was the Starter Female Political Comedy writer-in-residence at the National Theatre of Scotland.

Uma is a graduate of École Philippe Gaulier and a previous participant of the Royal Court's Young Writers' Programme and the Traverse Theatre's Young Writers' Programme. In 2014, Uma won the New Playwrights Award from Playwrights' Studio Scotland. Her play *Exodus* had its premiere at the Traverse Theatre in August 2022.

Awards include: Kavya Prize 2022, Shakespeare is Dead International Selection 2024.

She works as a staff nurse with NHS Scotland.

The Great Replacement was first performed in June 2023 at Òran Mór.

CHARACTERS

FI
Early 60s, She/Her, white or white-passing

LU
Early 30s, She/Her, white or white-passing

KAL
Early 30s, He/Him, brown

SETTING

Scenes 1—4 take place in the kitchen of Fi's flat.

Scene 5 takes place outside.

"'Civilization's going to pieces,' broke out Tom violently. 'I've gotten to be a terrible pessimist about things. Have you read The Rise of the Coloured Empires by this man Goddard?'

'Why, no,' I answered, rather surprised by his tone.

'Well it's a fine book, and everybody ought to read it. The ideas is if we don't look out the white race will be- will be utterly submerged. It's all scientific stuff; it's been proved'

'Tom's getting very profound,' whispered Daisy, with an expression of unthoughtful sadness."

F. Scott Fitzgerald, *The Great Gatsby*

ONE (PRODIGAL CHEQUE)

*an alternate offer—zipping into a cocoon

The sound of a few frogs builds to a cacophony.

And then, FI's kitchen.

FI is at her table. A phone or tape recorder in front of her. She sits up straight and presses play.

TRACK: Re-wiring Your Mind for Total Positivity. Series Two, Tape Four. Take a deep breath.

FI takes a deep breath.

Now let it out. That's it. Let all those worries melt away. Happiness is a choice. Choose it. Place your hands out in front of you. I want you to draw a bubble. All the way around yourself. That's it. Step into your bubble. How does that feel? Inside of this bubble, you are safe, you are worthy, you are loved. Everything is within your control. Nothing can penetrate this bubble.

A knock on the door.

FI: Oh.

FI opens it. An unexpected visit from her daughter, LU.

LU holds a box.

FI: Oh, Lu. What a surprise.

LU: Hi Mum.

FI: Come in. It's been a while. You're looking well.

LU: Thanks. You've got a new table.

FI: Well, I bought it last year. Isn't it beautiful? My pride and joy. Aside from you, of course. Did you manage to get parked?

LU: Yeah.

FI: There is a whole situation with the parking. What's in the box?

LU: It's a frog.

FI: A frog?

LU: I've borrowed him from my lab to lend to someone.

FI: How lovely. Come in. Maybe your friend wants to wait in the corridor?

LU: It's fine. It's in a case. It's sealed.

FI: Of course I would say let it out. But. You know. The table.

LU: It can't be let out. It's an invasive species.

FI: So. Um. Did you come to show me the frog?

LU: No. I was just in the area. I have some news.

FI: Oh?

LU: Marie and I are planning to have a baby.

FI: (*moved*) Oh.

LU: Marie has told her Mum. Who, of course, has gone and told absolutely everyone. I know you see each other at the Zumba.

FI: Oh, I've stopped all of that.

LU: I just thought you should hear it from me first.

FI: Wow. I just thought with you being. You know.

LU: — Gay.

FI: I'd kind of given on the idea of having a grandchild. The table. It's a bit delicate. Had I have known I might have. Oh, never mind. I'm delighted. Its good timing. With my retirement. Congratulations. Wonderful news.

LU: Thanks.

FI: Are you? Is one of you pregnant.

LU: No not yet. I'm going to try to do it.

FI: Oh, how wonderful!

LU: Well, fingers crossed. There's no guarantee I'm even fertile.

FI: Lu. Don't take this the wrong way. But...

LU: What is it?

FI: I know you can be sensitive.

LU: Just say it.

FI: How would you know if you are fertile if you haven't been having sex with a man?

LU: Right, lovely. Thanks Mum.

FI: You'd think they would teach you this in postgraduate biology.

LU: I just meant with the ticking clock.

FI: No sense in worrying about it. How will you?

LU: Sperm donor. Turkey baster.

FI: Very progressive.

(Beat.)

I'm delighted. I really am.

(Beat.)

LU: Well, fingers crossed. I just dropped by to let you know about the baby.

FI: Please. Sit down. Stay for a moment.

Against her better judgement, LU sits down, squirms.

FI: This is wonderful news. It really is. And how's Marie?

LU: Maybe let's not talk about it.

FI: It's just I don't see much of anyone any more. I have everything delivered. So I don't get many updates.

LU: They're fine.

FI: She does hold a grudge.

LU: They hold a grudge.

FI: Well, on a more positive note, it's just occurred to me that this is one of the great upsides of being gay. You get to choose, in a calm and rational manner, the genetic input for your future offspring. You can engage in mindful procreation.

LU: Mindful procreation?

FI: To select the traits and characteristics that would best balance out your own.

LU: That's just called eugenics.

FI: Call it what you want, but all I am saying is that you have the opportunity to procreate considering all of the available evidence and information. Without the distraction of—

LU: Love?

FI: Oh please, Lu. You're young. Love is just glorified eugenics. With all that heightened emotion and hormones, people sometimes get it very wrong.

LU: Did you get it very wrong, Mother?

FI: No. You're perfect. In every way. If a little stubborn.

LU: You surely can't blame him for that.

FI: What I mean to say is, given that this act of procreation will not be based on hormones and emotions, it's a good chance for us to sit down together and agree on a certain set of criteria.

LU: That's not going to happen.

FI: Well, is Marie going to have input?

LU: Marie is my partner and will be a parent of this child. We've already chosen a sperm donor. And not just a sperm donor. He's going to be involved.

FI: Oh. Well. What is there left to say?

LU: How about congratulations?

FI: Well done.

LU: OK. You know what? I'm going to go.

FI: Please. Don't go. Have a biscuit.

LU: Since when do you have biscuits?

FI: I have seaweed thins.

Against her better judgement, LU tries one, it's predictably disgusting.

They do tend to stick to your teeth. Look, I just wanted to say, I know that mistakes have been made. You are not the mistake. I'm just acknowledging that some mistakes in general may have been made in your childhood. Mistakes that I may have somehow played a role in.

LU: ...

FI: And, I'm sorry. I really am. We may not always see eye to eye but I think you've grown into a remarkable woman. And I think that you'll be a great mum.

LU: Right. I wasn't expecting that.

FI: Now that I've retired I've been thinking quite a lot. I meditate. Vigorously. Self-improvement, you know. I'm thrilled about this. I really am, I'd like to be a part of this child's life. From the very beginning. I could help you with childcare, whatever you need, really. Nothing would mean more to me. Would that be OK?

LU: I guess we can take it as it comes.

FI: Tell me about this donor.

LU: He's a close pal. I don't think you've met. He's a musician.

FI: Oh. Lovely.

LU: He's from Paisley.

FI: Oh, Paisley. Very nice. They have a very large B&Q.

LU: His name is Kal.

FI: Oh, Kal! I've heard of this Kal. You used to go on about him.

LU: Kal Kandasamy.

FI: Lovely. The New Scotland.

(Beat.)

I'm very happy for you.

LU: Good.

FI: Delighted.

LU: Great.

(A standoff)

FI: I do think a lot of thought needs to go into a decision like this.

LU: A lot of thought has gone into this decision.

FI: A colleague of mine, his son has just taken a post in Endocrinology at the Royal. Good broad shoulders. A gay. I'm sure he wouldn't mind giving you some. You know.

LU: Ew. Just. Ew.

FI: There's no rush to make any big decisions.

LU: 'We' are not making any decisions.

FI: It's just... well, you can't say anything in these days.

LU: Then don't. We had an understanding.

FI: This isn't politics. This is personal. Is it too much to ask, in this day in age, to have a grandchild that vaguely resembles you?

LU: You didn't even have a prospective grandchild until ten minutes ago, and anyhow, the child will still vaguely resemble you.

FI: You know what I mean.

LU: I don't actually. I'm going to go.

FI: Please. Wait. (*whips out her cheque book*) Let me write you a cheque. I know money is a bit tight, cost of living and all, you'll be clearing space, preparing a nursery. The costs will add up. I want this child to have everything they need to thrive. Here.

FI holds out a cheque. LU hesitates.

LU: (*barely*) Thanks.

Against her better judgement, LU takes the cheque.

FI: I'd like to meet him. This Kal.

LU: I don't know. We'll see.

TWO (DISASTER SAMOSAS)

Outside, LU and KAL approach FI's flat.

LU wears a mildly political T-shirt.

LU: I can't believe I let you talk me into this.

KAL: I've always wanted to meet your Ma. This is important. If we're going to do this, we're going to do this properly. Me, You, Marie, the baby, your Ma. One big happy unconventional family, right?

LU: Oh God. It's just. You don't understand what she's like.

KAL: I've listened to you go on about your Ma for about 10 years now.

LU: I do not go on about her!

KAL: You do.

LU: The damage with Marie is irreparable. But I thought, you, you get on with everyone. She's all I've got.

KAL: Yeah. That's why we should do this.

LU: We have a fragile peace. But there are rules. She got into all sorts of conspiracy theories during the pandemic. I haven't seen much of her since. Don't engage. Don't try and use logic. Just starve it of air. Move on.

KAL: Got it.

LU: No politics. No talking about what happened with Marie. No substance whatsoever to any conversation.

KAL: What about your T-shirt?

LU: Totally fair game.

KAL: Mind games.

LU: Welcome to the clan. Ah-

LU goes to ring the doorbell. Turns around.

KAL: Where are you going?

LU: I can't do this. I just had a moment. An out of body experience.

KAL: What?

LU: I had the feeling of looking down at myself from above. You know when you know something is a terrible idea and you are watching yourself going through the motions carrying out this terrible idea and what you really need to do is just—

KAL rings FI's doorbell.

LU: Kal!

FI opens the door.

FI: Ah, how lovely!!

KAL: You must me the famous Mrs. Mackay.

LU: Kal, this is my, uh, Mum. Mum this is Kal.

FI: Please. Call me Fi. Did you get parked okay? We have a situation.

KAL: Yeah, it was fine.

FI: Come in! Come in!

KAL: What a lovely home.

FI: Thank you.

KAL: Oh, is that a Mbira?

FI: It is.

KAL: Mind if I have a look?

FI: Please.

KAL absorbed in instrument.

FI: *(whispers to LU)* Gosh. Lovely shoulders.

(Beat.)

Wine! We need wine. You're looking very. Healthy.

LU: No politics.

FI: Sure.

(Beat.)

What a lovely top.

LU: Thank you.

FI: *(whispers to LU)* You know, if it were me, I wouldn't be using a turkey baster.

KAL re-emerges from playing the instrument.

LU: Ew. Ew. Oh God.

KAL: Everything OK?

LU: Yeah, yeah.

FI: I've got a whole collection of thumb pianos. There are more in this drawer.

KAL: Oh cool!

FI: Lu's great great grandparents were based in east Africa. They were avid collectors.

KAL: Lu has never mentioned that.

FI: I bet there's a lot she hasn't mentioned.

KAL: It's a pleasure to finally meet you, Ms. Mackay. I've heard so much about you.

FI: Oh dear. Let's be honest Lu and I haven't always seen eye to eye. Lu has got a certain perception of me, shall we say. But rest assured it's not the whole picture.

KAL: Well, I look forward to seeing the, uh, whole picture. I mean.

FI: For example. When Lu first told me she was gay. Do you remember this story?

LU rolls her eyes.

LU: Can we just—

FI: —I knew already. Obviously. I mean. But. Do you remember what I said? Good. I said good. There were too many of us straights, I said, and it will do well to redress the balance.

KAL: That's very progressive of you, Mrs. Mackay.

LU: Well done, Mother.

FI: This was before it was so fashionable. It's lovely of you both to come. So you're a musician.

KAL: Guilty as charged.

FI: What do you play?

KAL: I trained classically to play the sitar. But lately I've been immersed in a bit of side project.

LU: Kal has become a bit of a TikTok sensation.

KAL: I've been making music on my computer and mixing with wildlife sounds.

LU: He has quite the following.

KAL: What's not to love about a brown guy vibing with animals? I've borrowed a frog from Lu's lab to make a recording.

FI: Oh! The frog. Well it sounds very interesting. I'm glad there's a market for that.

KAL: Me too. I still drive an Uber on the side.

LU: He's being modest. One to watch.

FI: The landscape of the arts is changing isn't it?

KAL: What kind of music are you into, Ms. Mackay?

FI: Oh, I like a bit of Tchaikovsky.

KAL: Me too. Well I like anything beginning with chai.

LU: That was terrible.

KAL: Thanks. Seriously though. Symphony No. 6, his Pathetique is unreal. The guy had a tough life. Repressed homosexual, possible suicide, the guy never really believed in his music. At the time he was: "Too Russian for the West, too Western for the Russians."

FI: So how did the two of you meet?

KAL: Third year of uni. Developmental biology. I was sat there in class, pencils sharpened, keen as ever. Lu comes and sits in the seat next to me. And just starts chomping her way through the biggest sandwich I've ever seen in my life. It dawned on me that this person does not give a flying fuck what anyone thinks of her. We've been pals ever since.

FI: That sounds like our Lu. Well, it's very exciting, this 'unconventional family' business. Kal, did you not fancy having a family the more conventional way?

KAL: It's crossed my mind. I've never been convinced that a conventional family is right for me. Lu and Marie will make great parents. When Lu asked me to be a donor, to be a part of an unconventional family, it just felt right. I felt like it made sense.

FI: And what about your parents? Are they excited about this 'grandchild'?

KAL: We don't speak often. My dad worked overtime driving a taxi to provide for us all, only for me to drop out of biomedical sciences to make music and drive an Uber. I think he just wanted to be able to tell people I was doing something good in the world. But I was miserable. All I ever think about is music. Maybe it's selfish. I don't know. We're civil. But I don't think they'll be too impressed by the unconventional family idea.

FI: Maybe you can let them be the judge of that.

KAL: Don't know. Maybe.

FI: It's honestly such a treat to have you both here. Well. Let's raise a glass, shall we? I must say. When Lu first told me she was planning on having a baby, it was a surprise. I totally given up any notion of ever becoming a grandmother. Of course these days you can't even encourage anyone to do anything so... The point being, I'm delighted. I'm over the moon really. And it's good timing for me with my retirement. Lu, you are going to be a wonderful mother. Along with your partner, of course. And Kal, now we've only just met, but it's been a pleasure—

LU: —Thanks. Mum. That was a nice toast.

FI: I'm not done. Kal, thank you for coming over and taking the time to introduce yourself. And, of course, for your prospective contribution to the course of affairs. Really, I just wanted to say how happy I am. As for having a mixed-race child? Well, all I have to say about that is: if it's good enough for the Royal Family, it's good enough for me!

LU: —Because that's going so well.

FI: Ours is a time of such immense change. And I'll be the first to admit that I sometimes struggle to wrap my head around it all. But, as far as I'm concerned, you're you, she's with a they, and the baby will be lovely and I am extremely open-minded about all of it. Cheers!

KAL: Cheers.

FI: Now. Who's hungry? I've made samosas.

KAL: You made these?

FI: Sure did. They're a bit spicy, mind. I thought I'd start practicing for this grandchild.

KAL: Now we're talking. This kid is going to like a bit of spice!

LU: What are the little red dots on the end?

FI: Oh, I don't know. Little specks of lovely.

KAL: They tell you if they are meat or veg.

FI: Well, I procured the samosas.

KAL: They're delicious.

FI: I had them delivered. I have everything delivered nowadays. So convenient.

KAL: Excellent choice.

FI: And, you know what I was thinking as I plated these up?

Who knows, someday the samosa might be the national dish of Scotland.

KAL: I think it would take quite a lot to displace the haggis.

LU: To be fair, the vegetarian haggis is already doing quite a good job of it.

FI: What times we live in. Even the sheep intestines are going woke. So. Kal. Where are you from?

KAL: But, if you're asking where I'm from from? My parents came here from a dusty wee village a few hours southeast of Mumbai.

FI: Have you ever thought about going back?

LU: Back where? Why would you even ask that?

FI: It was just a question.

LU: I knew this was a bad idea.

KAL: Hey, it's OK, Lu, just chill.

FI: I meant on holiday. To visit Or... I don't say everything in the most PC of ways.

KAL: No need to be PC around me. We're practically family. Aren't we?

FI: Of course.

KAL: I decided to do it once, you know? Go back to my country. Not long after Lu and I met.

LU: Oh yeah. That was a funny time.

KAL: You heard that every so often growing up. You know. 'Go back to your country'. You hear it less these days. So, I thought I'd give it a bash. "Went back" to "my Country". I didn't tell my parents. It was something I had to do alone. I just rocked up, heartbroken, with a rucksack, battered copy of James Baldwin's Notes of a Native Son, and a sitar. I was obsessively learning the sitar at the time. Part of me hoped an ancestral connection to land would help with my playing. But folk there said I spoke the language with a Scottish accent. My teacher said my compositions sounded foreign. I thought of your man, Tchaikovsky. "Too Russian for the West, too Western for the Russians." And it was hot. Just like relentlessly hot. I was expecting to have some sort of transcendental experience, but just ended up homesick with heatstroke and a bad stomach. I missed my pals. I missed the people. I missed it pissing it down with rain. In the end, I had to come to terms with the possibility that my deep-rooted connection to land is to Paisley town-centre.

LU: You've not played much sitar since.

KAL: I'm giving it a rest.

LU: It's a shame. I love your stuff. You should look him up.

FI: Who was the girl?

KAL: What.

FI: You said you were heartbroken.

KAL: Oh. Can't remember.

FI: Well, I think it's great that you feel that way about Paisley. Do you know what I did the other day? I sent off for one of those ancestry tests.

KAL: Oh, how interesting!

FI: One of those spit in the tube, send it of in the post it tells you your ethnicity according to your genetics.

LU: Ethnicity is not genetic. It's a human construct that correlates with particular genetic variations.

FI: Well, for all intents and purposes, we come from pure, beautiful genetic stock. I just thought it would be interesting for the both of you, as you embark on this journey.

LU: There is no such thing as a clear-cut biological racial category. But why ask scientist?

FI: I think it tells us something interesting about who we are and where we've come from.

KAL: Ah it's the great question though, isn't it? Do I owe more to being a ball of inherited pre-programmed nucleotides, or am I my dreams volition and experiences?

You know what I always thought would be interesting? One thing I've always noticed. You take a cross section of any section of society: races, classes, political stripes, whatever, and you get roughly the same proportion across the board, of people who are extraordinary, a fair chunk who are decent and ordinary, and at the very bottom you get this small proportion that are just total, for lack of a better word, arseholes. What if you could identify the gene for that? That would be good, wouldn't it? Round them all up, knock on their doors. 'Sorry mate, turns out you're a bit of a dick, get in the van'. And, because the people dealing with it would be screened and wouldn't be arseholes, they'd be decent about it. Take them all to some lovely arsehole rehab facility in the mountains. We could call off the wars, avert climate catastrophe, sort out a fair distribution of resources. The identification of that gene. That would be true progress. What do you think, Lu? Is it viable?

LU: If there was a trait for arsehole, it would be polygenic.

FI: What does that mean?

LU: It means there's no one gene for arsehole.

KAL: Such is the tragedy of the human condition.

FI: So lovely to have you here. Who needs a drink?

FI tops up wine glasses.

I saw a photo on the internet the other day. Of children in a primary school in the city centre. A politician had gone to visit. And I have to say... very few of the children were white.

LU: I think we should go.

FI: It was just an observation.

KAL: It's a fair observation. Scotland has an aging population. There are demographic shifts, especially in the city-centre. It's OK to talk about it. Healthy even.

FI: More wine?

LU: — (*downs her wine*)

FI: The world is changing. I find it so interesting. Don't you? Population dynamics.

LU: Since when are you interested in population dynamics?

FI: Am I not allowed to have interests? I've been following this topic on TikTok.

KAL: You're on TikTok?

FI: I like to get my information from a wide variety of sources on social media.

LU: Social media is literally the opposite of a wide variety of sources.

FI: What do you mean?

LU: I'd imagine that your feed would be made up of a narrow subset of provocations to stoke your basest interests and anxieties.

KAL: As is yours. And mine.

FI: The point is... population demographics are shifting.

LU: Demographics are always shifting. That's the basis of life on earth.

FI: Did you know that according to some projections white people could become a minority in their home countries, by the latter half of this century?

KAL: To be fair, by then we all might be too busy battling tsunamis to be stressing about people's skin colours.

LU: Climate change isn't funny, Kal.

FI: There are certain theories, however.

KAL: What sort of theories?

LU: Kal. Don't.

FI: You know what? It doesn't matter. We're here to celebrate. Drink up!

KAL: What sort of theories?

LU: Kal? Honestly?

FI: There are theories that the decline of the white race is being intentionally coordinated by a group of elites. Have you heard of The Great Replacement?

LU: On what planet? Is it remotely acceptable?

FI: It was just a question, Lu.

KAL: It's OK, Lu. Calm down.

LU: Calm down? 'No politics! 'Sure, sure'. 'No politics'. 'Sure thing!' And yet. Lo and behold, here we are agreeing to discuss deadly neo-Nazi conspiracy theories in preparation for the birth of my mixed-race child. You calm down!

KAL: It's important to talk about these things.

LU: No, it's important to starve these things of air and light.

KAL: The world is changing. Your mum's got anxieties. She's seeing things online. It's important to address it in real life.

FI: An entire generation unable to have a proper conversation.

KAL: Let's just hear her out.

LU relents.

FI: Why don't you have some more wine?

LU: Seriously? Fuck my life. You know what? Whatever.

LU downs her wine. FI tops up LU's wine glass.

FI: Enjoy it while you can, sweetheart.

KAL: Let's just hear her out.

FI: The Great Replacement theory is gaining a lot of traction in America.

LU: Oh yes, America. That country famous for being indigenously white.

FI: The idea is that this is all intentional. That it's being actively promoted.

LU: By an elite cabal of communist lizards.

FI: Well, they aren't necessarily lizards. Or communists for that matter.

KAL: Well, if it is being carried out by a bunch of Pls singing Ye Cannae Shove your Granny aff a bus', I've got time for it.

LU: It's just maths. Whiteness is the only ethnicity to be defined by hypodermic inheritance, 'the one drop rule'.

FI: What's that?

LU: It's an inherently racist ideology dating back to the 1600s that, somehow, continues to persist. People with the tiniest percentage of non-white ancestry are considered non-white. It just means that declining birth rates and inevitable mixing, the so-called "white" population is bound to decline over time. Our prospective child is literally The Great Replacement.

FI: I am, honestly, just so delighted about the child. I was hoping that ancestry test would arrive in time for today. But, alas.

LU downs her wine, increasingly drunk.

LU: Well, you know what? There is going to be a great replacement. Not a tribalistic fantasy implying that different races are different species. A real one. Lithobates catesbeianus. The American Bullfrog. You've both met. According to the Species Distribution Models I've been running, their populations are set to boom alongside global warming. We're talking exponentially. And I love reptiles. But these aren't the most pleasant of creatures. They don't out-succeed other species by skill or stealth. They just wait for an opportunity and suck the life out of what's directly in front of them. It's vicious, opportunistic ambush predators that are fit for endgame capitalism. They eat their own young. So nothing to worry about, it won't be the meek that inherit the earth, or people with melanin. But giant cannibalistic bullfrogs.

KAL: Why were you hoping that ancestry test would arrive in time for today?

FI: I thought it might be interesting.

LU: I'm going to be sick.

THREE (A TRIPTYCH OF UNTHOUGHTFUL SADNESS)

A.

LU gets home. Kicks off her shoes. A phone call from MAX, the head of her research department.

LU: Oh, hi, Max. Oh no, don't worry, it's not too late. Yeah, I just got in. Went round to see my Mum.

(Pause.)

Yeah. It was, um, lovely.

(Pause.)

Oh thanks. I'm pleased you feel that way. I mean what an honour to be published by such a prestigious journal. Took me a while to wrap my head around that software. Had a few late nights. I've just discovered energy drinks.

(Pause.)

Pond enclosures were a short-term solution. I would agree that we've reached the end of non-lethal measures. We need to start thinking about a cull. Mass extermination. God, it's so brutal, isn't it?

(Pause.)

Project Lead?

Um. Wow. Erm. Sure. I'm flattered. But. I'm just not sure if I'm the right—

(Pause.)

Oh, they can't outsource it to Intek. We both know that would be a disaster. Our department would be best placed to—

(Pause.)

Thanks, Max. Sure. I'll have a think about it.

B.

Night-time. KAL sits reading a battered copy of The Great Gatsby. *The frog sits next to him... illuminated.*

KAL: "'Civilization's going to pieces,' broke out Tom violently. 'I've gotten to be a terrible pessimist about things. Have you read The Rise of the Coloured Empires by this man Goddard?'

'Why, no,' I answered, rather surprised by his tone.

'Well it's a fine book, and everybody ought to read it. The ideas is if we don't look out the white race will be—will be utterly submerged. It's all scientific stuff; it's been proved'

'Tom's getting very profound,' whispered Daisy, with an expression of unthoughtful sadness." Unthoughtful sadness.

C.

Morning. FI dials the number for the 'Ancestry DNA Solution!'. Or is on hold.

FI: *(into phone)* Hiya! HI there. Yes. Well, there's been some sort of mistake. I ordered your product. *(reads)* The Ancestry DNA Solution. Exclamation Mark.

(Pause.)

Oh yes. It arrived. I followed the all the instructions. Spit into the little tube and put it in the post.

(Pause.)

The results have come back. Yes. I got the wee notification.

(Pause.)

The problem is that the results are incorrect. Quite funny actually.

(Pause.)

It says here that I'm 12% Senegalese. The problem?

(Pause.)

I'm actually quite familiar with my lineage. I just thought I'd take the test for my daughter, you know.

(Pause.)

Yes, I copied the pin number into the app very carefully. I checked it three times.

(Pause.)

I'm definitely... My Zumba instructor... tell you himself. Not an ounce of rhythm in these hips. You know what. This isn't about me. There is some poor Senegalese woman somewhere who has incorrectly received my results. She is sat at home pouring over my result thinking that her life in the conga line has been a fraud and she needs to learn Highland dancing.

(Pause.)

Well, there must be some mistake. There is just no possibility. That. My grandmother. Oh. Oh. Dear. Bye now. Cheery bye.

FI shoves the paper test result in the drawer.

FOUR (A DANCE)

FI's kitchen.

FI is on a yoga mat, listening to 'meditation mantras' online.

MANTRA TRACK: Take a deep breath. And repeat after me. "Everything will work out in the end. If it's not all right, it's not the end".

FI: Everything will work out in the end. If it's not all right—

A knock at the door.

FI opens the door. It's KAL.

FI: Kal. What a surprise.

KAL holds the frog.

KAL: I was in the area.

FI: Christ. I get more visits from this frog than I do my own family.

KAL: I was on my way to return him to Lu's lab.

FI: Do come in.

KAL enters.

FI: About the other night... I wanted to... Um... I have a habit of saying the first thing that pops to mind. It's not the current fashion.

KAL perhaps thumbs her mbira.

KAL: There's just one thing that's been playing on my mind. Why were you interested in having an ancestry test? Why now?

FI: I don't think people should be made to feel guilty about wanting to know a little bit more about their heritage.

KAL: Aye, but was it just about that? You'd said this thing about being from pure genetic stock. And I was just trying to work out what you meant by that. I wanted to give you the benefit of the doubt.

FI: I just thought it would be interesting. To be honest. I don't know what I think anymore. Lu isn't speaking to me. She needs space. What is it with your generation and space?

KAL: She's pissed off with me as well.

FI: Oh?

KAL: She thinks I was goading you on.

FI: And were you?

(Beat.)

KAL: Yeah. I suppose I was.

(Beat.)

KAL: There's something compelling, isn't there? About people's hatred.

FI: I don't hate anyone.

KAL: It's rare to see it face-to-face anymore. I could spend hours on the internet, reading hateful comments. There's a part of me that wants to bathe and lavish in it. Like a pig rolling in filth.

FI: I understand that. I do. Things are easy for me now. But that wasn't always the case. Lu's father left me when she was quite young. Just up and left. What was he thinking, I know. See now it's the migrants. In the nineties, it was the scroungers. They especially had it in for single mothers. I remember being in the shops at the end of the day, barely making ends meet with a stroppy little toddler. You'd see the headlines. 'Single Mothers. The Scourge of a Broken Britain'. I bought them, when I could. I'd read them at the end of the day, exhausted at the kitchen table. Every last vicious word. Positive mental attitude. That's what I've always believed in.

KAL: It has its limits though.

FI: Please. Help yourself to a biscuit.

KAL tries a seaweed thin. He doesn't like it. He feeds it to the frog.

Poor thing. Invasive species. I suppose it will have to be exterminated somehow.

KAL: Did you get the results of your ancestry test in the end?

FI: Oh. Oh, Yes.

KAL: And?

FI: And oh, you know. More or less as expected.

KAL: What do you mean more or less? Did you hit the jackpot and get a dash of Viking?

FI: Very funny.

KAL: I'm just trying to understand, Mrs. Mackay.

FI: Well, I will say, I do appreciate you making the effort. Will you have a cuppa then? We can talk about something completely different!

KAL: Sure.

FI: Have a nice wee chat about Tchaikovsky and thumb pianos?

FI goes to make tea.

KAL goes to get second Mbira. Takes it out. Shuts the drawer.

(Pause._

KAL re-opens the drawer.

He reads the letter.

Puts it back. A moment.

FI re-enters with tea.

FI: Right. Let's talk about music.

KAL: Just to go back for a second. To this ancestry test.

FI: Oh, it doesn't matter.

KAL: I've got to admit, I'm just a bit surprised. It's just that I had this feeling.

FI: What sort of feeling?

KAL: That you might be...

FI: That I might be what?

KAL: It's just that we people of colour normally have a sense of intuition about these things.

FI: Perhaps you were mistaken.

KAL: And... And I had gotten that notification on my radar.

FI: What radar?

KAL: Oh, I really shouldn't say. It must have been an error of some sort.

FI: What radar?

KAL: I've already said too much. Unless of course you were a non-white individual.

FI: What if I was?

KAL: Then the notification on my radar would have been correct.

FI: Fine. Well. It was. I'm still coming to terms with it all.

KAL: I suppose it's a lot to take in. Welcome to the dark side, Mrs. Mackay.

FI: To think all this time, I've been ticking the wrong box on the diversity monitoring forms.

KAL: Nightmare.

FI: Well, it's just the tip of the iceberg really My daughter hates me. I'm at a loose end with my retirement. And there's this whole situation with the parking. I try to tell them not to park there and they just look right past me like I'm invisible. And suddenly the one thing I could reliably count on to give me my bearings in the world is ripped out from under my feet.

KAL: Well, that's a lot. I mean you've got a lot going on.

FI: Anyhow. Positive mental attitude. I guess when you think about it, I have done remarkably well for a woman of colour. So. What is this about? Tell me about this Radar?

KAL: It's, um, a part of a network.

FI: And what is the network called?

KAL: The Rise of the Coloured Empires. The aim is in the title.

FI: Tell me more.

KAL: We meet online. Every second Friday 16:00 Greenwich Mean Time. The British Empire once covered the same surface area as the moon. Yet here we all are in our little boxes on Zoom. Aboriginals and indigenous, Hindus and Muslims, Zionists and Palestinians. All conflicts set aside with the sole aim of unleashing a tidal wave of colour on the white western world.

FI: Fridays at 16:00s is a terrible time for a meeting. Most groups of humans, regardless of race or creed, tend to be preoccupied around then.

KAL: We are pretty dedicated to the cause.

FI: And tell me. How dedicated are you, personally, to this cause, Kal?

KAL: Oh very.

FI: I suppose the promotion of mixing genetic material is key to your aims?

KAL: Naturally.

FI: And I suppose the fusion of genetic certain types of material is particularly ideal. The fusion of our genetic material, for example. Would be top priority.

KAL: I suppose.

FI: Are you uncomfortable?

KAL: Nope. Not all.

FI: Well, then, I guess there's not much more to say.

KAL: Guess not. Um.

A standoff. KAL relents, cracks a smile, perhaps. They share a moment of mutual recognition and respect.

FI: I see you've been rifling through my drawers.

KAL: I was just looking for a mbira. Whatever it does or doesn't mean to you, Mrs. Mackay, the good news is you're still human.

KAL leaves the flat without frog. A moment between FI and the frog.

KAL: I forgot my, um, frog. You know, I think it's a shame. If it weren't for all of this. I think we'd really get on.

FIVE (BOBO LIVES ON)

Glasgow Green. LU and KAL have nets and are chasing the escaped frog.

LU: I cannot believe you would!

KAL: I know, but...

LU: I gave you very specific instructions.

KAL: I know. OK. I know. I had a moment.

LU: Like I get that you're a TikTok star but I have got actual responsibilities. Such as not destroying an entire ecosystem.

KAL: I brought a net. I just didn't think he would be so. Jumpy. Just thought I'd let the wee guy stretch his legs.

LU: Are you OK?

KAL: I'm fine.

LU: You're obviously not fine. You're wandering around Glasgow Green playing 'Free Willy' with a frog.

KAL: It's been a strange morning. Your mum said this thing earlier about extermination and—

LU: —You went to go see my Mum?

KAL: I was having a bit of a wobble. I had some questions.

LU: You were having a bit of a wobble so you went to see my highly reactionary Mum?

KAL: I can relate to him you know. Bobo.

LU: Who's Bobo?

KAL: The frog. Bobo. He's not meant to be here. Am I? Like who is meant to be anywhere?

LU: Get a grip, Kal. You're not a frog.

KAL: I mean, he's a human being.

LU: He is... categorically... not a human being. What is up with you?

KAL: I've been up all night. I honestly didn't think catching him again would be that hard.

LU: I told you how dangerous he is.

KAL: You know you can buy these guys from exotic pet dealers online.

LU: Don't even. I'm not going to ask why you were looking.

KAL shrugs.

How long have you been out here for?

KAL: Pure ages.

LU: We used to hang out here.

KAL: I know.

LU: The world felt so different then. I'm ovulating. I mean just so you know.

KAL: Oh. Right.

LU: You're having doubts.

KAL: I've been up all night and have just spent four hours jumping around a park with a net.

LU catches the frog.

LU: Got him!

KAL: What's going to happen to him?

LU: Bobo will spend the rest of his life in captivity.

KAL: Poor guy.

LU: I loved frogs when I was a kid. I could spend hours, hunched over in the woods, searching for them, and just staring in fascination. I became an ecologist because I loved them so much. And now it's somehow my job to mass exterminate them.

KAL: That's brutal, Lu.

LU: I shouldn't have subjected you to my Mum. It was a mistake.

KAL: It don't think it was a mistake.

LU: Really? Look at the state of you. I've been there.

KAL: I like your Mum. There's something about her.

KAL shrugs, is he provoking/ teasing LU?

LU: Straight people are such fucking degenerates.

KAL: Yeah, well, maybe it's muscle memory. Remember fourth year? We spent every waking hour together. We sat here. I was beside myself. It could've never have happened. But...

LU: What was I meant to do?

KAL: You could have given me a fucking hug. What am I doing with all of this? You know? You, your Mum, this baby?

LU: Do you still—

KAL: No. It was a long time ago. And we've both moved on from all of that. But... when you asked me to be a donor, it felt right. I want to be free to make music, to stay up till five in the morning tinkering. It felt like something that could tether me to this world.

LU: We've always said we were practically family. And now, we're trying to be a family. You're my best pal. And whatever it does or doesn't mean, I just want my child to have your qualities as a human being. I've spent my whole career thinking... imagining dystopian futures, heartbroken at everything we've done to this planet. Then we started talking about this baby... And all of a sudden I see lochs and glens and playparks and alongside all the horrors, there's this beautiful world I've dreamed of. Against the rising tide of hatred and intolerance, I see kindness and the beauty of ordinary people. Bigots are few and far between. They're clowns. Literally men in sheets. They just need to be cut off and starved of light. It was a mistake to get my Mum involved.

KAL: It wasn't a mistake. She's not a monster. She's just isolated. She feels invisible and powerless. She spends too much time on the internet, down digital wormholes. She doesn't know what she believes, it's all just algorithmically inflamed baseless outrage. Just like everyone else in this world. It's all just divide and rule. People need to talk to each other.

LU: No. I don't see the logic of giving it any space. I've tried. I have. The stuff with Marie, it's all too painful. Maybe you can be the go-between. The buffer zone.

KAL: (*sighs*) This beautiful world you dream of, Lu. I hate to break it to you but it's full of humans... who don't know how to talk to each other. 'Not everything that is faced can be changed, but nothing can be changed until it is faced.'

LU: By that logic, maybe you should pick up your sitar again. And by that logic, maybe I should meet your family. Maybe I can be your go-between?

KAL: Now that... is definitely a terrible idea.

LU: Well, maybe we can give it a try.

// SPLIT SCENE

FI's kitchen.

FI is at her table. A phone or tape recorder in front of her. She sits up straight and presses play.

TRACK: Re-wiring your Mind for Total Positivity. Series Two, Tape Five. Take a deep breath. Place your hands out in front of you. Draw your bubble. That's it. Step back inside. How does that feel? Inside of this bubble, you are safe, you are—

FI: Oh. Sod it.

FI shuts off the track, exits her bubble, and the door of her house, into the light.

The sound of a few frogs builds to a cacophony.

END

Aodhan Gallagher
Write-Off

A Play, A Pie and A Pint Team Choice

The current staff of A Play, A Pie and A Pint nominated *Write-Off* for the collection.

Aodhan Gallagher is a playwright and screenwriter from Glasgow, who trained at the Rita and Burton School of Dramatic Writing at New York University, Tisch School of the Arts. Upon returning to Scotland, they participated in Playwrights' Studio Scotland 2019/20 Mentorship Scheme, Dundee Rep Stripped Festival and Glasgow Film Festival 2023/24 New Talent Mentorship Scheme. As a screenwriter, they have written episodes for BBC's *River City* and worked as a story-liner for 110 episodes of the series. Aodhan's debut play *Write-Off* was produced as part of A Pie, A Pie and A Pint's Spring 2023 season at the Òran Mór and Traverse Theatre.

Write-Off was first developed through the Playwrights' Studio Scotland Mentorship Scheme 2019/20 and Dundee Rep Stripped Festival. It was then selected by Jemima Levick for A Play, A Pie and A Pint's Spring 2023 Season, performing at the Òran Mór in Glasgow and Traverse Theatre in Edinburgh.

CHARACTERS

FREDDIE

50s (he/him). A best-selling novelist

BEN

24 (he/him). An aspiring novelist

SETTING

Freddie's home in Morningside, Edinburgh. His Study

TIME

Present Day

SCENE 1

Lights up.

FREDDIE (50s) speaks directly to us, and a DICTAPHONE.

FREDDIE: So... this man... he... he wasn't afraid of dying. He was always better with endings, than he was with beginnings. So, let's start from the beginning.
Right, he's your typical working-class Scottish guy, who... who's living in the rubble and... he's running out of time to... But he was... and so...

Lights up on the rest of the space.

We're in FREDDIE's study in his flat in Morningside, Edinburgh. FREDDIE stares at the back wall, covered in POST-IT NOTES.

FREDDIE: So...

He keeps staring, then suddenly...
Frustrated, he destroys his storyboard on the wall.

A KNOCK on the door.
FREDDIE checks his watch.

FREDDIE: It's open!

We hear the front door open.
FREDDIE tidies up.

FREDDIE: In here.

Eventually, BEN (24) enters.

BEN: Mr. Atkinson, hi!

FREDDIE: Call me Freddie. We're both adults here. Ben, isn't it?

BEN: That's me!

BEN extends his hand, FREDDIE shakes it.

FREDDIE: How old are you?

BEN: Twenty-four.

FREDDIE: Hm. You look a lot younger.

BEN: I can show you my provisional if you like.

BEN laughs, FREDDIE doesn't.

FREDDIE: Let's get started, shall we? We're already running a bit behind.

BEN: Yeah, I'm so, so sorry I'm late. I couldn't find the building.

FREDDIE: You don't have Google Maps?

BEN: Edinburgh isn't the easiest to navigate.

FREDDIE: Isn't that the point of Google Maps?

BEN: There's so many alleys.

FREDDIE: Not an Edinburgh native, then?

BEN: Stirling.

FREDDIE: Sorry to hear that.

BEN: You're from Leith, aren't you?

FREDDIE: You've done your research.

BEN: Yes.

FREDDIE: So, what's my middle name?

BEN: I'm sorry?

FREDDIE: If you've done your research, what's my middle name?

BEN: Oh, I—

FREDDIE: Not very thorough research then.

(Beat.)

BEN: Just so you know... I'm, like, really bad at knowing when people are kidding and when people are—

FREDDIE: Sit down.

BEN: OK.

They both sit.

FREDDIE: Do you have your CV with you?

BEN: I do!

BEN goes into his bag.

He hands over a DAMP CV.

FREDDIE: This is damp.

BEN: It was raining earlier. My bag got—

FREDDIE: Best to keep something like this in a folder.

BEN: I didn't know it was going to rain.

FREDDIE: You live in Scotland.

(Beat.)

You completed your undergraduate degree at Glasgow University, yes?

BEN: Yes, I wrote my dissertation on queer hauntology.

BEN waits for a reaction. FREDDIE doesn't give one.

BEN: Essentially, analysing how we remember the AIDS epidemic.

FREDDIE: My understanding was that you want to be an author, not an academic.

BEN: I'm just giving a bit of background. I've been following your writing for years.

FREDDIE: You're a fan, then?

BEN: I think I read your first novel when I was twelve.

FREDDIE: That doesn't count.

BEN: I'm sorry?

FREDDIE: A twelve-year-old doesn't have the intellectual capacity to understand my books. As far as I'm concerned, you didn't read it.

BEN: Right.

FREDDIE: What book was it?

BEN: The Londoners.

FREDDIE: Hm, that's a good one. You really missed out.

BEN: I'll be sure to re-read it.

FREDDIE: What's your personal favourite of mine?

BEN: I suppose 'The Rude Awakening'. I like that it has a female protagonist.

FREDDIE: Why should that matter?

BEN: I'm a lot more interested in stories that aren't exclusively about moody, straight, white guys who smoke cigars and cheat on their wives.

Again, BEN laughs and FREDDIE doesn't.

FREDDIE: So, you're one of Maria Williams' students?

BEN: She's my thesis project adviser.

FREDDIE: Maria's a good friend of mine, she recommended you profusely.

BEN: She's incredible.

FREDDIE: Shame she's stuck teaching now.

BEN: Why's that a shame?

FREDDIE: The spider's web of a 9-to-5 job... it's poison for a writer.

BEN: But writers need to support themselves while they—

FREDDIE: Writing isn't supporting yourself?

BEN: In an ideal world.

FREDDIE: There's nothing ideal about Maria's situation.

BEN: But...

BEN stops himself.

FREDDIE: Say what you have to say.

BEN: Not everyone is interested in commercial success.

FREDDIE: Do you really believe that?

BEN: I'm interested in being the best I can be.

FREDDIE: What do you do for work at the moment?

BEN: I'm still a student.

FREDDIE: What were you doing for the two years between undergraduate and postgraduate?

BEN: Well, I mean, there's always that post-graduation adjustment period where—

FREDDIE: Waiter or shop assistant?

BEN: Waiter.

FREDDIE looks down at BEN's CV.

FREDDIE: Ah yes, here it is! Frankie and Benny's! Well, at least you got to wear a nice uniform.

No response.

FREDDIE: You didn't fantasise about writing a best-seller while serving tables? That's Maria's problem, you see. She writes gorgeous prose, comes up with these weird and wonderful ideas, but it just *doesn't sell*. None of her stuff is palatable, because she has a habit for preaching.

BEN: Preaching?

FREDDIE: I don't know what she's teaching you in class, but a writer's main job is to *tell the story*, it's as simple as that. You don't have to enlighten us, or be arrogant enough to assume that your views are interesting... just *tell the story*.

BEN: And you don't think Maria does that?

FREDDIE: I think it's a common thing among some female writers, which I know I'm not supposed to say, I'm not saying they push an agenda but...

BEN: What kind of agenda?

FREDDIE: You're getting very defensive.

BEN: A feminist one?

FREDDIE: There are plenty of exceptions, I love Margaret Atwood's stuff, but that's because there's a point behind it, there's a *story*.

BEN says nothing.

FREDDIE: If you're easily-offended, I'm probably not the best person to be around.

BEN: You're... you know... you're entitled to your opinion.

FREDDIE eyes BEN for a moment. Is he sincere?

FREDDIE: Has Maria told you anything about this job?

BEN: She said you need someone to conduct research for your next novel. Someone around my age?

FREDDIE: Well, not research, per-se. Basically, the work would consist of —

BEN: Wait. Do you mind if I take notes?

FREDDIE fires him a look.

FREDDIE: Be my guest.

BEN goes into his bag and pulls out a NOTEBOOK. He keeps rummaging.

BEN: Do you have a pen I could borrow?

FREDDIE sighs and rummages in his drawer. BEN picks up a PEN from his desk.

BEN: Are you using this one? Could I?

FREDDIE: That's my—fine. Yes, that's fine.

BEN: You said it *isn't* actually research-based then?

FREDDIE: I'm assuming you know it's been a while since my last best-seller. 'The Hour Glass,' back in 2019. Brilliant book, despite the backlash. "Culturally insensitive" and "misogynistic" and "gratuitous". One critic from The Guardian wrote a full fuck-off essay on it.

BEN: I know people have a lot of opinions about you.

FREDDIE: I've always written gritty stories. Murder, hate crimes, rape... You name it! It's all ugly, it should be written ugly.

BEN: But there's a brutal gang rape in it.

FREDDIE: And?

BEN: Well, as a man, have you considered the optics on that?

FREDDIE: Optics?

BEN: I think there's a few things people might be upset—

FREDDIE: Young people.

BEN: Excuse me?

FREDDIE: Young people are upset about it. People my age could handle grit. Irvine Welsh, Bret Easton Ellis, Chuck Palahniuk, They were all about pushing the envelope, now it's all about getting "triggered". I went to give a guest lecture at Glasgow Uni last month. All these undergraduate lit students were sitting there, with their chai tea lattes, their puffy, oversized shirts, their hats that sit on the top of their heads like an unrolled condom and don't even cover their ears...

FREDDIE takes a look at BEN.
He's wearing the exact outfit he's describing, even the HAT.

FREDDIE: These wannabe-hippy, lit students are sitting there while I'm speaking, looking at me like I'm Harvey Weinstein, just waiting for the Q&A to come, and a sea of hands shoot up. First, it's some Scandinavian girl in corduroy dungarees, who says: "I just have to say, I really think your treatment of women in your latest book and throughout your career is just so..." And she starts crying. She starts fucking crying! Over a book! So, I say: "is there a question?" And Jesus Christ, the room goes up in flames! "How dare you! I was sexually assaulted!" "You don't get it because you're an old white man!" All this over a book! Fiction. And I'm sure you've learned yourself, the industry is small.

When you've got mental people posting pictures of your book on social media, screaming "boycott!" you know... word travels fast. And it's infuriating, hearing words like... "racist" "misogynistic" "problematic," that's the worst one! Seems like it's impossible to appeal to anyone unless you're an Asian, transgender, disabled lesbian with—

BEN: Then why do you care?

(Beat.)

FREDDIE: Care?

BEN: If you think they're all snowflakes, why do you care so much about their opinions?

FREDDIE: My publisher cares.

BEN: I see.

FREDDIE: I can't stand being policed, being told something is offensive because it's got grit. I mean... 'A Clockwork Orange'! Imagine that was written today.

BEN: I think the time something is written... it's integral to how it's received.

FREDDIE: But it's a masterpiece! Does it stop being a masterpiece, when the words haven't changed, only the readers have?

BEN: Is that rhetorical, or...?

FREDDIE: My next book is going to be on the best-seller list.

BEN: And you want *my* help with that?

FREDDIE: My publisher is hesitant to move ahead with whatever I write next unless I consult a sensitivity reader. Do you know what that is?

BEN: They're becoming more popular.

FREDDIE: Get a real job, instead of censoring people.

BEN: But they're not there to censor, they're there to guide and—

FREDDIE: I said the day I hire a 'sensitivity reader' is the day I put down my pen for good.

BEN: And what did your publisher have to say about that?

FREDDIE: We came to an agreement. I suggested I bring on a young *assistant*, to be a fresh set of eyes. No one recommended anyone quite like Maria recommended you.

BEN: Really?

FREDDIE: You have something special apparently. And this would be a tremendous stepping-stone for you. You could add it to your CV.

BEN: Yes.

FREDDIE: If you can keep it dry. I'd say you'd be expected to do about five hours work per week. Sound reasonable?

BEN: Definitely.

FREDDIE: And you think you'd be a good fit for something like this?

BEN: I mean, there are so many writers I'd love to sit down with and be like: what were you THINKING?

BEN laughs nervously.

FREDDIE: Well, now's your chance.

BEN: Yeah.

(Pause.)

FREDDIE: I'm waiting.

BEN: What?

FREDDIE: What would you change about my writing?

BEN: Am I allowed to be completely candid?

FREDDIE: Please.

BEN: Well, in terms of the lens I'm coming from...

FREDDIE: What lens? Always be specific.

BEN: As a queer person... there's zero queer visibility in your novels.

FREDDIE: Just say gay.

BEN: I'm being inclusive.

FREDDIE: Besides, that's not true. There's a gay character in 'Brothers in Arms'.

BEN: Right, but... he's a serial killer. It's hardly favourable representation.

FREDDIE: And that's another meaningless soundbite. "Representation."

BEN: I just find it a bit disappointing, considering...

BEN trails off.

FREDDIE: Considering?

BEN: Aren't you gay yourself?

(Pause.)

FREDDIE: That's private.

BEN: Oh, come on.

FREDDIE: Did Maria tell you this?

BEN: It's one of those things in the lit world, like everyone sort of knows, but doesn't talk about it. Which, to be completely honest, in this day and age, I guess I really don't understand.

FREDDIE: So what if I am?

BEN: Well, I'd be interested to know why it doesn't factor into your writing.

FREDDIE: Because I'm not a gay writer.

BEN: But you're a gay man?

FREDDIE: Yes.

BEN: So you don't feel a responsibility to represent queer people in your work?

FREDDIE: You know, when I was your age, it was offensive to say—

BEN: Well, we've reclaimed the word.

FREDDIE: Who's we?

BEN: You don't feel the need to—

FREDDIE: I tell stories I want to tell, not the stories that are expected of me. My passion has always been gritty, psychological thrillers.

BEN: Why can't you write those books with gay characters?

FREDDIE: Because then they become "gay books". That's all people would see when they pick it up.

BEN: So say: This is the story I'm telling, take it or leave it.

FREDDIE: Well, I'd like them to take it. And if you're so passionate about it, feel free to write your own novel.

BEN: Clearly, you're offended.

FREDDIE: I don't get offended.

BEN: But you asked for my opinion and I gave it to you. Isn't that exactly what you're asking me to do?

FREDDIE: I'm not sure this is going to work out.

BEN: All I'm saying is... you have a platform! Use it!

FREDDIE: I'm a writer, not an activist. It's not my job to drag faggots out the closet.

BEN is outraged. Long silence as he processes. FREDDIE studies his reaction.

FREDDIE: Thank you for your time, and I wish you the best of luck. My pen, please.

BEN: If this is how you speak to people, you deserve everything you get.

FREDDIE: You want to talk about "reclaiming words" Try that one out! We are faggots!

BEN: Stop saying it!

FREDDIE: If we can't say it, then who can?

BEN: No one should.

FREDDIE: Do you want an apology? A musical number? Tell me what I can do to get you out the door!

BEN: I'm not going anywhere. Either you hire me—

FREDDIE: Why would I—?

BEN: Or I'll have no reason to keep what you said to myself.

FREDDIE processes this furiously.

FREDDIE: You're blackmailing me. Really?

BEN doesn't flinch.

FREDDIE bursts into laughter.

BEN: I'm serious.

FREDDIE: Oh, I know! That's why it's funny.

BEN: I'll put it on social media, I'll let people know what happened today. Like you said, the lit industry is small.

FREDDIE: I'll take my chances.

BEN: After your publisher has actively told you to make a change to your reputation, you really think this is going to do you any favours?

FREDDIE: Look, Bill, Ben, whatever the fuck your name is... it's your word against mine.

BEN: Looking at you and looking at me, my track record against yours—

FREDDIE: You don't even have a track record!

BEN: Who are people more likely to believe?

FREDDIE: This clearly isn't about a part-time job. What do you really want here?

(Pause.)

They stare each other down.

BEN reaches into his bag and pulls out a MANUSCRIPT. He throws it down on the table.

FREDDIE: What's this?

BEN: A novel I finished last year.

FREDDIE: A novel is never finished.

BEN: My latest draft, then.

FREDDIE: And what are you suggesting I do with it?

BEN: Give me some feedback.

FREDDIE: And?

BEN: Well, I'm sure you know a lot of people in the industry.

FREDDIE: Aw, bless, I bet you got all excited when Maria told you about this interview, eh? You graduate next month and this was going to be your big chance! Were you hoping I'd read your novel, recommend it to a publisher, then you'd travel around the world for the book tour, win the Man Booker Prize, and be reading about all of this on your Wikipedia page in ten years' time?

BEN: Well, I suppose that would be best-case scenario.

FREDDIE: It doesn't work like that, you wait your turn.

BEN: Maybe this is my turn.

FREDDIE: Okay, Ben... you're saying if I read your novel, you'll keep your mouth shut? You won't go around saying I called you a faggot, or that I badmouthed Maria Williams, you won't add fuel to the fire. Is that what you want me to agree to?

BEN: Yes.

Their stares linger.

Then, FREDDIE reaches into his pocket and pulls out his DICTAPHONE. He clicks it. Checkmate.

FREDDIE: Well, you can fuck off.

BEN: What's that?

FREDDIE: An antique from a bygone era.

BEN: I don't... wait... is that, like, a Dictaphone or something? Did you just *record* me?

FREDDIE shrugs obnoxiously.

BEN: Oh my God! Who actually does that? That's, like, fucked-up.

FREDDIE: Poetry at its finest.

BEN: How much did you record?

FREDDIE: Enough to make it very difficult for you to—

BEN: You won't use that. If people think you record everyone you speak to—

FREDDIE: Well, I was interviewing you. I've never conducted a job interview before. Do people not usually record their applicants?

BEN: Not without their permission.

FREDDIE: Ah, see, I didn't know that.

BEN: It doesn't help you. People will still know what you said, your career will still—

FREDDIE: At least I have a career to ruin. And you're right, I *do* know a lot of important people. People who listen to my opinion.

BEN: Are you threatening me?

FREDDIE: You didn't threaten me a few minutes ago?

(Long pause.)

Backed into a corner, BEN thinks.

Again, FREDDIE studies him.

BEN: I've never done anything like that in my life.

FREDDIE: I obviously bring out the worst in you, so let's both do ourselves a favour and—

BEN: You won't find anyone better than me.

FREDDIE: That's a bold statement.

BEN: I'm more than qualified to do this.

FREDDIE: There's plenty of *qualified* people out there.

BEN: You have to admit I'm brave. I could have really played you, walked on eggshells around you, told you exactly what you wanted to hear, without you even knowing it. I'm smart enough to do that. But I stood up to you, pushed back, even when I was making you uncomfortable.

FREDDIE: I don't need anyone to educate me.

BEN: You need someone who challenges you, who isn't afraid of you.

FREDDIE turns his back on BEN.

FREDDIE: The only person who knows what I need is me.

BEN: Then tell me! What do you need?

FREDDIE: Someone who listens to me.

FREDDIE didn't know he was going to say this.

BEN: Then I'll listen.

FREDDIE turns back to BEN.

FREDDIE: No.

BEN: Why?

FREDDIE: Every time I open my mouth, you're waiting for me to say something wrong.

BEN: I can work on that.

FREDDIE: I can smell the Glasgow Uni off you.

BEN: I can work on that too. Look!

BEN dramatically removes his "unrolled condom HAT".

He throws it in the BIN.

BEN: I wasn't lying when I said I'm a fan of yours. I mean, you're not, like... my favourite writer to walk the face of the earth or anything but... your work always spoke to me. I find it so painful. Underneath all the violence, there's this yearning, loneliness, and, like... vulnerability. I could tell from your writing that you were gay. Even though you never explicitly say it. I'm just saying, like... I feel connected to you, and I don't get that with many authors.

FREDDIE: Why should I believe you?

BEN: I have no reason to lie.

FREDDIE: You're an opportunist.

BEN: I'm not asking you to singlehandedly launch my career. All I'm asking is... to be taken seriously for once. It would be nice to have someone, someone whose work I've genuinely admired, point me in the right direction. Does that make me an opportunist?

FREDDIE says nothing. Is he thinking about it?

BEN: Look, if you weren't going to hire me, you'd have kicked me out by now.

FREDDIE: I've tried!

BEN: I'll help you out, you help me out, what is it going to take for you to say yes?

FREDDIE: You trying to solicit me now?

BEN: What? No. I have a boyfriend.

FREDDIE: Does he have a better sense of humour than you?

BEN: Well, he's American, so—

FREDDIE: God, you're both fucked then.

BEN smiles, genuinely a bit ticked by this.

FREDDIE softens just a little bit.

FREDDIE: Does he live over here?

BEN: We're long-distance.

FREDDIE: A little bit young for that, are you not?

BEN: Can't help who we fall in love with.

This hits FREDDIE. He thinks. This time, BEN studies him.

FREDDIE: Say you were in my shoes, what would you do next to appease Joe Public?

BEN: Does this mean I have the job?

FREDDIE: Answer the question.

BEN: I'd release an apology.

FREDDIE: To whom?

BEN: Do you have Instagram?

FREDDIE: Do I look like I have Instagram?

BEN: Twitter?

FREDDIE: I only really use it for news.

BEN: Post something, acknowledge the criticism you've been given, let people know you're sorry.

FREDDIE: I think apologies are nonsense. All that social media shit... it's not for me. Actions speak louder than words.

BEN: So what's your action?

FREDDIE: Using my words. Writing my best novel yet.

BEN: That's not going to automatically fix everything.

FREDDIE: If you help me take on board what people have said—

BEN: Do you even have an idea?

FREDDIE: Of course I have an idea. I always have ideas.

BEN: Good, then hit me.

(Beat.)

FREDDIE: Right now?

BEN: This can't be the first time you've made a pitch.

FREDDIE: I'm not "pitching" anything to you.

BEN: I'm just trying to do my job.

(Pause.)

FREDDIE can't believe this guy's nerve (but kind of likes it).

FREDDIE: So... so, there's this guy

BEN: Uh-huh.

FREDDIE: And he's your typical, Scottish working-class guy...

BEN: Got you.

FREDDIE: And he's at a turning-point in his life where... okay so, he finds out he has a lymphoma.

BEN: Cancer?

FREDDIE: That's right. And so...

FREDDIE gets lost in his thoughts.

FREDDIE: Actually, two seconds, let me get my notes.

FREDDIE gets his notes from the BIN.

FREDDIE: So, he's been a gangster most of his life, and his ex-wife and daughter have a restraining order against him. But when the cancer diagnosis comes along, he tries to get back in touch with them, and his wife and daughter still want nothing to do with him. But then, at his lowest point, he meets this Polish prostitute. And they form this odd, semi-romantic relationship, and decide to go on this wild crime spree together, so it's still a thriller but at its heart...
It explores the connection between sex and death.
It's really a story about a man who... under very unexpected circumstances... learns to love for the first time. Even though his days are numbered.

(Pause.)

BEN: Hm.

FREDDIE: Did you seriously just "hm" me?

BEN: No, no, it's an interesting idea, it's just... don't you think this kind of story has been written before? By *every* male writer to go through an existential crisis? Sad, straight, white guy who has made a lot of bad decisions confronts his mortality and emotionally redeems himself by having sex with younger women. And these kinds of stories always try so hard to be edgy.

They always want to be Nabokov or Hemingway or Bukowski, who were probably complete arseholes, and anyone who tries to copy them just comes across as a self-absorbed, masturbatory narcissist.

FREDDIE: Why don't you tell me how you really feel?

BEN: If you wrote something more personal—

FREDDIE: I happen to relate a lot to the main character.

BEN: A heterosexual gangster?

FREDDIE: Okay. Let me guess, you love all those gay writers, Alan Hollinghurst, Edmund White, Jeanette Winterson... who tell "poor-me" stories about their own lives, and conveniently change the main character's name. It's all about "coming-out," having volatile sexual tendencies, that's the kind of story you think I should be telling?

BEN: Maria always tells us in class that the further you go into the personal, the more you'll explore the universal.

FREDDIE: You said your favourite book of mine was 'The Rude Awakening'. That's probably the least personal thing I've ever written, I just got into the protagonist's mindset and—

BEN: And she was abused the whole way through it by—

FREDDIE: That doesn't happen to women out there?

BEN: Yes, but *women* can write about those experiences with sensitivity and empathy.

FREDDIE: I'm not interested in sensitivity and empathy.

BEN: Have you even tried it?

FREDDIE: And what? Be like everyone else? Write to appeal to oppression, that's what it's all about now, eh? Who's going to write the next big thing about gays, the next big thing about race, women, the working class... I mean, sometimes I think I'd be better off if I weren't a middle-aged white man.

BEN: That's creating a narrative that minority writers only get selected because—

FREDDIE: I didn't say that.

BEN: It's racist, and it's—

FREDDIE: Yeah, that's it. I'm racist.

BEN: I'm not calling you a racist, I'm pointing out—

FREDDIE: I'd love to keep chatting, Ben, but I'm having Nigel Farage over later, so...

BEN: You can't just say whatever you want without consequences. I mean... are you ever willing to be wrong?

FREDDIE: I'm sick of listening to how fucking high and mighty everyone is. Everyone thinks they're an expert, because their only area of expertise is themselves and how they look. Do you care more about being a good person or people thinking you're a good person? People are so scared of saying the wrong thing that they're not saying anything at all.

BEN: But don't you still think it's important to be socially and culturally aware?

FREDDIE: Then, what will we all talk about? How *socially* and *culturally* aware we all are? Are those really the stories you want to tell?

BEN: I don't want to be the kind of writer who doesn't listen.

(Pause.)

FREDDIE: Where I grew up was rough as fuck, full of junkies, scum, people wanting a fight for the sake of a fight. Whenever I looked at them, whenever they shouted "wee fairy Freddie" as I walked past, I'd just get this rage bubble up inside me. I hated how they were so... ugly. Repulsive, inside and out. From the way they spoke, to their football strips, to the way they smelt, and spat on the ground—

BEN: I mean, this is sounding a little—

FREDDIE: Classist, I know, but how could I not hate them? The only way I could stop feeling it, was to write about it, to understand it. Why they were calling me a "fairy", why they were constantly stabbing each other, and no matter how bleak things got, nothing would ever change. There's more than one way to experience empathy.

BEN: I disagree. Like, with my novel... I wrote it right after my Mum died.

BEN waits for a reaction. FREDDIE doesn't give one.

BEN: Breast cancer.

The same thing happens.

BEN: And so... So, it's about this boy, and yes, he's pretty much based on me, but, like... she died in my first year of uni. So, I was going out all the time, drinking constantly, drugs, having blackout one-night stands. I knew how self-destructive I was being. But I think what made it worse was that... I didn't have a community. Because, like.. I mean, it's totally not the same thing, but in the eighties, when queer people were in this constant state of grief, at least they had each other. At least there was some kind of... solidarity, you know? I guess that's what my novel is about. Like you said, that ugliness of grief, and yeah, sexuality, I guess.

FREDDIE takes the manuscript, looks at it, then throws it in the BIN.

It secretly crushes BEN.

FREDDIE: I don't have the time to read your novel.

BEN: That's—I know, that's not the point. I want to know more about *you*. The story only *you* can tell. I'm not saying you should write a book about why you've been in the closet all these years—

FREDDIE: There was no closet! You met me today.

BEN: But I'd read that novel. Just saying.

FREDDIE: Well, it's not going to happen. I don't subscribe to the notion that being gay automatically makes you interesting. I'm not into the whole "pride" thing. Don't need rainbows to be a... F word. You lot make me laugh, you all grow up—

BEN: Sorry, what's my lot?

FREDDIE: Young gays who grow up with parents who accept them, trying to act like they've drawn the short straw, thinking they're bloody martyrs, they weren't born when fucking meant dying.

BEN: Are you referring to AIDS?

FREDDIE: Am I—excuse me?

BEN: I mean, you must have been a young guy in the eighties and nineties so...

BEN waits for FREDDIE to interrupt. He doesn't.

FREDDIE: I don't like talking about it. Let's get back to—

BEN: How else can you keep the memory alive?

FREDDIE: Memory isn't always a good thing. Now, please—

BEN: This is what I wrote my undergraduate dissertation on. I'm proud of my history.

FREDDIE: How is it your history?

BEN: There's plenty of Jewish people who didn't live through the holocaust, but it's still their history.

FREDDIE: Tell yourself what you need to tell yourself.

BEN: See, this is what I can't stand about living in Scotland. When I went to New York to visit my boyfriend, queer people actually talk about being queer. Real, intellectual, complicated discussions, and they don't need to do a bump of mandy or gear to have them.

FREDDIE: No, they all hire therapists from the age of three instead.

BEN: They're more forward-thinking over there.

FREDDIE: America is a joke, and anyone who wants to live there is being sold a lie.

BEN: What people went through during the AIDS crisis, it's just... It's heart-breaking! Like, I could cry right now just thinking about it. That's why I've always wanted to live in a cosmopolitan city, like New York or San Francisco, or even London, I guess. To feel connected to that history. To be able to walk down the Castro, or step inside Stonewall, see the spaces that people lived in during the AIDS epidemic, experience that metropolis atmosphere, the nightclubs, the flats, the old bathhouses... to really get a deeper understanding of myself, and my identity and—

FREDDIE: I've been to New York and San Fran more times than I can count. They're the two most sickening places you'll ever go in your life. Full of people living off the backs of the people who died before them and pretending it was their battle when really it was won for them. A bunch of blonde, blue-eyed pricks sipping on cocktails, snorting overpriced cocaine and going to the gym every morning because healthy people seem to be the only ones who can have sex anymore. Typical fucking Americans! The worst people in the world! They think they own the AIDS crisis and gay liberation and oppression in general. Every book, every bit of analysis is all New York, all San Fran. God forbid someone cares about the tiny little country that hangs on the top of England. Or all the other tiny little countries where people were dropping left, right and centre. And, fucking hell, Edinburgh was the AIDS capital of Europe at the time. Did you know that? But no! Only America! America is the only place with angels!

Silence lingers. Where the fuck did that come from?

BEN: You're clearly a lot angrier than you care to admit, and you have a right to be.

No response.

BEN: I completely understand.

FREDDIE: No you don't.

BEN: I know it seems like the world has progressed, but I mean, gay-bashing is still a huge problem—

FREDDIE: Oh God, more politics, I need a paracetamol.

BEN: Are we just supposed to ignore the violence trans people still face? Just because it's better for us, doesn't mean—

FREDDIE: I understand that, thank you.

BEN: And, like, whenever my boyfriend comes here, I *never* feel comfortable holding his hand in the street.

FREDDIE: Put them in your pockets then. Read your books, write your dissertations, but, trust me, this... the world you're living in... this is as good as it gets.

BEN: Well, it's still not good enough.

FREDDIE: Learn some bloody resilience.

BEN: I have plenty of—

FREDDIE: Try living with the same disease for thirty years!

(Long silence.)

BEN: You mean... you have...

"AIDS" goes unsaid.

FREDDIE looks completely ashamed.

FREDDIE: Look, we've gone completely off-track here—

BEN: You have AIDS?

FREDDIE ignores him.

He tries to distract himself.

BEN: Like, full-blown AIDS?

FREDDIE: As opposed to half-blown AIDS, who the fuck marked your dissertation?

BEN: You've lived with it for *thirty* years?

No response. BEN processes this slowly.

BEN: So, you got it, like... like... *during* the epidemic.

FREDDIE: One of the lucky unlucky ones.

BEN: Does anyone know?

FREDDIE: I don't feel the need to talk about it. Besides, who really cares?

BEN: Readers will definitely care.

FREDDIE looks confused.

BEN: How many people have gone through this experience? This is your story, Freddie.

FREDDIE: My truth isn't a story. It defeats the purpose of fiction.

BEN: If you want a book back on the shelves, this is the way to do it.

FREDDIE: They didn't want it before, why should I give it to them now?

BEN: What do you mean?

FREDDIE hesitates.

FREDDIE: Back in the nineties, I did write about living with AIDS, about losing my partner. It was probably the bravest thing I've ever done. All of them told me the same thing, "Freddie. It'll never sell. It's not your audience." So, I've tried the whole "to thine own self be true" schtick, and I was told to get back in the closet.

(Silence.)

BEN: Your partner, what was his name?

Again, FREDDIE hesitates.

FREDDIE: Tony.

BEN: Did your family know about him?

FREDDIE: My family knew what they wanted to know. I wasn't even allowed to attend his funeral.

BEN: Seriously?

FREDDIE: It was a fucking horrible time, impossible not to hate yourself, but there's nothing that needs to be said that hasn't already been said.

BEN: I wouldn't be so sure about that.

FREDDIE: Please don't patronise me about this.

BEN: I'm not trying to—Really. I'm not.

(Pause.)

FREDDIE: I've looked through the comments online about me. One thing keeps coming up, that I'm just an "angry old man", and I just think: how true. I am angry, I've always been angry, even when I don't want to be. And if I stop being angry then... (*stops himself*)

I felt like I was going to change the world once too, then every week there was another funeral. And it was like overnight... I walked into a gay bar and felt ancient, diseased, in a room that only wanted a party. And I felt angry, I feel so... unbelievably...

FREDDIE stops himself.

He refuses to let himself get emotional.

FREDDIE: You know what? Why don't we schedule another meeting for another day. I've met you, you've got the job, through blackmail, but still—thank you for your—

BEN doesn't move, ignores him.

BEN: But think about it, Freddie. You got to go to gay bars when they were gay bars. Now... there aren't any parties worth going to.

FREDDIE: Not even in New York? With your boyfriend?

BEN: Do you really hate the place that much?

FREDDIE: Tony and I used to love it when it was actually New York, when it was the hub of experimentation.

(*Pause.*)

If you knew what he was like, you'd laugh your head off.

BEN: Why?

FREDDIE: He was a total poofter.

BEN shoots him a look.

FREDDIE: I know I shouldn't say that, but he said it all the time! Camp as Christmas, he was, and opinionated, stubborn.

Eye contact between them lingers.

BEN: Do you have a picture of him?

FREDDIE hesitates.

BEN: If you don't want to, it's totally—

FREDDIE: I'll show you.

FREDDIE goes over to his DESK.

He rummages around until he finds the PICTURE. He runs back over and shows it to BEN.

They sit close to one another.

FREDDIE: That's him.

BEN: Wow. He's beautiful.

Tender pause.

FREDDIE: Might look like a softy, but he was actually tough as nails. I remember one time he made me go to Echo and the Bunnymen—

BEN: What's that? A nightclub?

FREDDIE looks at him, frustrated by his age.

BEN: I'll Google it.

FREDDIE: Tony gets all dressed up like he's Pete Burns, and I'm in my standard jeans and T-shirt. We're waiting for a taxi home, and this arsehole walks past us, shouts all sorts of abuse at us, and I'm shitting myself obviously. But Tony walks right up to him, no insults, no cheek, just stares him down. Now, my heart sinks. I'm thinking this guy is going to kill us. But Tony just keeps staring, doesn't even flinch, and slowly but surely, the guy starts to walk away. Might have been a poofter, but nobody fucked with him.

BEN: Sounds like my kind of guy.

FREDDIE: I think he was everyone's kind of guy.

BEN: Were you in love with him?

FREDDIE gives an apathetic, but very sad shrug. His way of saying yes.

BEN puts his hand on FREDDIE's shoulder. FREDDIE looks startled, then settles into it.

BEN: Then show it, Freddie. Let yourself be with him again.

The eye contact intensifies. FREDDIE goes in for a kiss.

BEN pulls away from him immediately.

Silence.

BEN: What the fuck?

FREDDIE: I—

BEN: That is so not what—I meant you should *write* about—

FREDDIE: I know! I know what you meant, I'm an idiot, I'm a fucking—It was just...

BEN: What?

FREDDIE: I'm so sorry, I—

BEN: If I gave you the wrong impression—

FREDDIE: You don't have to—

BEN: It's completely inappropriate. You should know that.

FREDDIE: I do, honestly.

BEN: You're in a position of power here, technically.

FREDDIE: You touched me too, you know.

BEN: To *comfort* you!

FREDDIE: I just—I was caught up in—I know I had no right to... the things we spoke about, Tony, my condition... these aren't things I speak about often, to anyone really. Might sound mad to you but it's still hard to believe anyone cares. I didn't even know what I was doing there, until I was doing it.

No response.

FREDDIE: Look let's start completely fresh, pretend you never walked through the door.

No response.

FREDDIE: What can I do here?

BEN notices the MANUSCRIPT in the BIN.

He slowly picks it up and presents it again to FREDDIE.

BEN: You could read my novel.

FREDDIE looks taken back, wounded.

BEN: I really do want your feedback on this, and if you could help it get into the right hands... because all I need is a foot in the door.

FREDDIE processes this slowly.

FREDDIE: And if I don't read it?

No response. FREDDIE's hurt turns to fury.

FREDDIE: You wanted all this to happen, didn't you?

BEN: Excuse me?

FREDDIE: Do you really need attention that badly?

BEN: No.

FREDDIE: You'll do anything to feel relevant, use whoever you need to use. You wish you knew people dying of AIDS, you wish you knew what real prejudice felt like, don't you? You sit and look at me like I'm backwards and walk around like you already know everything. You think everybody is just waiting to hear all your big ideas? Wake up! You can talk, text and tweet all you want, but truth is, no one is listening to you. No one actually cares!

BEN: And who cares about you, Freddie?

No response.

BEN: Tell me! Who *actually cares* about you?

(Silence.)

FREDDIE: Go.

BEN: You've made assumptions about me from the second I walked in here.

FREDDIE: And you've made plenty about me.

BEN: Why can't you just read the fucking manuscript?

FREDDIE picks up the MANUSCRIPT. He crumples it, tears it, destroys it.

FREDDIE: I'm not responsible for your happiness, just like no one is responsible for mine.

BEN: Fine. Write another mediocre novel about men with wandering cocks, but we both know you're better than that, what you've actually lived through is a story worth telling, and I think the world should hear it.

(Pause.)

FREDDIE: Then have it.

BEN: What?

FREDDIE: It's yours.

BEN: I don't understand.

FREDDIE: If you love the idea so much, a lonely AIDS survivor, sad, old, pathetic, dying man who—

BEN: Dying?

FREDDIE: Who lost his partner, lost everything, living in the rubble... Go! Write it!

BEN: Freddie—

FREDDIE: I don't want it.

BEN: You said dying—

FREDDIE: That pen I let you borrow, Tony gave that to me. Keep it!

FREDDIE picks up the PHOTO from earlier. He throws it at BEN.

FREDDIE: This photo, keep that too!

FREDDIE goes over to his CABINET. He pulls out several JOURNALS.

FREDDIE: My journals, my thoughts, everything! Take it!

FREDDIE throws the JOURNALS viciously at BEN.

FREDDIE: I don't want any of it! Go! Write!

(Silence.)

BEN: Why did you say dying?

No response.

BEN: Freddie?

No response.

BEN: Do you have, like... like... complications from... do you have AIDS complications?

No response.

BEN: What, like, cancer?

Still nothing.

Then, the penny drops for BEN.

BEN: Lymphoma.

FREDDIE looks at him, surprised.

BEN: The story you told me earlier, about the man and the prostitute, he had lymphoma...

FREDDIE: That doesn't mean—

BEN: Do you have it?

(Pause.)

FREDDIE: I've beaten it before.

BEN: Then can't you—

FREDDIE: Doctors don't seem to think I'll be as lucky this time.

BEN: But you don't look... I mean, you don't seem particularly—

FREDDIE: It's early days.

BEN: I'm so—

FREDDIE: Don't say sorry.

BEN: Have you told anyone?

No response.

BEN: My mum took weeks to tell me and my family, and it only made things worse. I mean, writing another book should be the least of your priorities...

FREDDIE: I need to write.

BEN: You need to live.

FREDDIE: What's the difference?

(Silence.)

BEN: Can I ask you something?

FREDDIE looks at BEN.

BEN: Ignore me.

FREDDIE: Tell me.

BEN: Do you care about how you're remembered?

FREDDIE looks confused.

FREDDIE: You mean, like... when I...

"Die" goes unsaid.

FREDDIE: I try not to think about it.

BEN: But do you? Think about it?

FREDDIE: Constantly.

(Pause.)

BEN: I know a lot of people think you're the bad guy, but...

FREDDIE: If I thought in terms of good guys and bad guys what kind of storyteller would I be?

Their stares linger.

BEN: I'd never take your story from you.

FREDDIE looks away.

BEN: I honestly don't care about being a part of the process. If your publisher asks, just lie and say I reviewed some pages. I won't even tell people I met you. I mean it.

No response.

BEN: Tell your story, Freddie. What have you got to lose?

FREDDDIE stares off into space, unresponsive.

BEN, at last, takes this as his cue to leave.

He starts packing up his things.

FREDDIE: Do I have your email?

BEN: What?

FREDDIE: Your email address. Do I have it?

BEN: It's on my CV.

FREDDIE looks at the DAMP CV.

FREDDIE: Think it might have gotten smudged in the rain.

BEN: Then, I'll write it down.

BEN writes his email address down on his NOTEPAD. He tears out the paper and hands it to FREDDIE.

BEN: Oh, and here's your pen back.

FREDDIE takes the PEN and examines it for a moment.

FREDDIE: I'd like to send your email address to my publisher, just so they know I've taken their advice.

BEN: Of course.

FREDDIE: If you're interested... once I get to work, I could send you some of my pages.

BEN: Yeah?

FREDDIE: Nothing too serious, it would just be nice to...

FREDDIE trails off.

BEN: Well, I'd love to read them.

They awkwardly stare at each other, unsure what to do or say.

FREDDIE: I should probably—

BEN: Oh, yeah! Right. I'll leave you to it.

BEN picks up his bag and smiles innocently. Just as he turns to leave, he turns back slightly.

BEN: And let me know if you ever want me to stop by.

FREDDIE: Why?

BEN: Just to check you're okay.

FREDDIE: I'm fine.

BEN: I know, but—

FREDDIE: You don't know me.

BEN: I don't think that's true.

(Pause.)

BEN: I look forward to the pages.

BEN goes to leave.

FREDDIE: Thursdays.

BEN: What?

FREDDIE: Thursdays.

BEN: Thursdays are good for me too! I mean, I have class in the mornings, but after that... yeah, like... Thursdays are good.

(A beat.)

So... thank you.

FREDDIE: For what?

BEN: Time.

(Pause.)

Thank you for your time.

Lights down.

THE END

Ann Marie Di Mambro
Rachel's Cousins

Previous Artistic Director's Choice

Morag Fullarton and April Chamberlain, Co-Artistic Directors (2016-2021) nominated Ann Marie Di Mambro's play for this collection.

YOU *CAN* CHOOSE YOUR FAMILY

Ann Marie Di Mambro has written extensively for the stage, screen and radio in a career spanning more than thirty years. Her stage play *Tally's Blood* enjoyed a sell-out revival tour in 2023 and is on the school curriculum. Other stage plays include *Ae Fond Kiss* and *Only the Lonely* for A Play, A Pie and A Pint, *Brothers of Thunder* and *The Letterbox* which are also studied in schools. She's written for all of the BBC flagship television shows and also *The Inspector Lynley Myseteries* and *The Coroner* and has been regular writer on *River City* since the show began.

Rachel's Cousins was first performed on 2nd April 2018 at Òran Mór.

CHARACTERS

RACHEL
late 30s/early 40s. Lawyer

MARION
late 30's/early 40's. Rachel's cousin

JOSIE
Marion's sister/Rachel's cousin

ALEX
40-ish. Rachel's lover. Also her boss.

SETTING

Glasgow, present day.

SCENE ONE

RACHEL's house. RACHEL comes in, high heels in her hand. Slips them on, checks her appearance—wee black dress, make-up lovely. She scans the room, smiles to herself.

Knock on door.

ALEX: *(OOV)* Rachel...?

She quickly runs her fingers through her hair as ALEX lets himself in, suited and suave.

ALEX: Hey...

RACHEL: Hey...

A long moment as they look at each other.

ALEX: You're really OK?

She nods.

ALEX: Oh come here...

And they are in each other's arms.

ALEX: Oh thank God... Thank God... I've been so scared... Oh God, I've missed you.

RACHEL: I'm sorry. I didn't mean to shut you out. I just... I had to deal with this in my own.

ALEX: I know... I know...

He gives her a wee box.

ALEX: I didn't know what to get you, so...

RACHEL: You didn't have to get me...

She takes out a bracelet

RACHEL: Oh Alex... It's...

ALEX: Put it on.

He fastens it on her wrist.

ALEX: Wear it to work tomorrow.

RACHEL: What? My first day back?

ALEX: So I can see it on you. Touching your skin.

RACHEL: And if they ask where I got it?

ALEX: I won't tell if you won't.

Their eyes meet. It's charged.

RACHEL: I love it, Alex. Thank you.

They kiss, it's tentative but mounts. His hand moves from her waist to her breast. She jumps back.

RACHEL: Alex!

ALEX: Sorry... I'm sorry...

RACHEL: It's OK.

ALEX: I forgot... It just felt so... You look so... I'm sorry.

RACHEL: No. It's me. I'm not ready to... ready for... I can't even look—*there*—myself yet. I even keep my bra on in the shower.

ALEX: I'm sure it'll get easier.

RACHEL: Maybe once I get the nipples on them.

ALEX: Yes, well, I... will you have to go back into hospital?

RACHEL: Yes but it's a minor procedure. They tattoo on the areola.

RACHEL is on familiar territory. But ALEX squirms.

ALEX: OK.

RACHEL: Then they create the nipple by taking skin from my inner thigh and grafting it onto my... Is this making you uncomfortable?

ALEX: I... No... Not at all. But you know I can't stay.

RACHEL: It's alright.

ALEX: It's this parents' night. If I miss another one Miriam will—

RACHEL: —I said it's alright.

They kiss.

ALEX: I'll see you tomorrow. (*Nods to bracelet*) Wear it.

RACHEL: Yes, boss.

She salutes. Playfully he picks up a cushion to chuck at her, sees a letter under it. He picks it up. RACHEL reacts.

RACHEL: I'll take that.

ALEX: It's from the hospital.

RACHEL: It's not that important.

ALEX: You've not opened it.

She reaches for it, he keeps hold.

ALEX: Rachel?

RACHEL: It's just a blood test.

ALEX: But... you said you'd got the all clear.

RACHEL: I have.

ALEX: So why you scared to open it?

RACHEL: I'm not. Not really. I'm being silly. I'm just not ready to—

ALEX: —you big baby!

He rips it open.

RACHEL: Alex...!

He turns away from her to read it. His face falls.

ALEX: Oh Rachel. I'm so sorry.

He gives her the letter. She reads it, gutted. His phone rings, he glances at the screen.

ALEX: Shit!

He puts it in his pocket, letting it ring out. He looks at RACHEL who is reading the letter.

ALEX: I've heard of it. Vaguely. I don't know anything about it really. But I guess it's not the best news, eh?

The ringing stops.

RACHEL: I... Well... no... I...

ALEX: You going to be alright?

RACHEL: I will be. It's OK.

His phone beeps.

ALEX: Shit! Woman!

He looks at his watch, looks in the direction of the door.

RACHEL: You better go.

ALEX: I hate leaving you.

RACHEL: I told you. It's OK.

He hovers.

ALEX: Look, if it were any other time. But Rory's been having some problems at school and—

RACHEL: —It's alright, Alex. Please. I need to be on my own to process this anyway.

ALEX: I'll see you to-morrow.

A quick kiss and he's gone. RACHEL reads the letter again, deeply shaken. She takes a deep breath and heads out.

SCENE TWO

MARION's house. MARION comes in, worried looking. She picks up some pictures, flicks through them and sighs, undecided.

JOSIE: (*OOV*) It's only me.

MARION quickly puts the pictures away. JOSIE comes in, coat on, with a couple of fish suppers.

JOSIE: Don't know about you, but I'm hank.

MARION flicks her a nervous glance.

MARION: Kevin get away alright?

JOSIE: Yeah.

MARION: He's hardly been back.

JOSIE: It's overtime. (*Off MARION's look*) Now don't start, Marion.

MARION: What?

JOSIE: Just don't. Alright. You're meant to be cheering me up. Here.

She hands MARION a bottle of wine from her bag..

MARION: Lambrini?

JOSIE: Kevin gave it to me.

MARION: Went to town, didn't he?

JOSIE points, warning. MARION puts her hands up, backing off, picks up remote control.

MARION: Right. We watching this? It's the judges' houses.

X Factor music and soundtrack. They unwrap their chips, pour wine etc. JOSIE gets remote control and pauses the TV.

JOSIE: I need a pee.

MARION: You do this every time. Could you not have went before we sat down?

Doorbell.

JOSIE: Who's that?

MARION: Hold on. I'll use my X-Ray vision.

JOSIE: I'll go.

MARION's ears prick up as she hears voices. JOSIE comes in.

JOSIE: You will never guess...

RACHEL comes in. MARION's mouth falls open.

MARION: Good God. It's Lady Penelope.

RACHEL: Hello Josephine.

MARION: I'm Marion. She's Josie.

RACHEL: Oh, I'm sorry. It's been a wee whiley.

MARION: "A wee whiley?"

MARION and JOSIE share look, amused.

RACHEL: Is this a bad time?

MARION: Aye, it is. We're the middle of The Times crossword.

JOSIE: *(laughs)* Ha ha... Times crossword.

MARION: I thought you needed to pee.

JOSIE: In a minute.

RACHEL: I'm sorry for barging in.

MARION: What you doing round here anyway? Slumming it?

RACHEL: Eh... No... I...

(*Beat.*)

Will my car be safe out there?

Cheek! JOSIE and MARION share another look.

MARION: Should be. I don't suppose you'll be long.

JOSIE: You want some chips?

RACHEL: No, thank you.

MARION: Glass of wine?

RACHEL baulks at the Lambrini bottle.

RACHEL: I... Eh... I'm driving.

MARION: A cup of tea?

RACHEL: No. Thanks.

JOSIE: You want to sit down?

RACHEL: Thank you. No.

MARION: Oh, sit on your arse, Rachel. You'll not catch anything.

RACHEL sits on the edge of JOSIE's seat, the TV comes on full bung.

RACHEL: Oh!

She's sat on the remote. She fishes it out. Marion takes it and silences the TV.

MARION: So... Do we get twenty guesses or..?

RACHEL: I'll come to the point. I've had cancer.

MARION:	**JOSIE:**
Oh, I'm sorry...	Oh that's ..

RACHEL: No. I'm fine now. Absolutely fine.

JOSIE: Well, that's good, eh?

RACHEL: Breast cancer. I've had a double mastectomy.

JOSIE: Ooooh...

They both look at RACHEL's boobs.

JOSIE: Those implants?

RACHEL: Not exactly. They're made from my own fat?

MARION: Really? They can do that?

RACHEL: It's a new procedure.

JOSIE: They're lovely, aren't they, Marion?

MARION: They are that.

(Beat.)

JOSIE: Going to let us see them?

RACHEL: No. No way. Please. I'm here for a very specific reason. You know what—I'd rather stand.

She gets up, keen to get this over with. JOSIE sits back down.

RACHEL: My mum died of cancer. As did yours I believe... What I'm saying is there's a high incidence of cancer in our family.

JOSIE: I'm sorry, I'm really going to have to pee.

She gets up, eyeballs RACHEL's boobs as she passes.

JOSIE: They really are lovely. Mind if I just...

She has a wee squeeze.

RACHEL: Hey!

JOSIE: Sorry. *(To MARION)* They feel dead normal.

MARION: Away you go and pee.

RACHEL is losing patience:.

RACHEL: Look, can you hold off for one minute? This is important.

As RACHEL talks JOSIE is standing, struggling to hold in the pee.

RACHEL: There is a gene... That's something in our bodies that's passed down from generation to generation—

MARION: Duh!!

RACHEL: It's called BRACCA2. It can have a flaw which means you have a higher risk of breast and other kinds of cancer.

JOSIE is crossing her legs.

RACHEL: Because of our family history I got tested for this genetic flaw. And it's positive. Now I've been advised to inform all my family members to get tested.

JOSIE: Oh fuck!

RACHEL: *(To JOSIE)* It's just a straightforward blood test.

JOSIE: It's no that. I've started to wet myself.

MARION: Josie! Go!

JOSIE: I'll be right back.

JOSIE limps to the toilet. RACHEL wants away. She hands MARION some leaflets.

RACHEL: Anyway, I won't keep you. This leaflet explains it all. I brought quite a few, so you could give them out round the rest of the family. Especially the women...

MARION: Sorry?

RACHEL: The women in the family. They should all be told.

MARION: Why don't you tell them yourself? There's a cousins' night next Friday.

RACHEL: A what?

MARION: A cousins' night. Last Friday of the month, we all meet up. You should come. Explain it all.

RACHEL: No I couldn't. Really. I've got a lot on at the moment. now. In fact, I need to go now.

MARION: Hold on. You can't just drop a bombshell like that and then just swan off.

RACHEL: As I said, it's straightforward. Just go to your GP and take it from there.

MARION looks on in disbelief as RACHEL hurries out. Stay on RACHEL for a beat.

She lets out a sigh of relief as she fishes out her car keys and clicks her car open. In the background, MARION gathers up the chip papers etc. and exits

Enter JOSIE, on the phone. She is carrying one of the leaflets

JOSIE: Is there no chance you can get away early? Or just a few days off... I mean all the overtime you've been doing... I've had a health scare, Kevin, I'm really worried. I need you here... Can you at least ask? Please?

The call ends. She looks at the leaflet again.

Lights down.

SCENE THREE

RACHEL's house. RACHEL comes in, with some folders. She sits on the couch and starts to leaf through.

Knock on door.

RACHEL: It's open.

JOSIE: It's only me...

RACHEL's mouth fall open.

JOSIE: You don't mind, do you?

RACHEL: I... I... What are you...?

JOSIE: I went to your office but they said you were working from home.

RACHEL: (*Horrified*) You went to my office?

JOSIE: Oh, would you look at that view?

RACHEL: Look, Marion.

JOSIE: Josie.

RACHEL: Josie, I am actually working. I've got exams coming up and—

JOSIE: This is an amazing flat. You're doing alright for yourself, aren't you, doll?

RACHEL: Please don't call me doll.

JOSIE: I call everybody doll.

RACHEL winces.

RACHEL: I... did you want something in particular?

JOSIE: This BRACCA2 thing. You disappeared before I got the chance to ask you about it.

RACHEL: I can't tell you any more than is in the leaflets.

JOSIE: I've made an appointment for the test. So's our Marion. And we've spread the word, like you asked us to. At the cousins' night.

RACHEL: Oh... that...

JOSIE: They all turned up. Even Linda Burns and she never goes to anything. And Shirley, you know, Auntie Margaret's eldest, you know she's over 100 days sober. And our Laura—turns out she's a lesbian by the way. Her man's been that good about it.

She clocks the sofa, has a feel.

Is that suede? Oh so it is.

Her phone rings.

JOSIE: Oh it's our Marion. Hey, Marion, you'll never guess where I am. Where are you?... Oh you're dead near.

RACHEL is gesticulating wildly but JOSIE turns her back.

JOSIE: Come on up. Rachel won't mind.

Lights down.

Then lights up. MARION is there. RACHEL looks on helplessly as they nose about the place.

JOSIE: Feel that, Marion. It's real suede.

MARION: It is an'all.

JOSIE: And look at the view. You can see the campsies.

RACHEL: I don't mean to be rude. But I do need to get on.

JOSIE: No worries. A quick cup of tea and we'll be out your hair. Milk two sugars for me.

MARION: Just milk in mine.

RACHEL: I don't actually have any milk. Or sugar.

MARION: (*Posh voice*) In that case we won't actually bother. Actually.

JOSIE giggles. MARION looks round the flat.

MARION: Some place right enough. You just live here yourself?

RACHEL: Yes.

MARION: Must be great. No screaming weans.

JOSIE gets a leaflet from her bag.

JOSIE: So, Rachel, I've been reading up on it. And I've discussed it with Kevin. He is worried sick about me, so he is. Anyway I've decided, if I'm positive I'm going for a mastectomy.

MARION: Same here. (*Sings*) Tit tit titsy good-bye...

JOSIE: What's she like?

RACHEL is appalled.

MARION: (Sings) All night long I've been kissing
Your left tit cos the right one's missing, oh boy!

JOSIE: (In quick) A double mastectomy.

(Beat.)

MARION: (Sings) I... I who have nothing...

JOSIE laughs.

RACHEL: (*Voice raised*) Oh will you both just—

MARION: What?

RACHEL: BRACCA2 isn't funny. Cancer isn't funny.

MARION: I know. I nursed my mother through cancer. She died in my house.

RACHEL: I'm... I'm sorry.

JOSIE: (To RACHEL) Look, it's just her way of coping.

MARION: No harm in laughing, Rachel. People do it all the time.

RACHEL sighs, looks at her watch.

MARION: But I can moan, if you'd rather. The life I've had.

JOSIE: She's no had it easy, have you, doll?

RACHEL would react to the "doll" but what's the point?

MARION sits. So does JOSIE. RACHEL's heart sinks.

MARION: I'm on my own with three kids. Bleeding me dry so they are. I might as well have called them Gimme, Gimme and Ah Want. I've got one wage coming in and my hours have just been cut. Again. And now this BRACCA2 thing hanging over me. Hanging over my kids. Honest to God, Rachel. I don't know how much more I can take.

RACHEL: Well I'm... sorry.

MARION: You have no idea. Just last week, I... Well, I tried to finish it.

RACHEL: What?

MARION: You know. End it all. I just felt so...

Her voice trails off. RACHEL glances at JOSIE who is hanging on every word. RACHEL is being drawn in despite herself

RACHEL: God... Marion... I'm so...

MARION: Everything just seemed so bleak... So pointless...

JOSIE: You should've called me.

MARION: It's not like I planned it or anything. I'd just come off the late shift. It was dark. The station was dead quiet. The platform was empty. And suddenly the idea came to me. From nowhere. Just get out. And you know what. In that moment. It felt right. And I was dead calm so I was. I just climbed down onto the track and I lay down. And I waited...

RACHEL: Oh my God...

MARION: ...and I waited...

RACHEL: ...but you thought what it would do to your children?

MARION: No, hen. The train was late.

Eh? MARION laughs. JOSIE laughs, relieved.

JOSIE: What's she like?

MARION points at RACHEL.

MARION: Your face!

JOSIE: (*To MARION*) You had me going there.

RACHEL: That is not funny.

MARION: Oh, lighten up.

RACHEL looks at her watch.

RACHEL: I really do have to get on.

JOSIE: So, Rachel, you not got a man yet?

RACHEL is speechless.

JOSIE: I mean you're getting on a bit. You must be ages with me.

MARION: Oh wheesht. There's more to life than having a man.

(*Beat.*)

Mind you, what do I know? Last time I'd a man in my bed he was a corpse.

JOSIE: (*To RACHEL*) Oh, listen to this.

RACHEL: No. I'm sorry. I'm not listening to any more of your stupid stories.

MARION: It's about my late husband. He died in his sleep.

RACHEL: Oh... sorry. I did hear something. But not till after the funeral. I'm sorry I never—

MARION: —They said it was like a cot death.

RACHEL: Oh that's...

MARION: We were in this caravan in Prestwick. Belonged to a mate of his. Anyway, me and Des had just had sex. First time in ages. He was that grateful, the soul. He says, "Am I in the wrong caravan?" So, we're lying there, after, you know, and he asks me what I want to do the next day and I says, "Surprise me." That's the last words I ever spoke to him. Well, he surprised me right enough. Biggest surprise of my life.

RACHEL: I really... don't know... that's...

JOSIE: She's not had sex since, have you Marion?

MARION: No. That was four years ago and since then I've had this real fear of...

RACHEL: Intimacy?

MARION: No. Caravans.

Silence.

Then MARION and JOSIE laugh.

RACHEL: I don't believe... So, your husband didn't die in his sleep, in a caravan?

MARION: Course he did. You think I'd make up something like that?

RACHEL: You're sick.

JOSIE spies a Get Well Soon card, picks it up.

JOSIE: "Get well soon. From everyone at the office." They've all signed it... Oh, that's sad. You mean you just ONE card? From your work?

MARION sees one, face down, picks it up.

MARION: No look, there's another one. "Thinking of you. Love you. Alex." Aww...

RACHEL: Will you please stop touching—

JOSIE grabs the card from MARION.

JOSIE: Oh, there's an Alex on this one... Let me see... (*She compares cards*) They look the same.

MARION grabs the card back.

MARION: Let me see... Oh yes... So, you and Alex? Wee office romance?

RACHEL: Give me that.

RACHEL grabs the card from MARION.

MARION: Ah... I'm guessing... He's married?

RACHEL: That is... that is...

MARION: Look. She's went all red.

RACHEL puts her hands on her cheeks.

JOSIE: I'd kill Kevin if he looked at another woman. I'd cut his balls off. I'd— (*To MARION*) How'd you know he's married?

MARION studies RACHEL.

MARION: (*To RACHEL*) No ring on your finger. Living alone. No pals. On account of always keeping herself available for *him*. And they'd just tell you you're a mug. Plus... you look the type.

RACHEL: How dare you?

MARION: Let's see... You keep your legs shaved. And your oxters. Your nails done, your roots done. Your flat tickety-boo. Because you never know when he might show up.

RACHEL is speechless. ALEX lets himself in.

ALEX: (*OOV*) Rachel. I've just got a few minutes...

RACHEL: Alex I...

He stops as he sees them. JOSIE nudges MARION and mouths "ALEX".

ALEX: Oh, sorry... I didn't realise you had company.

RACHEL: They're just leaving.

MARION: So you're Alex?

JOSIE: Pleased to meet you. We're Rachel's cousins.

RACHEL winces, mortified.

ALEX: Really? Well, I'm Rachel's boss and she's supposed to be working from home.

JOSIE: That a fact?

ALEX: That's why I'm here.

MARION: To check up on her?

ALEX: To see if she needs help. With her studying.

JOSIE: Ah... right... "studying". Marion.

MARION: We'll get out your hair and let you get down to it.

MARION and JOSIE get up to go.

JOSIE: Keep her hard at it.

MARION: Flat out.

JOSIE: See you again, Rachel.

MARION: Nice meeting you, Alex.

They head out. MARION clocks his wedding finger and catches JOSIE's eye and points to her own wedding finger. JOSIE nods, she clocked it too. RACHEL lets out her breath.

ALEX: Nice.

RACHEL: I'm so sorry about them. But I had to tell them about the BRACCA2 gene.

ALEX: Yes... Well...

ALEX has something on his mind.

RACHEL: I normally have nothing to do with them.

ALEX: Just forget about them.

RACHEL: The last time I saw them was my mother's funeral. And I'm sure they only came to that for the free alcohol.

(Beat.)

ALEX: So, Rachel... How are you?

RACHEL: I've been better.

ALEX: Listen... I...

RACHEL: I thought I was done with cancer. Hospitals. Surgery. Waiting for results. Now this BRACCA2 gene's pulled me right back in.

ALEX: You'll be alright. You've already lost both your—

RACHEL: —It's not just breast cancer. There's cervical cancer. Ovarian cancer. I'm considering getting a hysterectomy. It's not as if I'm going to have a baby is it? Remember I had that pregnancy scare a couple of years ago and you totally panicked.

ALEX: I didn't panic.

RACHEL: And an oophorectomy. *(Off his look)* My ovaries removed.

ALEX: I'm sure you'll make the right decision. For you.

RACHEL: I'm sorry. This is all getting too heavy. I'm glad you came.

She kisses him. He tenses. She pulls back, gives him 'question mark' eyes.

RACHEL: What?

ALEX: You know how I feel about you.

RACHEL: Ye-es? *(Where is this going?)*

ALEX: Listen...

A warning bell goes off for RACHEL.

RACHEL: I'm listening.

ALEX: Miriam and I got called to the school yesterday. Rory's got some real behavioural issues. Look, I won't go into detail. Bottom line is Miriam blames me. We talked and she feels... oh, this isn't easy.

RACHEL: Easy for who?

ALEX: Oh, come on. Don't be—

RACHEL: (*Int*) I'm not "being" anything. I get it. You need to spend more time with your family. Which leaves you and me . Where?

ALEX: I never ever said I would leave her, did I?

RACHEL: And I never "ever" asked you to. Did I?

A lull.

ALEX: Look, I don't want to lose you.

RACHEL: You just want me to wait in the wings till you get bored with your wife again?

ALEX: I don't want to lose you from the firm?

RACHEL: To ease your conscience?

ALEX: Jeez-o, Rachel. Because you're an excellent lawyer.

The fight goes out of RACHEL.

ALEX: There's a salaried partnership coming up and if you pass these solicitor-advocate exams I want you to apply for it.

RACHEL: I...

ALEX: Say you'll think about it. Please.

And he goes. She could cry.

Lights down.

Lights up on JOSIE. She unfolds a letter, her hands shaking. As she reads it her face falls.

JOSIE: Oh no...

Lights down.

Then up again on JOSIE, on the phone.

JOSIE: It's pretty serious, Kevin, we need to talk about it. It's not just about me... Well, I thought me getting my breasts off and replaced with false boobs affects us both. As a couple... That we should discuss it... What?... It's not about their size. It's about me getting major surgery... Or living with the prospect of getting cancer... I'm not asking you to give up the rig... I know. I know how hard you work... No, I don't suppose it is urgent... Yes... It can wait.

Miserable, she ends the call.

SCENE FIVE

Law firm. Enter ALEX, very smart in lawyer's gown, carrying a wig. Rachel approaches.

RACHEL: Alex.

ALEX: Yes, Rachel?

They look at each other for an awkward moment.

RACHEL: I... Em... I need a couple of days off next week.

ALEX: That should be fine.

RACHEL: It's for a procedure. A minor procedure.

ALEX: Take whatever time you need.

RACHEL: Thanks.

She would head off. He stops her.

ALEX: So, how is it going? All that.

RACHEL: Fine. Thank you. Getting there.

ALEX: You're looking well.

RACHEL: Thank you.

(Beat.)

How's Rory?

ALEX: Good. Good. Got his highers coming up.

(Beat.)

So your exams must be immanent.

RACHEL: Week after next.

ALEX: Well if I can help at all. Even just as a sounding board.

RACHEL: That's kind of you. I'll... bear it in mind.

She walks off, aware he is looking at her. He watches her go, longingly.

SCENE SIX

Hospital reception area/coffee shop. JOSIE, deeply worried, coat on, holds a plastic coffee cup. RACHEL comes in, with wee overnight case. JOSIE sees her and tries to duck but RACHEL's seen her.

RACHEL: Josie... ?

JOSIE fakes surprise.

JOSIE: Oh, Rachel, I never saw you there.

(Beat.)

What you doing here?

RACHEL: Getting nipples grafted on.

JOSIE: Oh... right.

RACHEL: So how about you?

JOSIE: I... well, I've changed my mind about the mastectomy.

RACHEL: But you tested positive?

JOSIE: Me and Marion both. A few of us did.

RACHEL: I'm sorry.

JOSIE: Our Linda's negative.

RACHEL: Linda Burns? She's the lesbian?

JOSIE: No, Shirley's the alkie. Laura's the lesbian. She's positive by the way. She's going in for a hysterectomy.

RACHEL: But you're—

JOSIE: —just going to get regular check-ups. You know mammograms, cervical smears and that.

RACHEL: Well, that is an option.

JOSIE: I know I was all for it but Kevin hates the thought of me going under the knife. This has knocked him for six. But he's been a rock. I don't think I'd've got through it without him.

RACHEL: So... What are you doing here?

JOSIE: Waiting for our Marion.

RACHEL: She seeing the consultant?

JOSIE: (*A bit cagey*) Yes.

RACHEL: About surgery?

JOSIE: Probably, aye, I would think.

RACHEL: Well, there's no rush.

JOSIE: I think there is. She found a lump.

RACHEL is affected.

JOSIE: On her breast.

JOSIE could cry.

RACHEL: It might not be that serious. If she's found it early. The important thing is she's getting medical help.

JOSIE: Everything bad happens to her. And she just takes it. You know what she said. If this is cancer she'd rather it was her than any the rest of us because she can handle it. I feel so bad.

RACHEL: I think you're over-reacting. You need to wait and see what the doctors say.

JOSIE: It's not that... It's... Oh God, Rachel, I've done something terrible.

RACHEL is at a loss.

RACHEL: I'm sure it can't be that bad.

JOSIE: I lied.

RACHEL: What?

JOSIE: About BRACCA2.

RACHEL: You lied about...?

JOSIE nods. RACHEL is struggling to take it in.

RACHEL: You mean you don't have it?

JOSIE: No.

RACHEL: You're negative?

JOSIE: Yes.

RACHEL: It doesn't make sense. Why would anyone—

JOSIE: —because I wanted to have it, alright?

RACHEL: But why?

(Beat.)

JOSIE: He hardly talks to me anymore. He's never at home. Takes all the overtime that's going.

RACHEL: Who?

JOSIE: Who do you think? My husband.

RACHEL: But you just said—

JOSIE: —yeah, I lied about that too.

RACHEL is speechless.

JOSIE: See, I thought maybe, if there was something wrong with me, it would give him a shake. I'd go in for surgery, he'd realise how much I meant to him.

RACHEL: So you lied to get attention?

JOSIE: Not attention. Affection. I wanted him to... *Cherish* me.

(Beat.)

You must hate me.

RACHEL: I don't hate you.

JOSIE: I lied in my teeth. To my man. To my sister. To my cousins. What am I going to do, Rachel? Tell me what to do.

RACHEL: Oh I don't think I'm—

JOSIE: —Rachel, please. I'm begging you.

RACHEL: You need to tell the truth.

JOSIE: You off your head!

RACHEL: You going to keep this lie going? Pretend you're going in for consultations?

JOSIE: You're right. God, I'm so stupid.

RACHEL: You're not stupid. You just didn't think it through. But you need to tell the truth. Starting with Marion.

JOSIE: Will you come with me?

RACHEL: Me?

JOSIE: Please, Rachel. She might not kick off if you're there.

Lights down.

MARION: *(Shouts. Furious)* What the fuck!!!!!

Lights up.

RACHEL is looking on, awkward, embarrassed, at the ding-dong between MARION and JOSIE.

MARION: You lied? You told a bare-faced lie?

JOSIE: I'm sorry.

MARION: You pure stupid lying wee cow.

RACHEL: I don't think there's any need...

MARION: You got a death wish or something? You should be on your knees pure thanking God you're alright.

JOSIE: I know... I know...

MARION: You any idea what it's like for the rest of us. Knowing we've got it. Knowing we could pass it on to our kids? And you're what? Jealous? Want in on the act?

You're... you're... I can't even look at you.

JOSIE: I am so sorry.

MARION: Aye, so you said.

Silence.

JOSIE, helpless, gives RACHEL an appealing look.

JOSIE: Rachel...?

MARION: What you doing here anyway? Enjoying the show?

JOSIE: Please, Rachel.

RACHEL: I... Just... (*Off JOSIE's look*) Look, Marion, the thing is Josie was acting in an emotional state which was exacerbated by personal problems and she... She deserves the benefit of your understanding and compassion.

SHIRLEY: Pile of shite!

JOSIE: Shhh... Go on, Rachel.

RACHEL: Well, as you just witnessed, she's made a full and frank confession. Of her own volition. And she is taking full responsibility for her actions and is showing genuine remorse.

JOSIE: I really am sorry, Marion. And... and... everything she just said there. But I won't blame you if you never want to speak to me again.

Long moment.

RACHEL can't bear it. She looks appealingly at MARION, her tone up..

RACHEL: Come on, Marion.

MARION: What?

RACHEL: Say something.

MARION: Like what?

RACHEL: I don't know. Something funny.

MARION: I can't think of anything funny right now.

RACHEL: Just... you know... crack a joke... ease the tension? Isn't that what you do? Oh, here's something funny. It's a true story actually. This Scottish High Court Judge was hearing a plea in mitigation... This is pretty funny... the lawyer was laying it on a bit thick about the potential prison sentence hanging over his client like "the sword of Damocles". And as quick as anything the Sheriff said, "Pity he didn't think of that before assaulting someone with the Knife of Stanley."

She laughs awkwardly. They don't.

RACHEL: The knife of Stanley. You know... A Stanley knife?

Tumbleweed.

MARION: Anyway...

MARION looks at JOSIE, her tone softer now.

MARION: Why did you do it?

JOSIE bites her lip.

MARION: Because of Kevin?

JOSIE nods. MARION sighs.

JOSIE: You hear about these couples that don't have children. They're just wrapped up in each other. You know... devoted.

(Beat.)

I thought it would be alright not having kids because we'd be one of those couples. Only we're not. I told a lie to get a reaction and I did. Just not the one I wanted.

MARION: Do yourself a favour, hen. Tell him to—

JOSIE: —I can't. I still love him.

MARION: Josie, please. The way he treats you.

JOSIE: I know but—

MARION: But what?

JOSIE: I don't want to be on my own.

MARION: You're not going to be on your own. You've got me.

She puts her arm round JOSIE. They've forgotten about RACHEL who looks on, excluded.

MARION: You've got all of us. The whole family. We'll all rally round. Remember what my Mammie used to say, "We might not have much but we're rich in blood."

RACHEL slips out, unnoticed.

JOSIE: I know. I know all that. But...

MARION: Oh Josie...

JOSIE: What?

MARION takes a moment.

MARION: There's something you need to see.

She goes to the drawer [or wherever] and takes out the pics from earlier. Her heart is racing. She takes a deep breath and holds them out.

MARION: Just remember, I did it for you.

Lights down.

SCENE SEVEN

Law firm. Enter RACHEL, with lawyer's gown and carrying wig. She pulls an unopened letter from her pocket, goes to open it, changes her mind. She hears ALEX come in and shoves it back in her pocket.

ALEX: (*Approaching*) Well?

RACHEL: Well what?

ALEX: Any news?

RACHEL: About what?

ALEX: Fine, you know. I heard the results were out.

RACHEL: Well... No... Not mine.

ALEX: What's that in your pocket?

The edge of the envelope can be seen.

RACHEL: What?... Nothing?

ALEX: That right there.

RACHEL: Alex... Don't...

He grabs for it. She resists but both enjoy the tussle. He wins, gets the envelope, holds it out of reach.

RACHEL: Give me that.

ALEX: The Law Society. I knew it.

RACHEL: Alex...

ALEX: You've not even opened it.

RACHEL: Well, no I was...

ALEX: You big baby!

RACHEL: Don't you dare...

She protests as he rips it open and reads and his face falls.

ALEX: Rachel, I'm so sorry...

RACHEL: It's OK. I'm OK. (*She's gutted*)

ALEX: You sure?

RACHEL: I just feel I've... Let the firm down.

ALEX: Don't be silly. I'm sure you tried your hardest.

RACHEL: I'd like to sit them again, if that's alright with you.

He winces.

ALEX: I don't really think there's much point.

RACHEL: (*Gutted*) Oh, right.

ALEX: Because you've passed.

RACHEL: What?

ALEX: You are now a qualified solicitor-advocate.

RACHEL: Let me... (*She grabs the letter*)... You... You... That's not funny.

He laughs and hugs her.

ALEX: Oh come here. Congratulations.

She pulls away.

RACHEL: Thanks.

ALEX: You'll be a shoe-in for this partnership.

RACHEL: Really?

ALEX: The timing couldn't be better. What with the partners' dinner on Friday.

(*Beat.*)

Why don't I come and pick you up?

RACHEL: I'm not sure.

ALEX: I've missed you, Rachel.

He kisses her. She likes it.

RACHEL: Don't.

ALEX: Can you honestly say you've not missed me?

She groans, very tempted. He slips his arm round her waist, leans in.

Knock on door. MARION enters.

RACHEL: Marion...

He looks round, horrified to see her.

ALEX: Oh Jeez... you again.

MARION looks at his crotch.

MARION:

Is that a scroll in your pocket or am I interrupting something?

He glances at RACHEL. She shrugs. He sighs.

ALEX: I'll leave you to it. (*As he passes MARION*) Don't be keeping Rachel off her work now.

He goes.

MARION: You and him still at it?

RACHEL: No. (Off her look) No!

(*Beat.*)

So what are you doing here?

MARION: Girl on reception sent us through, seeing as we're family.

RACHEL: Us?

MARION: Josie's went to the toilet. She'll no be long. (*Lowers her voice*) She's in some state. Over that man of hers. But we've pure got him this time.

RACHEL looks at her watch.

RACHEL: I don't mean to be rude but you can't just turn up—

MARION: —Our Josie needs some legal advice...

RACHEL: Then she should make an appointment.

MARION: To speak to her cousin?

This pulls RACHEL up. She tries to be nicer, changes the subject.

RACHEL: I'm sorry, I should've asked. Your biopsy? How did it go?

MARION shrugs.

MARION: Breast cancer.

RACHEL: I'm sorry.

MARION: (*Shrugs*) Just your Donald. (*Off RACHEL's look*) Your luck. Your Donald Duck.

RACHEL looks blank.

MARION: Anyway, they were going to do a lumpectomy but, under the circumstances—that's my new favourite phrase by the way. Under the circumstances you know, BRACCA 2, they'll do the... (*She winces and indicates her boobs*)... off!

RACHEL: Both of them?

MARION: Well yeah. I says just lob the other one off as well, Doctor, save me keeling over.

RACHEL: That can't actually happen... (*It dawns on her*) Oh? Right, I see.

MARION: I mean, I could die or I could lose all my hair. But least I get a boob job on the National Health, eh?

She laughs, RACHEL is not amused.

RACHEL: You can drop the funny act, Marion. It's just you and me here. You can admit to being scared.

(*Beat.*)

MARION: I'm bloody terrified.

RACHEL: It's alright. I won't tell anyone.

MARION: It could be worse. They said it's non- aggressive. It's at an early stage. And the thingway is very good.

RACHEL: The prognosis?

MARION nods. JOSIE comes in. She picks up the heavy atmosphere.

JOSIE: You've told her then?

MARION: No yet. *(To JOSIE)* Show her. *(To RACHEL)* Wait to you see this.

JOSIE gets pictures out her bag, shows them to RACHEL. MARION looks on, expectantly.

RACHEL: What am I looking at?

JOSIE: Kevin.

MARION: Doing the dirty.

JOSIE: See. That's him going into her flat.

RACHEL: Whose flat?

JOSIE:	**MARION:**
Hers.	His bit on the side.

RACHEL: Where did you get these?

MARION: Me and our Laura took them. Followed him so we did. I knew he was up to something.

JOSIE: And that's him coming out. With her.

MARION: Lying, cheating scumbag. Telling her he's doing overtime on the rigs. I says no unless they've struck oil in Partick.

JOSIE: That's him shutting her curtains. You can see her in the background.

RACHEL: And what do you hope to achieve with these?

MARION: What do you mean? That's proof of adultery right there.

RACHEL: I'm sorry. But it's not.

MARION: Eh?

RACHEL: For it to work they would have to prove physical relations took place. And these don't.

MARION: Why else would he be shutting the curtains?

JOSIE: Hold on. I found this.

She hands RACHEL a piece of paper.

JOSIE: It's a receipt. For a hotel. Double room. Look at the price!

RACHEL: It still doesn't prove anything.

MARION: Oh come on.

RACHEL: Look. The point is nobody really uses proof of adultery now. Besides, you don't need all this if you want to end your marriage. (*To JOSIE*) That is what you want, isn't it?

MARION: Absolutely.

RACHEL: Josie?

JOSIE nods, not trusting herself to speak.

MARION: So what does she need?

RACHEL addresses her questions to JOSIE.

RACHEL: Tell me this. Has Kevin been a good husband?

MARION: No way. Pure torn-faced bastard.

RACHEL: Josie?

JOSIE: Well... No, he's not.

RACHEL: He's lied, he's uncommunicative. He's made you unhappy and his behaviour has been unreasonable. Am I correct?

MARION AND JOSIE: Yes.

RACHEL: Has the marriage broken down irretrievably?

MARION: Abso-fucking-lutely.

RACHEL: Marion, please.

MARION: It's just the way we are, OK. If one of us gets cut, we all bleed.

JOSIE: Yes it has. Broken down. The marriage.

RACHEL: Then that's enough to go on.

JOSIE: For what?

RACHEL: A divorce.

JOSIE's stomach is churning at the word.

JOSIE: Oh God... Oh God...

RACHEL: That is why you're here isn't it? For legal advice?

JOSIE: Yes, but...

She is struggling not to cry.

JOSIE: You know what hurts the most? No him sleeping in my bed after he's been in hers. No that I wasn't enough for him. It's the lies... I told a lie and it nearly killed me. But he's lied and lied... All this time... How little he must think of me...

The tears come and they are sore. RACHEL squirms.

RACHEL: Can I... get you a glass of water?

MARION: God you're useless. See when someone cries, you're supposed to give them a hug.

MARION pushes past RACHEL to get to JOSIE and hug her. RACHEL looks on, helpless.

MARION: There there. It's alright. Shhhh.

RACHEL: Can I get you anything?

JOSIE composes herself.

JOSIE: Just tell me what to do.

MARION: Kick him out.

JOSIE: Rachel?

RACHEL: Tell him—

MARION: —he's a useless prick.

RACHEL: Just say—

MARION: —get it right up you.

RACHEL AND JOSIE: Marion!

MARION: Sorry... sorry...

RACHEL: Don't enter into any discussion, alright?

She puts her hand up to keep MARION quiet.

JOSIE: OK.

RACHEL: You need to act with decorum. Simply tell him, "This marriage is over. We are separating. And you'll be hearing from my lawyer."

JOSIE: This marriage is over...

RACHEL: We are separating...

JOSIE: And you'll be hearing from my lawyer. I've got it.

(Beat.)

My lawyer?

RACHEL: Just say it, Josie.

JOSIE: You mean...?

RACHEL: I better get on. I'm due in court. Good luck.

She lifts her wig and leaves.

MARION: You going to do it?

JOSIE: Yes.

MARION: When?

JOSIE: Now. Before he goes back to the rig.

MARION: You want me to come with you?

JOSIE: Best not. She says to act with decorum.

MARION: Fair do's.

She heads out, practising the lines.

"This marriage is over. We are separating. And you'll be hearing from my lawyer .."

Lights down.

SCENE EIGHT

RACHEL's flat.

Lights up on RACHEL as she enters, carrying her coat which she puts down. She looks lovely, as she did in first scene. She puts in her earrings [or something].

Doorbell.

RACHEL: (*Shouts*) It's open.

She flicks her fingers through her hair as ALEX comes in, suited and super-suave, carrying a bottle of champagne.

RACHEL: Hi. I'll get my coat.

ALEX: Hold on. There's plenty of time. I got this to toast your success.

RACHEL: I don't think that's—

ALEX: Relax. One glass.

He knows his way around, as he talks he opens the bottle, gets glasses etc.

I know the interviews aren't till next week but the real interview's tonight.

RACHEL: No pressure then.

ALEX: The dinner's an excuse to see you in a social situation, see how you fit in with the partners.

(Beat.)

I won't sit beside you. I'll have to mingle, talk to everyone.

He hands her a glass.

ALEX: Cheers.

RACHEL: Cheers.

It's charged.

ALEX: But we all agree. You're the candidate to beat. You're an excellent lawyer. You've been with us since you were a trainee and you got your solicitor-advocate qualifications first go. And you know I'll support you in any way I can.

RACHEL: Thanks. I won't let you down. Drink up. I'll call a cab.

ALEX: Wait.

RACHEL: What?

ALEX: I got you something.

RACHEL: Alex...

ALEX: Sssshhh... Here.

He hands her a small box, watches as she opens it. She gasps.

RACHEL: You shouldn't have.

ALEX: I wanted to.

She takes out a necklace.

RACHEL: It's beautiful but really—

ALEX: —I want you to wear it tonight.

He takes if from her and fastens it on her, slowly, his fingers touching her neck.

ALEX: I want to look over and see it on you. Touching your skin.

He turns her round, admires her.

ALEX: You're so lovely.

RACHEL: Alex... I'm not sure this is a good idea.

ALEX: Shhh... Don't fight it.

He kisses her. She lets out a soft moan.

ALEX: You feel the same, I know you do.

They kiss again. She doesn't resist.

ALEX: That's why I've booked us a room. In the hotel.

They kiss.

ALEX: And you can keep your bra on. I don't mind.

His phone rings. He groans

ALEX: Sorry. I better take this.

He moves away, lowers his voice. His tone very dry. He is not looking at RACHEL but she is listening intently.

ALEX: Yes, Miriam?

RACHEL tenses. Her dislike building as she registers what he is saying.

ALEX: ...I'm still at the office then I'm going straight out... I did tell you. You really need to listen to your messages... Well no, because none of the other wives are going... (*softening her up now*) Oh, by the way it's going to be a late one. And there's a breakfast meeting first thing. So best I just stay over at the hotel... I know, it's a drag... I'll see you tomorrow.

He heads back over to RACHEL.

ALEX: Now where were we?

RACHEL: You lying, cheating scumbag.

He yells as she chucks the champagne in his face.

ALEX: For God's sake, Rachel. Get me a... I need a...

He looks round frantically, grabs a tea-towel to wipe himself.

RACHEL: That woman's given you the best years of her life and you talk to her like she's an idiot.

ALEX: My good suit!

RACHEL: Lying to her face. Buying me expensive gifts and trying to get into my knickers.

ALEX: Oh please. You've been gagging for it.

RACHEL is furious now, closing in on him, voice raised. She keeps her posh accent throughout.

RACHEL: I've been a selfish, ignorant cow. Never once thought what I was doing to your wife. I've a good mind to go see her right now and tell her I'm sorry.

ALEX: You do that and I swear I'll—

She lets rip. Right up close.

RACHEL: You'll what? Fire me? Well, go on then. Fire me. Fire me right now?

A long moment. A gleam in his eye.

ALEX: Are you as turned on as I am?

RACHEL: What? No! No way!

He reaches for her and she recoils.

RACHEL: Get your hands off me, you sleazy big bastard.

ALEX: Careful...

RACHEL: My flesh is pure crawling so it is. You useless prick.

ALEX: Hey! Just you remember who you're talking to.

RACHEL: Oh I do. And you know what? You can stuff it. Stuff your job. Stuff your partnership. Stuff your fucking necklace!

She pulls it off and chucks it on the floor, grabs her coat.

RACHEL: And you can get it right up you.

She storms out. ALEX, on his knees, picking up the bits of the necklace.

Lights down.

SCENE NINE

MARION's house. It's Cousins' Night. MARION and JOSIE are nicely dressed. Wine and glasses and nibbles laid out etc. JOSIE is very pleased with herself.

JOSIE: "This marriage is over. We are separating and you will be hearing from my lawyer.

MARION: Good for you.

JOSIE: For once I didn't say too much, I didn't go on. I said exactly what Rachel told me to say and I'm so proud of myself.

Doorbell.

MARION: Here they come... I'll get it.

She heads out.

MARION: (*OOV*) Rachel?... You coming in?

RACHEL and MARION come in. RACHEL is wearing the same dress as in previous scene and carrying her coat, not really sure why she's there.

MARION: You're just in time.

RACHEL: For what?

JOSIE: Cousins' Night.

MARION: Last Friday of the month, remember.

RACHEL: Oh I... I didn't actually. I'm—

MARION: You should stay anyway.

JOSIE: I did it, Rachel. Exactly like you said. I finished with him.

RACHEL: So did I?

JOSIE puts up her hand for a high five. RACHEL ducks then realises her mistake and puts her hand up for a high five but JOSIE has now put her hand down and it's an awkward moment for RACHEL with her hand in the air.

JOSIE and MARION share an amused but affectionate look.

MARION: So, Rachel, if you've no come for the Cousins' Night what brings you here?

RACHEL: I... I don't really know... I was just... I've made such a mess of... (*fighting down sobs*) I didn't want to be on my own and I . I... really don't have... anyone to... to...

The sobs come. JOSIE and MARION are gobsmacked.

JOSIE: Is she crying?

MARION: She is. I think she is.

RACHEL: You two are useless. See when someone cries you're supposed to give them a hug.

JOSIE and MARION share a look and rush over to RACHEL and the three of them hold each other in a hug.

THE END

ALSO AVAILABLE FROM SALAMANDER STREET

All Salamander Street plays can be bought in bulk at a discount for performance or study. Contact info@salamanderstreet.com to enquire about performance licenses.

A Play, A Pie and A Pint Vol One
Paperback ISBN: 9781913630225
eBook ISBN: 9781913630232

6 plays from Òran Mór: *A Respectable Widow Takes to Vulgarity* (Douglas Maxwell), *Toy Plastic Chicken* (Uma Nada-Rajah), *Chic Murray: A Funny Place for A Window* (Stuart Hepburn), *Ida Tamson* (Denise Mina), *Jocky Wilson Said* (Jane Livingstone and Jonathan Cairney) and *Do Not Press This Button* (Alan Bissett)

Group Portrait in a Summer Landscape
by Peter Arnott
Paperback ISBN: 9781914228933
eBook ISBN: 9781914228957

An intense and riveting play set in a Perthshire country house during the Scottish Independence referendum of 2014. A retired academic and political heavyweight invites family and former students together for a dramatic reckoning.

Placeholder by Catherine Bisset
ISBN: 9781914228919
eBook ISBN: 9781914228940

Profoundly thought-provoking, this solo play about the historical actor-singer of colour known as 'Minette' offers an exploration of the complex racial and social dynamics of what would become the first independent nation in the Caribbean.

O is for Hoolet by Isabel McFarlane
ISBN: 9781913630126
eBook ISBN: 9781913630133

A solo show about the Scots language—stories, interviews, memories, characters and attitudes—to challenge and disrupt our expectations and prejudices about language.

www.salamanderstreet.com

www.ingramcontent.com/pod-product-compliance
Lightning Source LLC
Chambersburg PA
CBHW020049170426
43199CB00009B/218